BEACON
BIBLE
EXPOSITIONS

BEACON BIBLE EXPOSITIONS

BEACON BIBLE EXPOSITIONS

VOLUME 7

CORINTHIANS

by
OSCAR F. REED

Editors
WILLIAM M. GREATHOUSE
WILLARD H. TAYLOR

BEACON HILL PRESS OF KANSAS CITY
Kansas City, Missouri

Permission to quote from the following copyrighted versions of the Bible
is acknowledged with appreciation:

New American Standard Bible (NASB), copyright © The Lockman
Foundation, 1960, 1962, 1963, 1968, 1971.

New English Bible (NEB), © The Delegates of the Oxford University
Press and the Syndics of the Cambridge University Press, 1961, 1970.

Revised Standard Version of the Bible (RSV), copyrighted 1946, 1952.

The New Testament in Modern English (Phillips), copyright © by J. B.
Phillips, 1958. Used by permission of the Macmillan Co.

Weymouth's New Testament in Modern English (Weymouth), by
Richard Francis Weymouth. By special arrangements with James
Clarke and Co., Ltd., and by permission of Harper and Row,
Publishers, Inc.

The Living Bible (TLB), copyright © 1971, Tyndale House Publishers,
Wheaton, Ill.

New International Version (NIV), copyright © 1973 by New York Bible
Society International.

The New Testament in the Language of the People (Williams), by
Charles B. Williams. Copyright 1937 by Bruce Humphries, Inc.;
assigned 1949 to Moody Bible Institute, Chicago.

The New Testament (Knox), by R. A. Knox, © 1944 by Sheed and Ward,
Inc., New York.

The Bible: An American Translation (Goodspeed), by J. M. Powis Smith
and Edgar J. Goodspeed. Copyright 1923, 1927, 1948 by the University of Chicago Press.

The Amplified New Testament, copyright 1958 by the Lockman Foundation, La Habra, Calif.

Dedication

To Grace
wife, mother
and gracious companion

Contents

Editors' Preface

No Christian preacher or teacher has been more aware of the creating and sustaining power of the Word of God than the Apostle Paul. As a stratagem in his missionary endeavors, he sought out synagogues in the major cities where he knew Jews would gather to hear the Old Testament. No doubt he calculated that he would be invited to expound the Scriptures and so he would have a golden opportunity to preach Christ. That peripatetic preacher was confident that valid Christian experience and living could not be enjoyed apart from the Word of God, whether preached or written. To the Thessalonians he wrote: "And we also thank God constantly for this, that when you received the word of God which you heard from us, you accepted it not as the word of men but as what it really is, the word of God, which is at work in you believers" (1 Thess. 2:13, RSV). Strong Christians, and more broadly, strong churches, are born of, and nurtured on, authentic and winsome exposition of the Bible.

Beacon Bible Expositions provide a systematic, devotional Bible study program for laymen and a fresh, homiletical resource for preachers. All the benefits of the best biblical scholarship are found in them, but nontechnical language is used in the composition. A determined effort is made to relate the clarified truth to life today. The writers, Wesleyan in theological perspective, seek to interpret the gospel, pointing to the Living Word, Christ, who is the primary Subject of all scripture, the Mediator of redemption, and the Norm of Christian living.

The publication of this series is a prayerful invitation to both laymen and ministers to set out on a lifelong, systematic study of the Bible. Hopefully these studies will supply the initial impetus.

—WILLIAM M. GREATHOUSE AND
WILLARD H. TAYLOR, *Editors*

The Corinthian Correspondence

Religion is life, and for that reason, any complete expression of Christian doctrine must discover its correlative in Christian ethics. William Baird reflects this truth in speaking of the Corinthian situation by suggesting that "the epistle which deals with pagan reveling also describes the table of the Lord; the epistle which discusses emotional babbling also announces the word of the Cross; the epistle which decries intellectual cynicism also proclaims the hope of the resurrection."[1] Throughout the Corinthian Epistles, and with design, Paul confronts individual life concerns, probes the depths of theological understanding with respect to them, and then applies his findings to the issue at hand. In these remarkable letters, Paul moves from the sanctuary, to the study, market, shop, home, and street.

Today as Yesterday

The study of the Corinthian letters is particularly important to the urban Christian. The rise of contemporary Western culture is in part the story of her cities. Her technological advance—progress beyond man's wildest dreams—centers in the glass-enclosed skylines which thrust their way into the sky like towers of Babel. The congested freeways, the smog-filled atmosphere, and the suburban sprawl have become symbols of a faceless society. There *are* reasons why atheistic existential philosophy arose as the dominant philosophy of a secular society.

One needs only to read *The Lonely Crowd, The Organization Man,* or *Future Shock* along with the daily media to see the devastating mobility, the racial issues, and the multiplicity of social problems which have arisen because of the urban explosion.

The Christian Church has responded both positively and negatively to these crises. She has retired to the suburbs with the people but left the millions in the inner city with very little help except from well-meaning zealots whose commitment much of the time has not been balanced by either theological understanding or cultural awareness. "The sons of the city were left to grow up under the foreboding shadow of the tenement rather than the steeple of the church. Little wonder that many of them preferred the 'Egyptian Dragons' to the Christian Endeavor, the young people's society, or the Boy Scouts."[2]

However, the suburbs have fared no better. The dawn of a new day among the affluent has turned for many into a spiritual indifference—the heart of secularity. As one Californian growled, "This is what we do on Sunday. It is our life-style. We will adjust our budget to the energy crisis rather than give up our weekends at the beach and in the mountains. We plan to live as we please." It might just as well have been in Wisconsin, Missouri, Tennessee, or New York.

Today, the good life has become our enemy rather than our benefactor; and while technology has freed us from the past, its very goodness has become perverse in a profoundly demonic way. As a result, a reorientation of values is taking place with shattering consequences. Rollo May suggests that "our society is sick because it has lost its language by which it communicates the meaningful crises of life. Thus New York City (for example) is a city of terribly lonely people who can get together only when they are drugged, or drunk, or in bed."[3] No wonder there is a kindred feeling when the posture of Corinth is reviewed culturally. It is the image of contemporary society—the problems are the same.

But while the problems are the same, so is the hope. This is God's world. The very culture which is finally opening men to communication is the culture which will open the way to redemptive possibilities through the Cross. The very conflict between culture and religion—so characteristic of both Old and New Testament history—may form the ground upon which renewal can come.

The City of Corinth

Does the Bible have anything to say to the problems of the church in an urban society? Nowhere was the setting more appropriate than Corinth. It was a relatively new city, having been rebuilt by Julius Caesar after its destruction in 146 B.C. It was soon populated by colonists from all over the Mediterranean basin, including Jews exiled from Rome. Robertson suggests that it was the "empire in miniature."

Rather than take the dangerous voyage around the peninsula, the sailors preferred to move their cargoes across the isthmus at Corinth, making the city commercially virile and culturally cosmopolitan. The cultural differences, however, stratified society and tended to crystallize the differences. Slave, freedman, merchant, and noble entered into a mix in buying and selling, but followed their own paths socially and religiously.

The pagans were a religious people with temples and images everywhere, reflecting both their indulgence of the gods of Mount Olympus and their involvement in the rites of the mystery religions. The festivals found the streets thronged with people in the worship of their gods. Corinth was infamous for the immorality associated with its worship. At times, over 1,000 temple prostitutes served its famed temple of Aphrodite.

Paul, who was in Corinth when he wrote to the Romans, said of many contemporaries: "They were filled with all manner of wickedness, evil, covetousness, malice. Full of envy, murder, strife, deceit, malignity; they are gossips, slanderers, haters of God, insolent, haughty, boastful, inventors of evil, disobedient to parents, foolish, faithless, heartless, ruthless" (Rom. 1:29-31, RSV).

The Corinthian Church

In the above cultural milieu, a strong Christian church was established in Corinth, with evidence of suburban groups growing from the mother congregation (2 Cor. 1:1; Rom. 16:1). The fellowship consisted of a variety of people and classes including both the affluent and the poor (1 Cor. 7:21; 1:26).

It is not surprising that a church with such a social profile should fall into difficulty, making necessary the extended correspondence between them and Paul—the "written residue" comprising some of the more important writings of the New Testament.

Very early in the life of the Corinthian church, word came to Paul of the critical problems within the fellowship. Evidently some of the report came through "Chloe's people" (1:11, RSV), along with a letter delivered to Paul with questions concerning ethical and ecclesiastical issues (7:1; 16:17).

It is the purpose of this expositional study to share not only what Paul says, but also what he means. Most Christians are not concerned with "meat offered to idols," wearing veils in church, or the Corinthian "women's lib" movement. Beneath these externalities are profound ethical principles which speak to every generation. The ethic of Paul is a protest against both the permissiveness and the legalism which were condoned by different segments of the Corinthian church. "His concern with the practical should not be construed as a banal particularism. Rather, the concern with particulars rests on the conviction that basic ethical concerns are relevant to every aspect of human conduct."[4] While there are textual-critical problems, we have elected to note them only insofar as they affect the expositional treatment of any particular passage.

*The First Epistle of Paul
to the*
CORINTHIANS

Topical Outline of First Corinthians

The Preface (1:1-9)
    Greetings (1:1-3)
    Thanksgiving (1:4-9)

The Problem of Division and the Life of Faith (1:10—4:21)
    Tensions in the Fellowship (1:10-17)
    The Word of the Cross and the Sufficiency of Christ (1:18-31)
    The Character of Christian Ministry (2:1-5)
    The True Wisdom of God (2:6-9)
    When Spirit Meets Spirit (2:10-16)
    Men of Flesh (3:1-4)
    Like People, like Priest (3:5-9)
    The Temple of God (3:10-17)
    All Things Are Yours (3:18-23)
    Stewards of the Mysteries of God (4:1-5)
    An Audacious Claim (4:6-21)

Moral Standards and the Life of Faith (5:1—7:40)
    Whatever Happened to Church Discipline? (5:1-13)
    Truths that Every Christian Should Know (6:1-8)
    Standards of the Kingdom of God (6:9-20)
    The Sanctity of Christian Marriage (7:1-16)
    Being a Christian Where You Are (7:17-24)
    Advice to the Unmarried (7:25-28, 36-38)
    Jesus Is Coming Soon (7:26-35)
    Counsels on Remarriage (7:39-40)

Secularism and the Life of Faith (8:1—11:1)
    Setting an Example (8:1-6)
    Christian Attitudes: The Strong Toward the Weak (8:7-13)
    The Magnificent Obsession (9:1-18)
    Openness Is Next to Holiness (9:19-23)
    The Conditions of Christian Existence (9:24-27)
    Scriptural Warnings and Divine Promise (10:1-14)
    Rules for Christian Discernment (10:15-33)
    A Remarkable Request (11:1)
    Some Concluding Remarks on Secularism

Public Worship and the Life of Faith (11:2—14:40)
    The Veiling of Women (11:2-16)
    The Lord's Supper (11:17-34)

Introduction

The Message of First Corinthians

First Corinthians deals with a number of subjects—differing loyalties within the church, sexual immorality among its members, legal disputes, marriage and divorce, food offered to idols, hairstyles, spiritual gifts, the Lord's Supper, death and resurrection.

The Epistle, rather than simply expressing Paul's ecclesiastical authority, reflects his intense love and affection for the congregation. It reminds one of the father and son relation in Hosea between God and the "chosen people."

The Corinthians are God's people beset by temptation. Paul is their pastor, deeply concerned for them. The Epistle reveals Paul as both pastor and counsellor. It shows his strength in love, his forbearance in matters of indifference, his strictness in issues of right and wrong, and above all his unwearied activity and wonderful endurance.

Uniquely, the Epistle points up the sharp ethical conflict between Christianity and paganism. "Principles relating to church discipline, to social relations and intercourse, to public worship, the nature of the church, and of the sacraments are here unfolded, not in abstract form, so much as in their application."[1] The book gives insight into the problems of establishing a church among non-Christians, and also delineates the conduct which should prevail within the church.

While First Corinthians is not a doctrinal letter like Romans or Galatians, every part of it deals with some profound theological issue. Christ is the Center of the message, and the glory of God the Father is the ultimate end. It is only *in Christ* that there is the saving revelation of God (1:17—2:15). Paul points out very clearly that Jesus was a Person in history, a Teacher who suffered betrayal, who died on a cross and was buried. Yet He was more than that. All things came into existence through Him (8:6). He was the *Rock* from which the Israelites drank in the wilderness (10:4). God raised Him from the dead, confirming Him as *Christ* and *Lord* (15:1-28). This Jesus will soon come again to consummate the new age (15:51-57).

Paul speaks personally of life in Christ, faith, and baptism. He does not speak in propositional *credos,* but in the life of the Spirit which flows from redemption *in Christ.* He proclaims deliverance from sin, but expresses it in the imperative as well as the indicative mood, indicating that it was supernatural in character, but not supramoral.[2]

Chapter 13 is the heart of the holy walk in Christ. The Spirit was given to build the Church in *love.* One should doubt the presence of the Spirit if this is not true (13:1-3). It is fascinating to see that the most thorough examination of love in the Bible is given from the pen of Paul rather than John the Beloved. The *Shema* of Deuteronomy (6:4-5) and the ethic of Jesus are set forth descriptively as the greatest of all graces. Love is the heart of the gospel. All other materials in the Epistle point to love as the answer in action to the issues of the Corinthian church. It is superior to tongues, prophecy, knowledge, miracles, and outward works of charity. The gifts are worthless apart from the inherent excellence and perpetuity of love.

The ideal is not of pagan but of Christian origin. The pagan had no idea of *agape.* Neither *eros* nor *philia* answered to the Christian understanding of *agape.* The Latin words *amor* and *caritas* (from which "charity" is derived) fell short of the Christian ideal.

It is not of charity that Paul is speaking, but love *(agape)*; not primarily an emotion, but a *life-style*—a commitment to a God-given ideal which was the heart of Christ's sacrifice on the Cross and an example in principle of what God expects of His people who are *in Christ*.

The whole Epistle is a study in priorities—and there is nothing greater than love *(agape)*. It is the supreme ethic.

Preaching and Teaching from First Corinthians

First Corinthians is a study in biblical ethics. Although Paul deals with practical matters, his understanding is theological in nature. He will usually begin with an everyday occurence, probe it theologically, and then apply the principle to the practical experience of every Christian.

The great personal and social issues of his day are the same issues the church faces today. And though the preacher and teacher must be careful not to confuse *particular* with *principle,* the rich insights of the apostle will speak vigorously to nearly every ethical dilemma.

The author readily admits that there are some areas of the Epistle which are difficult to understand exegetically and culturally. In these he has attempted to give suggestive exposition without dogmatic exegesis.

It is taken for granted that exposition is grounded in sound exegesis. The homiletical suggestions run parallel with Donald Metz's fine study in the *Beacon Bible Commentary.* The bibliography also points to many other excellent commentaries.

I recently heard a layman commend his pastor, "Sir, we thoroughly enjoyed the exposition this morning. Can't we have more?" The pastor hesitated for a moment and replied, "It costs too much in preparation!"

The answer was truer than he realized. Exposition takes work—and more work. But if a preacher or teacher will "catch the vision," he will gather up "twelve baskets full" and continue to gather after the work is over. The

Bible is the unfailing Source of preaching and teaching materials—whatever the subject.

First Corinthians has a great deal to commend to our secular society. God can speak through it to every community. Try it!

The Preface
1 Corinthians 1:1-9

Greetings

Can you imagine Paul sitting in a home with friends in Ephesus, studying the various reports before him from Corinth? Can you feel the tremendous pathos of Paul mingled with the spirit of authority as he replies to the questions asked and the problems presented? The apostle immediately answers the questions in a spirit which communicates both authority and love.

1 Corinthians 1:1-3

> 1 Paul, called to be an apostle of Jesus Christ through the will of God, and Sosthenes our brother,
> 2 Unto the church of God which is at Corinth, to them that are sanctified in Christ Jesus, called to be saints, with all that in every place call upon the name of Jesus Christ our Lord, both theirs and ours:
> 3 Grace be unto you, and peace, from God our Father, and from the Lord Jesus Christ.

1. *The Divine Calling* (1a). For Paul, apostleship meant an "inescapable vocation" (cf. John 15:16). It was not a calling to be assumed at his pleasure, but by God's design. The word *apostle* means literally a messenger and then a missionary. That calling *(klētos)* was the word of the *Lord* which had claimed him. There was a profound consciousness on the part of Paul that one greater than he had set him aside as an instrument for His purposes (Acts 9:15-16).

There was no question in Paul's mind that he was to speak with authority. His ministry was determined by God's will. He knew that his divinely appointed leadership would be questioned (4:9; 2 Cor. 4:1-15; 10—13). He also anticipated the false leadership assumed by those who abused the gifts of the Spirit.

His authority was given immediately through *Christ* on the road to Damascus (Acts 9). It was not by election, consecration, or ordination by the apostles before him. The calling is expressed more specifically in Gal. 1:1, "Paul an apostle—not from men nor through man, but through Jesus Christ and God the Father" (RSV).

There is for those who respond to the divine initiative an authentic mark of authority which comes from God. It is the "tap on the shoulder" (Peter Marshall). It is the deep personal awareness that this is for me. It is a call to high vocation from which a man never escapes. And while there are differing ministries (12:4-11; Eph. 4:11-13), there is one Initiator who makes clear in His own way those who are called.

I am aware of a "sacramentalism" which says that all men are called to sacred vocation—and in a sense this is true. But let no man hold lightly the work of the ordained ministry. Would that every man of the cloth had that "thumb in his back," that inescapable "Voice on the road to Damascus" such as the Apostle Paul had.

2. *The Fellowship of Sharing* (1*b*). It is just a small phrase, but it has tremendous application: "our brother Sosthenes" (RSV). The term "brother" was a common one among Christians (Matt. 23:8). Evidently Sosthenes was well known to the Corinthian Christians and was probably the ruler of the synagogue in Corinth, described in Acts 18:17. Whether so or not, he is numbered among the fellowship *(koinonia)* of Christians and a friend of Paul. Some even believed him to be the amanuensis (secretary) in this letter, as Timothy was in others.

"Brother" represents the term commonly used by Christians who in Jesus Christ are all sons of one Father.

The ordinary distinctions of sex, race, and class have ceased to exist (Gal. 3:28; Col. 3:11).

I sat on the platform of the first Billy Graham crusade in Boston and watched several hundred respond to the invitation. So intent were they that they came with little, if any, self-consciousness. Here was a burly laborer in overalls coming down the aisle with a mink-coated young lady. Here were black and white, rich and poor mingling together with no awareness of class or racial distinction. We sang hymns together on the elevated railway to Everett. All human distinction was lost in the common fellowship with one another and with Christ.

It always happens that way! Christian revival breaks the barriers and provides a common ground before the Cross. No wonder Paul sent greetings and included Sosthenes "our brother."

3. *The Nature of the Church* (2-3)

a. The Church is of God (2a). Paul is speaking to the *ecclesia*. The Church is "the commonwealth of God, an organized community of people who share a common experience in Jesus Christ, and who are united in love, faith and loyalty to him and to one another in the bonds of fellowship and service."[3] For Paul, the *ecclesia* was continuous in history, the living body of Christ. It was the continuing incarnation of Christ in His world.

One hesitates to use the term *invisible* as over against *visible* in any Platonic sense, since the visible church with all its impurities is properly speaking *the* church. F. W. Robertson illustrates the point by speaking of the Rhine River, muddy and discolored and charged with impurity. But it is no less *the* river. So is the Church of Christ. Corinth was truly the "church of God" with all its ambiguities. There were not two churches, but one, just as the parable of the vine did not speak of two vines, but one needing to be pruned. Corinth was called the "church of God" because it was God's church. It was God who elected them to membership on the ground of their faith, and they were His because He had bought them with blood (Acts 20:28).

b. The Church consists of the "sanctified in Christ Jesus" (2b). The verb *hagiazein* ("to sanctify") means both to cleanse from sin and to render sacred by consecration to God. Both concepts are united in the opening words of Paul. The church of Corinth had been cleansed by God for His own possession (cf. Titus 2:14). They had turned their back to evil ways and pagan habits. Something genuinely spiritual had happened to a large group of people as they were confronted by the claims of Christ. While Paul will censor many in the church for falling short ethically of that reality and will unfold the truth of *entire* sanctification as he reveals the life in the Spirit, we err if we do not see the church generically as that fellowship of initially cleansed believers, consecrated to the service and will of God (cf. 6:11).

It is imperative for us to recognize that all who are "in Christ" are sanctified both positionally and provisionally. Positionally, as justified they have a "cleansed" (1 John 1:7) and "perfected" relationship to God (Heb. 10:14). Moreover, they have been actually incorporated into Christ by the Spirit and therefore share His life and holiness (1:30-31). It is all of Him (Heb. 13:12), and we receive His sanctifying grace as an open door to a holy walk. This sanctification is a present reality in our life. It is not of ourselves, it is of Him—"in Christ." In Him we receive the gift of God's righteousness and are re-created by the Spirit.

Christ himself is the Source and Center of our sanctification. It must always be Christocentric if it is biblical. Paul is more than commendatory in his designation of "the church of God . . . sanctified in Christ Jesus." It is his deep and profound recognition that a vital spiritual change has taken place, and this forms the ground for his ensuing counsels.

Even Calvin recognized this change which seems to be more than "positional" when he remarked, "For if you do not by holiness of life show yourself to be a Christian, you may indeed be in the church, and pass undetected, but of it you cannot be. Hence all must be sanctified in Christ who would be reckoned among the people of God."[4]

c. The Church consists of those who are saints by calling (2c). The Corinthian church was called a fellowship of saints *(hagioi)*. Sainthood, biblically speaking, is not the pseudo-piety which we have popularly associated with the term. Believers are saints because they are outwardly consecrated and inwardly renewed. They are not "called to be saints" (KJV); they are "saints by calling" (NASB). They are not invited to be saints; they are saints by definition (cf. Rom. 1:7).

It seems contradictory that the Corinthian church should be corrupt in doctrine and practice and still be identified as "saints." Yet this is a useful lesson and a Pauline instrument for counsel, rebuke, and instruction, even to the point of exclusion from the fellowship (c. 5).

Not all are called to be apostles, but all are "saints by calling." It is by God's initiative. Christ's indwelling Spirit sanctifies, molds, and shapes believers into God's people. Sainthood is the point of departure for the Christian. Faith opens the door to a new life in Him. By the gift of grace we are enabled to perpetuate His spirit.

d. The Church consists of those who recognize Jesus as Lord (1:2d). The Christian is called into "community" where there are no boundaries ("who in every place"). It would broaden our borders and bless our spirit if we would sometimes lift our eyes to the horizons and see the multitude who stand and will stand before the throne of God. On that day "thousands of thousands" will stand, "saying with a loud voice, Worthy is the Lamb that was slain to receive power, and riches, and wisdom, and strength, and honour, and glory, and blessing" (Rev. 5:11-12).

The Church of God is as wide as the world. And the Church of God in Christ is that fellowship which proclaims Him Lord—*their Lord and ours.* William Barclay points out that "it is the amazing wonder of Christianity that all men possess all the love of Jesus Christ, that God loves each one of us as if there was only one of us to love."[5]

4. *The Divine Salutation* (3). All good flows from God. Our very existence is dependent upon His benevolence. Grace always indicates favor, and peace its fruit. Included in the scope of Paul's greeting is all that is of grace: justification, adoption, sanctification, and all the benefits that flow from them. And they always find their source in God our Father and in the Lord Jesus Christ.

It is appropriate that Paul should salute the Corinthians with "grace" and "peace," for they were defective in both. It is particularly significant that he should find the source of grace and peace in God, because the Corinthian arrogance tended to forget their ultimate dependence upon the Divine.

Grace and peace are central to Paul's theological understanding. God is grace (15:10; 2 Cor. 8:9), and His graciousness is revealed in His Son, our Saviour. Grace is conditioned only on our willingness to receive it, but the fullness of His grace is always available to the receiving heart. It is a marvelous word that defies definition. It implies a relationship which is as adequate as God himself and limited only by the unwillingness of our hearts to accept it. It is the unmerited love of God in action through Jesus Christ. What more can be said?

Peace is more than a frame of mind, a mood, or an atmosphere. It is not a debilitating dependence upon God, but an abiding strength, an awareness of the deep resources of God's grace and of the Spirit who works within us. It is the fruit of the Spirit which ends in well-being and confidence.

> *What a treasure I have in this wonderful peace,*
> *Buried deep in the heart of my soul,*
> *So secure that no power can mine it away*
> *While the years of eternity roll!*

> *Peace! Peace! wonderful peace,*
>   *Coming down from the Father above!*
> *Sweep over my spirit forever, I pray,*
>   *In fathomless billows of love.*[6]
>
> —W. D. Cornell

Thanksgiving

1 Corinthians 1:4-9

> 4 I thank my God always on your behalf, for the grace of God which is given you by Jesus Christ;
> 5 That in every thing ye are enriched by him, in all utterance, and in all knowledge;
> 6 Even as the testimony of Christ was confirmed in you:
> 7 So that ye come behind in no gift; waiting for the coming of our Lord Jesus Christ:
> 8 Who shall also confirm you unto the end, that ye may be blameless in the day of our Lord Jesus Christ.
> 9 God is faithful, by whom ye were called unto the fellowship of his Son Jesus Christ our Lord.

We might think that Paul's expression of thanksgiving for the church at Corinth is ironical when we continue to read the issues he was to face. Can one be genuinely thankful for a rebellious fellowship? Yes—Paul was!

He thanked God for the "grace of God . . . given in Christ Jesus" (4, NASB) and for the gifts (7) bestowed upon the church in great abundance. He was thankful that they were "enriched in Him in all speech and all knowledge" (5, NASB), and that their hope was in the Lord Jesus who would confirm them blameless (8) awaiting the soon coming of the Lord *(parousia)*.

This generous spirit of Paul was typical of the man who through all his suffering always rejoiced with his churches.

1. *He thanked God for the "grace of God given in Jesus Christ"* (4, NASB). Once again he speaks of the grace of God. In this particular context he is speaking of the spiritual gifts which God has given the church with great blessing and generosity. It is through *grace* that the Corinthians were "enriched in all speech and all knowledge" (5, NASB).

"Enriched" is a key word. We are enriched in Christ because we are members of His body and engrafted in Him, sharing everything that He has received from the Father. What a great thought! We are co-heirs with Jesus Christ (Rom. 8:17) and receive as He has received.

2. *He thanked God for the spiritual gifts given in great abundance* (7). The Lord not alone honoured them with great grace, but endowed them with the gifts *(charismata)* purposed for the ongoing of the body, the Church *(ekklē-sia)*. The scripture does not indicate an abundance which left nothing to be desired, but an adequacy until there was no want of gifts in awaiting the blessed *parousia.*

3. *He reminds them of the hope in God resulting in con-firmation and blamelessness* (8). After Paul tells them what he thinks of them, he defines the hope that is theirs for the future. It is the assurance through *grace* that God will keep them *blameless* until the Lord comes in that *day.*

While the confirmation came through the endowment of gifts (cf. Gal. 3:2-5; Heb. 2:4), blamelessness was the result of their calling (Eph. 1:4; Col. 1:22). They were called to be "holy and blameless before him in love" (Eph. 1:4). Paul in Colossians states it similarly but includes "beyond reproach," which is the heart of blamelessness. No charge can be laid against those whom Christ guaran-tees or confirms. As Donald Metz observes, "The blame-less life is the life of holiness."

4. *He reminds them of the confidence that they can have in God.* (9). The hope that Paul has given the church is not a vain boast. He goes back to the beginning. This faithful God called the Corinthians into the "fellowship of his son, Jesus Christ our Lord." "Fellowship" is a direct antithesis to the divisions within the church. The text seems to indi-cate either or both a fellowship *with* or *in* Christ. In any case the fidelity of God brings about what He has prom-ised—the unity of the body of Christ in which they are one. God is faithful. He can be depended upon. He is steadfast in His purpose. And our faith, as His gift, can be so simple

and trustful that the Spirit will confirm that faith in blamelessness until the end. Thank God for His faithfulness (John 10:27-30; Rom. 8:28-39)! How can we be "stedfast" (15:58)? Because God is faithful! We are in partnership with Him. It is a "family tie."

Alan Redpath remarks that it is God's intention that He share His interests with us in Christ. "Your interests are His: your mind and its development, your body and its sanctity, purity and holiness, your spirit and its graciousness, tenderness and love. Your concern is to be His glory, the wonder of His person, the majesty and greatness of His power."[7]

Nine times in nine verses Paul speaks affectionately of the Saviour. He will do it again and again. For Paul, Christ is absolutely central. "Paul lingers over the name," and so should we!

The Problem of Division
and the Life of Faith
1 Corinthians 1:10—4:21

Tensions in the Fellowship

Paul leads into the issue of schism within the church with tender appeal. "Now" *(de)* is adversative. It introduces a contrast to what he has previously said. Notice the vocabulary he uses as an example of response to a spirit of tension within the fellowship. "I beseech you, brethren, by the name of our Lord Jesus Christ" (10). There was nothing for Paul to gain in furthering a spirit of hostility. He came to heal and not to divide.

1 Corinthians 1:10-17

> 10 Now I beseech you, brethren, by the name of our Lord Jesus Christ, that ye all speak the same thing, and that there be no divisions among you; but that ye be perfectly joined together in the same mind and in the same judgment.
> 11 For it hath been declared unto me of you, my brethren, by them which are of the house of Chloe, that there are contentions among you.
> 12 Now this I say, that every one of you saith, I am of Paul; and I of Apollos; and I of Cephas; and I of Christ.
> 13 Is Christ divided? was Paul crucified for you? or were ye baptized in the name of Paul?
> 14 I thank God that I baptized none of you, but Crispus and Gaius;
> 15 Lest any should say that I had baptized in mine own name.
> 16 And I baptized also the household of Stephanas: besides, I know not whether I baptized any other.
> 17 For Christ sent me not to baptize, but to preach the gospel: not with wisdom of words, lest the cross of Christ should be made of none effect.

1. *The fact of division* (10-11). The information that came to Paul was not sent officially from the church, but through

the members of Chloe's household (11). Chloe was probably a wealthy Christian businesswoman.

Parties arose in Corinth, producing tension within the fellowship (10). Let us try to understand what these parties represented. You cannot read the Epistles without recognizing that there were different emphases among the apostles and Early Church leaders (for example, contrast Paul, Peter, and John).

Their mode of expression was not contradictory, but complementary. Their points of view were like the flashing sides of a scintillating jewel (see Acts 15, the Council of Jerusalem). Their differences actually formed a greater unity of the gospel beyond any one of them. Paul understood this, but the people did not and ranged themselves under different religious teachers as party leaders. The sin was obvious. Christ is incapable of division (13), and the oneness of the church was at stake. Jesus Christ was the Center of that unity—not religious leaders!

These divisions arose, therefore, because of a forgetfulness on the one hand of the common ground that the Corinthian church had in Jesus Christ, and secondly, because they gave their loyalties to certain religious leaders.

Paul was thankful that he was not the occasion of the tension (13-14). It was his Christocentric ideal for the church and his love for the people which made it possible to counsel in the face of division. It is always so with Christian leadership.

2. *The explanation of division* (1:12). The schisms in Corinth were not hostile sects, but competing divisions resulting in "alienation of feeling and party strife." Division can mean a rent (Matt. 9:16), or a difference of opinion as in John 7:43, or an alienation of feeling, an inward separation. In this case there was evidence of all three.

a. The party of Paul: Christian liberty and universality (12). Paul deprecated the use of his name as much as the other three. He viewed the tendency as pagan—exalting religious leaders to the status of a man having divine qualities. And while he could point to those converted under his ministry, he would not tolerate any schism in his behalf. In fact he was incensed: "Paul was not crucified for you, was he? Or were you baptized in the name of Paul?" (13, NASB).

While in Corinth, Paul taught the doctrines of justification by faith and the universal call and scope of the gospel with characteristic vigor. The gospel of Christian liberty was what he called "my gospel" (Rom. 2:16)—the truths which by revelation he had been given to preach. Probably those who said "I am of Paul" were principally Gentile. We suspect that some of the Pauline party may have been returning to pagan practices under the guise of Christian liberty.

Bultmann has remarked that "the Christian indicative always brings about the Christian imperative. They had forgotten that the indicative of the good-news brought the imperative of the Christian ethic. They had forgotten that they were saved, not to be free to sin, but to be free not to sin."[8]

b. The party of Apollos: the highly educated (12). Apollos was an Alexandrian Jew distinguished for his eloquence as a preacher and his literary culture (Acts 8:24). His rhetorical flair may have entranced some of the Gentiles in Corinth who were unimpressed by Paul's image and preaching style. I can hear them saying, "Never have we heard a pulpiteer like Apollos!" They were interested in intellectualizing the Christian faith into a philosophy.

While Paul was a dear friend of Apollos and appreciated his talents, his followers were loyal to what they mistakenly thought were his ideals and so perverted the gospel of Christ.

c. The party of Cephas: the legalists (12). I hesitate to call the Cephas party legalistic, since Paul and Peter had agreed in Gal. 2:6-10 concerning circumcision. The spirit of Peter did not lend itself to a spirit of legalism. However, since Paul deals so fully with food restrictions in the letter, it may be that this party represented the legalism which was so diametrically opposed to Christian liberty (Acts 15:28 ff.; cf. 8:1 ff.; 10:25 ff.).

It may have reflected a lack of sensitivity on the part of Peter's followers to the delicate balance established at the Council of Jerusalem (Acts 15). Willard Taylor reminds us that Paul speaks of Cephas (Aramaic) rather than Peter probably as a gentle rebuke hearkening back to his beginnings. The position of Peter's followers came from "weakness" rather than "strength" (Rom. 15:1-13).

Just as license in the name of Christian liberty can create schism in the body of Christ, so legalism in the name of the law can bring an unchristian spirit to the fellowship.

d. The party of Christ: the libertines. It is difficult to define this rent in the community of the church. Of one thing we are sure—the designation was not commendatory. They were as much to blame as the others.

Did they hold some exclusive claim to Christ denied to their fellow Christians (the Gnostics of 1 John)? Or did they oppose apostolic authority to claim complete religious and ethical freedom through a presumed special revelation from the Spirit? In any case, there seemed to be an exclusive arrogance which sanctified them in the midst of the fellowship. They set themselves up as superior to others.

3. *The rebuke in the face of division* (13-17). The whole passage is a not-so-subtle rebuke on the part of Paul. Phillips translates 1:13, "What are you saying? Is there more than one Christ?" Or, as TLB has it, "You have broken Christ into many pieces." "Paul was not crucified for you, was he? Or were you baptized in the name of Paul? . . . For Christ did not send me to baptize, but to preach the gospel, not in cleverness of speech, that the cross of Christ should not be made void" (13, 17, NASB).

Nothing eats at the heart of love more than a party spirit. "Christianity is love; party spirit is the death of love." Christianity is unity; party spirit is disunity. We must learn to love those who differ with us. It is that willingness to die for unity, coupled with a tolerance and love for others, that brings strength to the church. Let us not be crucified for the wrong principles.

4. *Counsels because of division* (17). During the apostolic age, truth stood immeasurably above external rites. "The apostasy of the church consisted in making rites more important than truth."[9] Paul made baptism subordinate to preaching (17). And while he recognized the importance of the rites of the Church (Rom. 3:2) and never undervalued them, he established a priority which is universal in its application to every age. The apostles were to proclaim the Good News. They were witnesses to the saving work of God in Christ. This was the indicative that called forth the imperative.

The Corinthians were too much inclined to revere words of "eloquent wisdom" (17, RSV), or an orator's cleverness. But this detracts from the cross of Christ and makes it seem an "empty thing" (Goodspeed).

We can identify the causes of strife in Corinth as false wisdom, pride, and perverted loyalties. What does Paul counsel? First, an understanding of divine wisdom; second, a call to humility; and third, a new loyalty to God. What more could Paul say to these confused Corinthians? Christ was "all in all." We would do well to take his counsels seriously today.

The Word of the Cross and the Sufficiency of Christ

1 Corinthians 1:18-31

18 For the preaching of the cross is to them that perish foolishness; but unto us which are saved it is the power of God.
19 For it is written, I will destroy the wisdom of the wise, and will bring to nothing the understanding of the prudent.
20 Where is the wise? where is the scribe? where is the disputer of this world? hath not God made foolish the wisdom of this world?
21 For after that in the wisdom of God the world by wisdom knew not God, it pleased God by the foolishness of preaching to save them that believe.
22 For the Jews require a sign, and the Greeks seek after wisdom:
23 But we preach Christ crucified, unto the Jews a stumblingblock, and unto the Greeks foolishness;

24 But unto them which are called, both Jews and Greeks, Christ the power of God, and the wisdom of God.
25 Because the foolishness of God is wiser than men; and the weakness of God is stronger than men.
26 For ye see your calling, brethren, how that not many wise men after the flesh, not many mighty, not many noble, are called:
27 But God hath chosen the foolish things of the world to confound the wise; and God hath chosen the weak things of the world to confound the things which are mighty;
28 And base things of the world, and things which are despised, hath God chosen, yea, and things which are not, to bring to nought things that are:
29 That no flesh should glory in his presence.
30 But of him are ye in Christ Jesus, who of God is made unto us wisdom, and righteousness, and sanctification, and redemption:
31 That, according as it is written, He that glorieth, let him glory in the Lord.

1. *The Word of the Cross* (1:18-29). In the face of division Paul brings the message (*logos* or "word") of the Cross. In it is the heart of the Christian revelation, and it deserves our closest attention.

What did Paul mean by the "word of the cross" (NASB)? It was not, for him, a matter of theological argument concerning a heavenly transaction. He was too close to the Crucifixion for that. It was, rather, a matter of experience. He was humiliated by his own former persecution of the followers of Jesus—a tragic error. Unlimited implications were involved in his encounter with Christ on the Damascus road. Where before he looked upon the Cross as a curse, now he saw it as carrying out the redemptive work of God (cf. Gal. 3:13).

a. The Cross is the touchstone of man's destiny (18). It is to the "word of the cross" that Paul calls the church at Corinth. It is central and fundamental to everything else he has to say. He is not willing to answer their questions until he has built a sure foundation: "God was in Christ, reconciling the world unto himself" (2 Cor. 5:19).

It was this gospel of the "glowing heart" that he preached to them—the gospel they so gladly received.

It is by the Cross that we stand or fall. "To those who are perishing" it is utter foolishness, but to those "who are being saved it is the power of God" (NASB).

Paul without apology divides humanity into two categories: the "lost" and the "saved" (cf. John 3:18). Those saved by Christ see in the Cross the redemptive act of God, graciously making possible their salvation (cf. 2 Cor. 2:15).

b. The Cross is the sole instrument of salvation (19-21). Paul calls the Old Testament to his defense when he quotes Isa. 29:14. He continues in v. 20 to challenge the "wise" of every class to disprove his thesis on "the word of the cross." He includes both the Greek sophist and the Jewish scribe. His argument here parallels the first three chapters of Romans, where he argues the powerlessness of man apart from the righteousness of God. It is impossible through human wisdom to come to a knowledge of God.

Kierkegaard expressed it beautifully: "The genius is what he is by reason of himself; an apostle is what he is by divine authority."[10]

c. The Cross is the infinite wisdom of God (22-29). The tragedy of the world's sin is that it has inverted divine values. What the world usually despises, God can use. What the world calls *foolishness,* God has transformed into divine *wisdom.* Man cannot save himself. And so, Paul builds his argument toward the all-sufficiency of Christ in vv. 30-31.

(1) The futile quest of the unredeemed (22-23). The Jews were asking for external *signs* to authenticate Christ's kingly power. The Greeks sought *wisdom* (dialectical skill) from anyone who aspired to be their teacher. Thus the Cross became a stumbling block to the Jew who could not fit it into his Messianic expectations, and folly to the Greek who could not accept as Lord one who was crucified.

(2) Divine insight to those who trust in Christ (24-26). Paul uses a paradox to drive the truth home to the believer. The very issue which the Jews and the Greeks could not make compatible with their understanding of God and His ways, he identified as both the "power" and

"wisdom" of God (24). To reach God through the Cross is utter folly to the unredeemed; but to those who have trusted in Christ, it is the pivotal fact of history.

And so it has ever been! God chooses the "foolish things of the world to shame the wise" (27, NASB). He uses the weak to confound the strong. This has always been His strategy.

One is often amazed at the insights of some who, though lacking formal education, are sensitive to the movings of the Spirit. The Spirit of truth leads them into "all truth"—even the truth that is Jesus Christ. Their simplicity is the opening door to godly wisdom.

What a marvelous thing it would be if we could recover the "wonder" of apostolic days. "The cross was Christ's way of conquest." It cut new ravines in history and captured the minds of men in a way totally unexpected by either Jew or Greek. As Wendland says, "The foolishness of God is indeed the true wisdom; . . . the weakness of God is indeed the true power of God."

The action of God on the Cross is how God acts. "The crucifixion is not God at his weakest, but God at his best."[12]

(3) The call to humility (26, 29). It has already been suggested that Paul counseled humility in the face of the Cross as one of the solutions to factionalism. In vv. 26 and 29 he asks what ground the Corinthians have for boasting. They are "nobodies." Not many of them are wise (kata sarka, according to the flesh or worldly standards). Not many are mighty (dunatoi, prominent people of power). Not many are of noble birth. It is against this background that Paul portrays the redemptive activity of God.

*From the cross of Calvary shineth the Light of
    Life so free.
Sinner, "Look and live," saith He; pardon is
    offered to thee.*

Why will you perish? He took your place,
  cancelled the debt for Adam's race.
Mercy's door is still ajar; come to Him just as you
  are.

—DAVID LIVINGSTONE IVES

2. *The Cross suggests the sole sufficiency of Christ* (30-31). "By His doing you are in Christ Jesus" (NASB). The whole Source of our life, both natural and spiritual, is in God. Our existence is from Him. Our salvation is His doing, not ours. He initiates, we respond. Our conversion is thus not of ourselves, it is of God. It is not because we are "wise," or better, or more diligent, or "noble." It is because He loves us, calls us, converts us. Here is the touchstone of evangelical theology: our salvation is from God, not of ourselves.

a. We are in Christ through Him. "You are in Christ Jesus by God's act" (30*a*, NEB). To be in Christ is to be united to Him as a branch to the vine (John 15:1-7), as the body to the head (John 12:12-27). This union is achieved consciously by faith (Rom. 8:1).

b. Christ is "all in all" (30*b*). The substantives "righteousness," "sanctification," and "redemption" are not correlatives of wisdom. They are aspects of the *wisdom* which the believer finds in Christ. The NIV translates it: "It is because of him that you are in Christ Jesus, who has become for us wisdom from God—that is, our righteousness, holiness, and redemption."

Christ is our *Righteousness*. It is by His sole merits that we are pardoned and accepted of God. When we stand before the judgment seat of God, Christ will answer for us. "I have suffered the loss of all things, and do count them but dung," Paul says, "that I may win Christ, and be found in him, not having mine own righteousness, which is of the law, but that which is through the faith of Christ, the righteousness which is of God by faith" (Phil. 3:8-9).

He is indeed our *Sanctification.* His Spirit is transforming us into His likeness "from glory to glory" (2 Cor. 3:18; see Acts 26:18; Rom. 8:9-10; Gal. 5:22; Eph. 2:5, 10; Heb. 12:14).

He is our *Redemption* as well. He is our Deliverer from evil—from guilt, sin, and hell. In certain contexts redemption has an eschatological meaning, referring to our final salvation. On the "day" of Christ He will bring about a "perfect salvation" for the people of God, for both soul and body (cf. Rom. 8:23; Eph. 1:14; 4:30; Heb. 9:12). Then we will be delivered completely from the evils of sin and introduced to the "glorious liberty of the children of God."

These marvelous blessings are all in Christ. Union with Him is the imperative—the necessary condition of our participation in these blessings. No, it is not of ourselves. Not by our own wisdom, strength, nobility, or goodness—but solely through His "grace" which makes possible even our trusting in Him. Christ is "all in all."

c. Our boasting can be only in Him (31). The end of God in bestowing all things upon the believer in Christ is that we may not claim any merit to ourselves, but will give God all the praise. Paul quotes Jeremiah in supporting his position that God is to be exalted (Jer. 9:23-24).

This runs counter to our human tendencies. Everything points to man's praise rather than God's. However, Paul observes that the heart of redemption points to the redemptive action of God in love in the face of man's sin. Our ability to choose is in Him by grace, our freedom is His gift. There is no boasting in our own ability.

It is a great thing that in our day celebration has become the center of worship, along with confession. Praise changes things! Paul believed it could change the Corinthians, and it can change us! When we catch the tragedy of our sinfulness and the picture of God's grace, then we are in a position to partake of His fullness. Praise be to God!

The Character of Christian Ministry

1 Corinthians 2:1-5

> 1 And I, brethren, when I came to you, came not with excellency of speech or of wisdom, declaring unto you the testimony of God.
> 2 For I determined not to know any thing among you, save Jesus Christ, and him crucified.
> 3 And I was with you in weakness, and in fear, and in much trembling.
> 4 And my speech and my preaching was not with enticing words of man's wisdom, but in demonstration of the Spirit and of power:
> 5 That your faith should not stand in the wisdom of men, but in the power of God.

The true character of Christian ministry is found in v. 2: "For I determined to know nothing among you except Jesus Christ, and him crucified" (cf. Gal. 6:14; 1 Cor. 1:23). Paul's only design in going to Corinth was to proclaim that "Christ died for our sins" (15:3). He was determined to keep the gospel out of the realm of Greek philosophy, Jewish legalism, and the oriental mystery religions. *Christ crucified* was the sum of the gospel. In this particular passage is found the character of Christian ministry.

1. *A decisive tone of personal conviction* (1-2). Paul's message was "the testimony of God" (1). He was not concerned about the preacher as much as he was the "word" (cf. 1:18). There is a note of irony in his opening words. He came not with "excellency of speech" or of presumed "wisdom," as the Corinthians had interpreted some who preached, but with a simplicity of utterance which was both "testimony" and "wisdom" (6-7). "The gospel was both the message to which the apostles bore witness and the divine revelation, previously concealed which they made known."[13] No wonder it bore a decisive tone of personal conviction.

2. *A selfless spirit* (2). "I determined not to know any-

thing." He emptied himself of all personal reference. He was not concerned about his future, his reputation, or his success. And this self-forgetfulness led to the source of his power. John the Baptist caught the spirit from Jesus when he said, "He must increase, but I must decrease." "That which is the temple of God must never have the marble polluted with the name of the architect or builder."[14]

Preacher, if you want to move men, speak convincingly of Christ rather than self and some will be kindled by the flame.

3. *A spirit of openness* (4-5). Openness of communication is indicative of life in the Spirit. Paul came not with any image (mask) to preserve. He came telling the truth in Christ. He came "in fear, and in much trembling" (3).

He came not with personal anxiety for his own safety, but with "the trembling anxiety to perform a duty." He came with a fluttering in the stomach for fear that he would not accomplish what he was ordained by God to accomplish. Every speaker knows that tremor—it is the "stuff" of greatness.

Paul depended not on "enticing words of man's wisdom, but in demonstration of the Spirit and of power" (4). What more can be said? Paul relied for success not on natural skill, but on the authenticating witness of the Spirit.

4. *A faith in the results* (5). It might have been easy for Paul to argue his case grounded in the superiority of the Christian over the pagan ethic. He was capable of doing so. He knew, however, that the conclusions might convince, but they could never bring saving faith.

A faith that is grounded on the authority of the church or addressed to the understanding alone is "unstable and inoperative." But a faith which seeks its foundation in the *demonstration of the Spirit* is "abiding, infallible, and works by love and purifies the heart."[15]

The True Wisdom of God

1 Corinthians 2:6-9

> 6 Howbeit we speak wisdom among them that are perfect: yet not the wisdom of this world, nor of the princes of this world, that come to nought:
> 7 But we speak the wisdom of God in a mystery, even the hidden wisdom, which God ordained before the world unto our glory:
> 8 Which none of the princes of this world knew: for had they known it, they would not have crucified the Lord of glory.
> 9 But as it is written, Eye hath not seen, nor ear heard, neither have entered into the heart of man, the things which God hath prepared for them that love him.

1. *That wisdom is not of this age* (6*b*). The wisdom that Paul speaks of is not "secular wisdom." Nor is it of the "rulers of this age" (RSV). It is not a wisdom controlled by a particular climate of thinking or education. That comes to naught. Its power is "doomed to pass away" (RSV).

Such thinking was not a rejection of reason, but a rebuke to those Corinthians who thought themselves to be equipped by the current philosophies and mystery cults to discern the wisdom of God. They really did not understand God's way of doing. Otherwise "they would not have crucified the Lord of Glory" (8).

2. *That wisdom is addressed to the mature* ("perfect," 6*a*). It is evident from Paul's words that some in the church had dismissed his message as elementary. Who are meant by the "perfect" *(teleioi)?* Is he speaking of advanced Christians as opposed to "babes in Christ" (3:1)? Is he speaking of the unbeliever as opposed to the believer? The contrast made is between the "wisdom of this world" and "the wisdom of God," and not between levels in the gospel. There is only one gospel, but levels of instruction as in c. 3.

In this context, he must have been speaking to the competent (mature)—"the people of God." He would not dismiss the mysteries of the faith as insights in incompetence, but God's way of declaring the gospel *(kerygma)*.

3. *It is the hidden wisdom of God, now revealed* (7-9). "That wisdom that came from God, once a covered secret,

but now uncovered" (Williams). There is an implied rebuke to arrogance in this passage. The revelation of God (the divine mystery) is the "word of the cross" (1:18, RSV). It is not what we have discovered but what God has revealed (cf. Eph. 3:2-12).

God in His infinite wisdom "predestined before the ages" (7, NASB) a plan "for our benefit." The *Amplified New Testament* translates 7*b* "for our glorification" (that is, to lift us into the glory of His presence).

Just think—God in His eternal knowledge and infinite wisdom ordained a plan for the glorifying of His people of God as "the climax of his saving purpose in the universe" (cf. Rom. 8:30). That plan was revealed in the Saviour crucified that we might attain through His Spirit a complete conformity to His will.

When Spirit Meets Spirit
1 Corinthians 2:10-16

> 10 But God hath revealed them unto us by his Spirit: for the Spirit searcheth all things, yea, the deep things of God.
>
> 11 For what man knoweth the things of a man, save the spirit of man which is in him? even so the things of God knoweth no man, but the Spirit of God.
>
> 12 Now we have received, not the spirit of the world, but the spirit which is of God; that we might know the things that are freely given to us of God.
>
> 13 Which things also we speak, not in the words which man's wisdom teacheth, but which the Holy Ghost teacheth; comparing spiritual things with spiritual.
>
> 14 But the natural man receiveth not the things of the Spirit of God: for they are foolishness unto him: neither can he know them, because they are spiritually discerned.
>
> 15 But he that is spiritual judgeth all things, yet he himself is judged of no man.
>
> 16 For who hath known the mind of the Lord, that he may instruct him? But we have the mind of Christ.

Until now Paul has mentioned the Spirit only occasionally, but at this point he begins to dwell on the Spirit's activities in the life of the Church as being instrumental to God's revealed wisdom.

1. *The words which the Spirit speaks in understanding* (10-12). The Spirit we receive is God's own Spirit which probes the "depths of God" (RSV). He knows what is in God as our spirit knows what is in us (11). Paul declares that the hidden wisdom of God is now made accessible through the Spirit to all believers.

It is the Spirit who communicates the truth about God (10). It is the Spirit who reveals the meaning of the gospel (12). It is the Spirit who convinces the hearer of the truth of the gospel (14). Those who are *in Christ* have received His Spirit "that we might know the things freely given to us by God" (12, NASB).

2. *The words which the Spirit speaks by comparative judgment* (13-16). The *words* which the man in Christ knows by the Spirit, he also communicates. These words are taught not by human wisdom but by the Spirit, clothing "spiritual thoughts with spiritual words." That is, the believer in Christ explains the things of the Spirit in the *words* of the Spirit.

Secular words are not the manner of spiritual speaking. The Holy Spirit himself will provide the words for spiritual speaking. Paul characteristically explains the issue and defines the matter by an antithesis between the *natural man* and the *spiritual man.*

a. *The natural man* (14). The natural man is the man who lives as though there is nothing beyond physical life. He is the secularist who assumes there is nothing beside human and material standards. A man like this cannot understand spiritual matters. He is blinded to the spiritual life. He is without God, the very Source of spiritual life. He is *psychikos* (that is, cannot transcend his own "psyche").

It is easy to fall back into the life from which we were rescued, to become so involved in the world that we believe there is nothing but this world. A man like that cannot understand the things of the Spirit of God.

b. *The spiritual man* (15-16). But there is also the

man that is *spiritual (pneumatikos)*. He is sensitive and obedient to the Spirit. His perspective sees an "other world" as well as "this world." He is guided by the Spirit and responds wholeheartedly to the rebuke of the Spirit.

The man who is *spiritual* discerns the things of the Spirit, though he is not understood by the *natural* man. His is the ability to judge what is true and good. He possesses spiritual insight inspired by the Spirit. "The right of private judgment in matters of religion is inseparable from the indwelling of the Spirit."[16] This is perfectly compatible with the subjection of the believer to his brethren, which Paul will later discuss in 5:9-12; 12:13; and Gal. 6:1.

3. *The words of the Spirit define the mind of Christ* (2:16). Hodge treats v. 16 syllogistically:

> No one can instruct the Lord.
> We have the mind of the Lord.
> Therefore, no one can instruct us.

It can be put another way. The Old Testament title *Adonai* (LXX, "Lord") is given to Christ (*kurios,* "Lord") in the New Testament. We have the *mind of Christ* because we have the *mind of the Lord* through His Spirit. "The same person who is revealed in the New Testament as the Son of God, was revealed in the Old as Yahweh (JHYH). This teaches how firm a foundation the believer has for his faith, and how impossible it is for any one taught by the Spirit to give up his convictions to the authority of men."[17]

What a bold statement! *We have the mind of Christ.* It does not mean that we know all that Christ knows. It does not mean that we understand all His thoughts. But it does mean (as the "knowledge of God" in the Old Testament meant an intimate communion) that the mind of Christ can bring us so close to Him through His Spirit until we see things in faith through His eyes. We are His men!

Men of Flesh

1 Corinthians 3:1-4

> 1 And I, brethren, could not speak unto you as unto spiritual, but as unto carnal, even as unto babes in Christ.
> 2 I have fed you with milk, and not with meat: for hitherto ye were not able to bear it, neither yet now are ye able.
> 3 For ye are yet carnal: for whereas there is among you envying, and strife, and divisions, are ye not carnal, and walk as men?
> 4 For while one saith, I am of Paul; and another, I am of Apollos; are ye not carnal?

Paul has preached the great goal of faith in Christ to the Corinthians. He knows that the highest expression of that commitment in the Spirit is necessary for their personal fulfillment. But they have fallen short of that goal. He now turns to a consideration of their failures and points out two main reasons why they have failed:

1. *They are carnally minded* (1, 3). The Corinthians are displaying a divisive spirit which is a product of their carnal-mindedness. They are lacking in mutual forbearance, sincerity, and humility. While they are recipients of the Spirit, the Corinthians still to some degree manifest the works of the flesh. The old self-life continues to corrupt their Christian existence and witness.

F. F. Bruce states the problem most succinctly, that carnal-mindedness should "persist in men who have received his Spirit is part of the paradox which finds expression in Paul's repeated injunctions to his readers to be what they are—to be in practical conduct what they are by divine calling as members of Christ" (saints by calling).[18]

2. *They are spiritually immature* (1-2). Paul urges the Corinthians to "grow up." He calls them "babes in Christ," unfit for "solid food" (NASB). This worldly and immature attitude is made obvious in their spirit and factionalism.

a. There is envying *(zelos)* and strife *(eris,* 3). Both of these are included in the works of the flesh in Gal. 5:20 (cf. 2 Cor. 12:20). While *eris* is always bad, *zelos* may be interpreted "zeal" (cf. 2 Cor. 7:7; 9:2; 11:2). But in this case it is associated with a competitive spirit. *Strife* speaks for itself ("squabbling," Phillips). Both jealousy and strife have led to self-assertion and unhealthy rivalries.

b. There are party divisions and wranglings (3-4). While there are four parties, Paul confines himself to a discussion of two. Since the problem of party spirit arose because of the perversion of a minister's function in the church, Paul immediately presented a corrective (5-9).

Factionalism and group antipathies are the denial of spirituality—the proof of spiritual infantilism ("babes in Christ"). How strange it is in the course of church history that intolerant, cantankerous sectarians have been notorious in their claims to spiritual superiority!

Claiming a high degree of sanctity, Christians have many times conducted themselves as *carnal* rather than Spirit-filled disciples of Christ. When onlookers can say, "I see no difference," Christians deny the very profession they make.

Spinoza, the Dutch philosopher, once asked sarcastically why Christians differed from others, not in love or joy or peace, or in the fruit of the Spirit, but only in theological opinions.

It is because this condition is far too current that the relationship of ministry to the church is so important. The key is in the hand of the minister. Paul deals with the issue autobiographically in vv. 5-9.

Like People, like Priest

1 Corinthians 3:5-9

5 Who then is Paul, and who is Apollos, but ministers by whom ye believed, even as the Lord gave to every man?
6 I have planted, Apollos watered; but God gave the increase.

7 So then neither is he that planteth any thing, neither he that watereth; but God that giveth the increase.

8 Now he that planteth and he that watereth are one: and every man shall receive his own reward according to his own labour.

9 For we are labourers together with God: ye are God's husbandry, ye are God's building.

1. *The corrective to a party spirit* (5-8). A minister is never an end within himself, but a servant, a trustee, a messenger, a herald of the gospel. While he is necessary, that necessity is always instrumental to the chief end—the propagation of "the word of the cross." It is thus completely out of order to make any of the ministers, including Peter, the head of a party. Both Paul and Apollos are simply ministers (*diakonoi,* Luke 22:25-27). They are waiters, attendants, servants, both to Christ whose gospel they bear and the Church to whom they belong and whom they serve.

The only service worth mentioning is that which builds upon the foundation of Jesus Christ—His person and work as well as His spirit, character, and purpose. "Other foundation can no man lay" (10-15). How much nobler than the later creeds is the first: "Jesus is Lord" (Rom. 10:9)!

2. *The differing functions in the unity of God* (6-9b). "Diversity in unity" is the law of God's working. We see it time and time again in Paul's writings. Ministers have different gifts: "I have planted, Apollos watered." But both are merely instrumental; it is God who "causes the growth" (NASB). And while the minister has his reward, his work is always judged by the way it builds on the true Foundation.

There are many pastors, missionaries, and teachers who labor without any seeming reward. Paul promises a reward which is *his own* (8). The rule of reward is not grounded in a man's talents but in his labor. This brings all men to a common ground before the Cross. Each must answer for himself in proportion to his fidelity to Christ and the gospel.

The Temple of God

1 Corinthians 3:10-17

> 10 According to the grace of God which is given unto me, as a wise masterbuilder, I have laid the foundation, and another buildeth thereon. But let every man take heed how he buildeth thereupon.
> 11 For other foundation can no man lay than that is laid, which is Jesus Christ.
> 12 Now if any man build upon this foundation gold, silver, precious stones, wood, hay, stubble;
> 13 Every man's work shall be made manifest: for the day shall declare it, because it shall be revealed by fire; and the fire shall try every man's work of what sort it is.
> 14 If any man's work abide which he hath built thereupon, he shall receive a reward.
> 15 If any man's work shall be burned, he shall suffer loss: but he himself shall be saved; yet so as by fire.
> 16 Know ye not that ye are the temple of God, and that the Spirit of God dwelleth in you?
> 17 If any man defile the temple of God, him shall God destroy; for the temple of God is holy, which temple ye are.

1. *The only service which has permanent worth is that which is in and for Jesus Christ.* No other loyalty can support the weight of the structure of the church. The warning to teachers is given in v. 10: "I laid a foundation and another is building upon it. But let each man be careful how he builds upon it" (NASB). There are two ways that a teacher can go wrong:

a. He can tamper with the *foundation* of the temple. "No man can lay a foundation other than one which is laid, which is Jesus Christ" (11, NASB). This metaphor is important when one remembers Peter's confession of the "Christ of God" (Mark 8:29). Was Paul asserting the centrality of Christ in His Church, or was he speaking of a particular error which threatened the Corinthian church? In one sense, Peter is represented as the true foundation of the church, though he was only "the primary bearer of the testimony on which the church rests." Later, all "the apostles and prophets," as primary witnesses to Christ, are represented as the foundation of God's temple (Eph. 2:20). Here, however, Paul is speaking of Christ himself—His life, death, and resurrection—as the Foundation. We dare not tamper with the Foundation!

b. He can use inferior materials in the *superstructure* of the temple (12-13). Paul speaks of two kinds of building materials: "Gold, silver, precious stones," and "wood, hay, stubble." The first category represents basic truths of the gospel. It is inferred that others had used inferior materials which would not stand in that day "because it shall be revealed by fire" (13).

The common house was made of wood, hay, and stubble. Paul carries the metaphor to its conclusion, probably remembering a fire that swept the city consuming the inferior buildings, but not destroying the temple made of gold, silver, and precious stones.

2. *The revelation of every man's work* (13-15).

a. Paul suspects that some are not building well and warns them of the day of judgment (13). In this life there may be a question as to the truth of a man's position, but in that day the truth of a man's work shall be revealed by fire, "and the fire itself will test the quality of each man's work" (13, NASB).

b. The rewards (14-15). There is a reward to those who build well, but loss to those who build with inferior materials.

On the day of judgment, if the materials stand the test, the laborer will receive the reward of his servantship. If his work cannot stand the test, he will find himself the loser.

c. Loss in the face of gain (15). Paul speaks of the salvation of those who build upon the true Foundation, but lose because of inferior workmanship (15). "Though he himself shall be saved, but only as through fire" (RSV) is admittedly a difficult verse to interpret. However, it does not speak either of eternal security or purgatory. The work which will be burned will be that of the servant who has not built solidly on the gospel.

It is plain from v. 12, "if any man shall build upon this foundation," that Paul is speaking of those teachers who have combined truth with error. It is not enough that a teacher should hold fast to the truth of Christ; he should also take care that he faithfully *teaches* "the truth as it is is Jesus." While he will be saved because of his personal faith in Christ, he may suffer great loss as a "man pulled to safety through the smoke and flames of his burning house . . . [for] his salvation depends on God's grace, not on his own works; but he would have nothing to show for all his labor."[19]

Milton's great lines ring as a tocsin in the ears of those who will listen:

The hungry sheep look up, and are not fed,
But, swoln with wind and the rank mist they
*   draw,*
Rot inwardly, and the foul contagion spread;
Beside what the grim wolf, with privy paw,
Daily devours apace, and nothing said.
But that two-handed engine at the door
Stands ready to smite once, and smite no more.[20]

3. *The holy temple: a justification for personal responsibility* (16-17). "Do ye not know . . . ?" (16, NASB) implies that they ought to have known. What has been discussed before now climaxes in a superlative affirmation. "You are God's temple and . . . God's Spirit dwells in you . . ." (16, RSV). The temple is not made with materials other than that which glorifies God through faith and obedience.

The Corinthians are reminded that with the indwelling Spirit of God, it is imperative that their building be compatible with its Foundation. When the Spirit is present within, seeing and hearing all things, it is absolutely necessary that the *temple* (body of believers) be *holy* (17).

Every believer is a member of the corporate temple of God. Any profaning of the *temple* is an offence against God and a sacrilege to the Holy Spirit who dwells in the Church. It is no wonder that Paul speaks out against quarreling and a party spirit which defile God's temple. Paul is not soft on those who would undermine the temple of God, but warns them of "destruction" to come by God himself.

The reasoning of Paul is apparent. God's temple is holy. You are that temple. Therefore, you must be holy. When one stops to remember that every one who confesses the name of Christ is a part of His temple, the Church, it places an awesome responsibility as well as a blessed privilege on that believer to walk holy and blameless before Him.

All Things Are Yours

The discussion of wisdom and folly comes to a close (though it will be illustrated and picked up in chapter 4 and then in 6:5; 8:1 ff.; 10:15; 12:8; and 13:8-12). Paul has shown the foolishness of a party spirit. He moves quickly to a conclusion and in the last two verses of the chapter is "carried away" in the wonder of a Christian's relationship to God in Christ.

1 Corinthians 3:18-23

> 18 Let no man deceive himself. If any man among you seemeth to be wise in this world, let him become a fool, that he may be wise.
> 19 For the wisdom of this world is foolishness with God. For it is written, He taketh the wise in their own craftiness.
> 20 And again, The Lord knoweth the thoughts of the wise, that they are vain.
> 21 Therefore let no man glory in men. For all things are yours;
> 22 Whether Paul, or Apollos, or Cephas, or the world, or life, or death, or things present, or things to come; all are yours;
> 23 And ye are Christ's; and Christ is God's.

1. *A self-delusion* (18-21). The Corinthian church was too much in love with "this world." Paul saw the real danger of substituting the wisdom of this world for the truth of God. They were in danger of self-delusion.

The imperative of v. 18 is graphically expressed: "Let him become a fool that he may be wise." Let a man renounce his own wisdom that he may accept God's wisdom. Our own righteousness, strength, and wisdom are worthless in God's sight. Paul is declaring that we must empty ourselves in order to be filled with the wisdom, righteousness, and strength of God in Christ. To take God's wisdom we must rid ourselves of any assumed self-adequacy, which is the heart of sin.

The infinite mind of God sees only folly in the wisdom of this world. The world believes the saving cross of Christ to be foolishness. It must then follow that the wisdom of this world is foolishness with God (2:19-20, 27). There are two reasons why this is true: (1) Wisdom may be said to be "folly" when it is used for wrong ends, and (2) much which passes for wisdom is indeed utter foolishness.

Both of these ideas are comprehended in v. 19. The knowledge of man is entirely inadequate to save men, and the speculations of men are utterly foolish in probing "the deep things of God." "Therefore let no man glory in men. For all things are yours." Or, let no man "repose his confidence" (Knox) in men, "for everything belongs to you" (Phillips).

The Corinthians rested their confidence in men rather than God. They followed after human teachers rather than the "Spirit of truth." They forgot their own dignity as believers in following others, forgetting that all things were theirs in Christ.

2. *A superlative promise—"all things are yours"* (22-23). These words are to be taken in the widest sense. The universe and all that is in it is yours. The people of God must not be unmindful of their heritage. All that is, is for the Church. That is why the actions of the Corinthians were full of folly. They were called to great promise, and they were sacrificing that inheritance for "pottage." All things are given to Christ, the Head of the Church, and to the body through Him. Paul is solicitous that the foundation and structure of the temple of God should not be profaned with inferior construction. Too much was at stake.

Paul is so concerned that he repeats his appeal in v. 22. Here is the climax of his argument: All is yours, so why waste your time serving a world which deals in foolishness? What difference does it make whether it is of Apollos, Cephas, or Paul "or life, or death, or things present, or things to come"? Why? Because all things belong to you, and you belong to Christ; and Christ belongs to God.

Nothing more can be said. The apostle has reached the limit of his argument. His mind, under the inspiring word of Christ, has soared beyond finite reason. The mysteries of God's wisdom defy man's definition.

> *When thou hast thanked thy God*
> *For every blessing sent,*
> *What time will then remain*
> *For murmurs or lament?*
> —R. C. TRENCH

1 CORINTHIANS 4

Stewards of the Mysteries of God

Paul has completed his formal criticism of the four parties in the Corinthian church (cc. 1—3). He now turns to the nature of Christian ministry—what it ought to be! What he says about Apollos and himself is intended to apply to all ministers. The description that Paul gives is a plea for trust and respect.

1 Corinthians 4:1-5

> 1 Let a man so account of us, as of the ministers of Christ, and stewards of the mysteries of God.
> 2 Moreover it is required in stewards, that a man be found faithful.
> 3 But with me it is a very small thing that I should be judged of you, or of man's judgment: yea, I judge not mine own self.
> 4 For I know nothing by myself; yet am I not hereby justified: but he that judgeth me is the Lord.
> 5 Therefore judge nothing before the time, until the Lord come, who both will bring to light the hidden things of darkness, and will make manifest the counsels of the hearts: and then shall every man have praise of God.

1. *Ministers are the servants of Christ* (1a). Again and again Paul will remind us that ministers are servants. While they are servants of the people, their first loyalty must be to Christ. *Servant,* as a word, has no significance in itself. The work that is done is not his, but the master's. The claims of the apostolic ministry turned on the fact

that there was no preference for self, pointing consistently to Christ.

The word translated "ministers" is not the usual *diakonoi* (3:5), but *hupēretas* (used only here). It originally described an "under-rower," that is, one who rowed in the lower bank of oars on a large ship. It came to mean "menial" service, but not always so.

The striking point was that Paul meant for the Corinthians to understand that the idea of entire subjection was to be retained. Ministers are the servants of Christ. Their authority is in Him. It is their business to stay so close to the Lord through His Spirit that they will consistently obey His commands.

2. *Ministers are stewards of the mysteries of God* (1*b*). It is as "dispensers" or directors of the household that ministers are called "stewards of the mysteries of God."

The mysteries are neither the sacraments nor the ordinances of the Church, but the truths of God's revelation. These truths are not discoverable through human reason and therefore are hid to man apart from the divine revelation. Yet they are truths (mysteries) into which men must be initiated. The mystery of God is the gospel (c. 2), and the true minister of God is primarily a steward of that gospel.

Ministers have no arbitrary power in the Church. Neither do they have any supernatural power endowed through the Church. Their function is that of a witness—one who represents another—even the Lord Jesus Christ.

3. *As stewards, ministers are to be found faithful* (2). The great demand on the servant of God is that he be a man of fidelity.

He must be faithful in "feeding the flock." He cannot adulterate nor substitute inferior goods for what has been given to him to dispense.

The simile is obvious. A minister as Christ's faithful servant must not arrogate powers to himself which are not his. Neither must he be less than true to the people he serves. Metz concludes his commentary on this passage by writing, "When all is said and done, the main requirement for a man who teaches or preaches is faithfulness to God and to the truth. Not eloquence in words, not brilliance in thinking, not magnetism in appearance—but day-by-day faithfulness is the demand."

4. *In the end, the minister is judged not by men, but by God* (3-5). The apostle is still sensitive (13) to the slander he has suffered at the hands of the Corinthians and particularly the charge of incompetence. Subtly he declares his authority as their pastor. He will not be judged by "any human court" (3, NASB). Neither is he his own judge. And while he was not *aware* of anything against himself, yet it is the Lord who will examine, and it is the Lord who will judge (5).

a. The Lord will reveal light from darkness (5). Since the Lord is the only Judge, we must await His appearance and neither assume His prerogative nor anticipate his decision. We are not to judge anything before the appropriate time *(kairos)*. That time is indicated in the next clause— "until the Lord come." He will do what we cannot do. "He will bring to light the things hidden in the darkness" (5, NASB). He will reveal the wickedness now *hidden*.

b. The Lord will disclose the motives of men's hearts (5*b*). He alone can discern the motives ("counsels") of men. Paul is reflecting the burden of the Sermon on the Mount which internalizes the Christian ethic. He will judge the heart and conscience as well as the act. "Paul appealed from the fallible judgment of shortsighted men to the infallible judgment of his omniscient Lord."

c. Each man's praise will come from God rather than man (5). While Paul will recognize the right and duty of the church to sit in judgment on the qualifications of her own members, he is now speaking of the "heart" which the church cannot judge.

Whether a minister is genuine or spurious, sincere or hypocritical, only God can judge. And the praise that the

minister deserves will come at the time of the *parousia.*
It may not come now—but God's promise is that it will
come then!

An Audacious Claim

Only Paul had the audacity to say, "Wherefore I beseech you, be ye followers of me" (16). It is the climax of
his final appeal in c. 4. In 11:1 he will repeat the appeal.
"Be imitators of me, just as I also am of Christ" (NASB).
It is not a note of arrogance, but a moving appeal to the
church to move toward the One whom Paul follows—the
Lord Jesus Christ.

1 Corinthians 4:6-21

> 6 And these things, brethren, I have in a figure transferred to myself
> and to Apollos for your sakes; that ye might learn in us not to think of
> men above that which is written, that no one of you be puffed up for
> one against another.
> 7 For who maketh thee to differ from another? and what hast thou that
> thou didst not receive? now if thou didst receive it, why dost thou
> glory, as if thou hadst not received it?
> 8 Now ye are full, now ye are rich, ye have reigned as kings without us:
> and I would to God ye did reign, that we also might reign with you.
> 9 For I think that God hath set forth us the apostles last, as it were ap-
> pointed to death: for we are made a spectacle unto the world, and to
> angels, and to men.
> 10 We are fools for Christ's sake, but ye are wise in Christ; we are
> weak, but ye are strong; ye are honourable, but we are despised.
> 11 Even unto this present hour we both hunger, and thirst, and are
> naked, and are buffeted, and have no certain dwellingplace;
> 12 And labour, working with our own hands: being reviled, we bless;
> being persecuted we suffer it:
> 13 Being defamed, we intreat: we are made as the filth of the world,
> and are the offscouring of all things unto this day.
> 14 I write not these things to shame you, but as my beloved sons I
> warn you.
> 15 For though ye have ten thousand instructors in Christ, yet have ye
> not many fathers: for in Christ Jesus I have begotten you through the
> gospel.
> 16 Wherefore I beseech you, be ye followers of me.
> 17 For this cause have I sent unto you Timotheus, who is my beloved
> son, and faithful in the Lord, who shall bring you into remembrance of
> my ways which be in Christ, as I teach every where in every church.
> 18 Now some are puffed up, as though I would not come to you.
> 19 But I will come to you shortly, if the Lord will, and will know, not the
> speech of them which are puffed up, but the power.
> 20 For the kingdom of God is not in word, but in power.
> 21 What will ye? shall I come unto you with a rod, or in love, and in the
> spirit of meekness?

1. *Irony and pathos* (6-14)

a. The church was not to think of her ministers more highly than the word authorized them to think (6; comp. Jer. 9:23-24).

Paul was deathly afraid of arrogance in relationship to the status of teachers in the church. What he had said about Apollos and himself was also true for the Corinthians. Barclay remarks that "there was always a wonderful courtesy of Paul. He had a way of including himself in his own warnings and his own condemnations." His form of communication was a *we* rather than a *you.* He shared with them rather than looking down upon them. His judgments had a persistent way of including himself.

It was to this end that the Corinthians were not to be "puffed up for one against the other" (6). They were not to be arrogant as students of a particular teacher. Their spirit was to be a spirit of humility.

b. The church was to judge itself by comparison with its true ministers (7-16). Paul begins wistfully and builds his irony to words of flame. He begins with a quiet reproach concerning favorites (6), but rapidly moves to a biting criticism of those who would assume any superiority in judgment (7). "For who maketh thee to differ from another?" A man has nothing in himself, but is a debtor to God's grace. Cyprian remarked that we must glory in nothing because there is nothing of our own.

So in vv. 8-10, Paul with biting irony shows how they are not what they assume themselves to be. "We are fools . . . but ye are wise. We are weak, but ye are strong; ye are honorable, but we are despised." They were acting as though they were already reigning with Christ (8, cf. Luke 22:29-30; Rev. 20:4). This was not a time to *reign* with Christ, it was a time to *suffer* with Him (1 Thess. 3:4). The people of God were still living between the Resurrection and the Second Coming.

While Paul was ironical to the point of sarcasm, he was not bitter. He hoped to shame the church into seeing their proper role as Christians and as members of the community of Christ.

Paul continues by contrasting the self-sufficiency of the Corinthians with the lot of Apollos and himself. We are "poorly clothed and are roughly treated and are homeless" (11, NASB).

Notice the wonderful antitheses of vv. 12-13. When "we toil . . . [and] are reviled, we bless; when we are persecuted, we endure; when we are slandered, we try to conciliate; we have become as the scum of the world" (NASB).

c. The church was to imitate Paul, not as tutor but as father (15-16). Paul was entitled to warn them as a father in Christ. He contrasts his place as a spiritual father with that of "ten thousand instructors in Christ." His relation preceded that of the instructor and was more intimate.

As a spiritual father in Christ, he pleads with them to follow his example. That is, he is not arguing his case against Cephas and Apollos, but he has spoken of himself as humble, self-denying, and self-sacrificing (10-13) for the cause of Christ. Imitate me as I imitate Christ (16, cf. 11:1), he says.

There is a holy audacity about his exhortation to the Corinthians. And yet in the face of all that he had written before, it was an expression of humility rather than arrogance. He loved the church with an all-consuming affection. He was heartbroken over the condition. He knew that the wisdom of the world would not suffice. Only the "word of the cross" could penetrate the arrogance of the Corinthians' hearts. "It is the apostle's appeal to vicarious suffering. As we have seen, it possesses the greatest lifting power in the world: if that appeal fails, what other is likely to avail?"[21]

> *Love so amazing, so divine*
> *Demands my soul, my life, my all.*

2. *Exhortation and promise* (17-21). "In order that you may know what my life-style is and whether I am worthy to be followed, I am sending Timothy, who is my beloved son, and faithful in the Lord. He will be a faithful witness to these things" (see v. 17).

Paul closes the chapter with a promise to follow Timothy to Corinth (19), not in the "words of those who are arrogant," but in the power of the Spirit. "For the kingdom of God is not in word, but in power" (20).

Evidently there were those who said that Paul would never visit the city again. Paul made it clear that he would return. He looked at Corinth as MacArthur looked at Bataan. "I will return." But he made it crystal clear that when he came it would not be to listen to their wranglings, but to demonstrate the power of the Kingdom.

Kingsley G. Rendell calls our attention to the three *wills* in vv. 19-21: "I will" (19), "if the Lord will" (19), and "What will ye?" (21). Paul will come with a rod, or in love and in meekness (21). It is up to the Corinthians how he shall come. It is up to every man whether God acts in judgment or in mercy.

Postscript

William Baird, in a brilliant opening chapter in *The Corinthian Church—A Biblical Approach to Urban Culture,* concludes that "inordinate loyalty to leaders still divides the church. In some circles it is more important to ask what a certain leader says than to ask what is the truth of God's Word."

We cannot create "personality cults" around men either dead or alive, supposing that "no one else can do the work of God so effectively as he." Paul speaks directly to the issues of our urban church. The wisdom of God is never to be confused with the wisdom of men. Our plans and projects must always stand under the judgment of God.

Any unity we achieve will be with a spirit of humility, recognizing that oneness comes with diversity.

The church cannot become a "ladder of social success." It cannot become a "patron of prestige" or privilege (4:13; Isa. 53:3). "The urban church needs to be on its knees confessing its sin and acknowledging the grace of God." When God makes a people new, He unites them in a oneness so personal and so compelling that if one member suffers, we also suffer with him; and when another is honored, we rejoice with him (12:26).

Christian leaders deserve honor, and rightfully so; Paul was clear at this point. But the kind of loyalty that "goes wrong" is that which divides—which forgets that "all things are yours."

A loyalty that goes wrong focuses on man and is a "blurring of God." "The job of Christian leadership," says Baird, "is loyalty to the Almighty—a kind of loyalty wherein leaders become transparent to the work of God. This is why Jesus Christ is the 'pioneer and perfector of our faith' (Heb. 12:2); he always pointed away from himself to God (cf. Mark 10:18); 'All are yours; and ye are Christ's; and Christ is God's'" (3:22-23).[22]

Moral Standards and the Life of Faith
1 Corinthians 5:1—7:40

The "word of the cross" came by Paul to a sex-saturated society in Corinth. Sin of all kinds and descriptions had a free run in the city. Corinth's stream of commerce and her mystery religions with their lack of moral standards led to a pervasive antinomianism (morality is grounded in individual judgment). The result was that anything was right in the "eye of the beholder." While there were outstanding examples of individual holiness among the pagans, there were no continuing ethical mores which could guide and judge a person's conduct.

The Corinthian church was composed of men from many moral backgrounds. In 6:9-11 Paul lists all of the major sins of an urban society and then drives the truth home: "And such were some of you."

From this, Paul does not shrink. He is willing to give ethical counsels as the spiritual father of the fellowship. An Episcopalian bishop recently said that the mood of celebration must be accompanied with personal ethical responsibility. He continued by exhorting his priests to use the Word in declaring that the Christian faith is wedded to the Christian ethic.

God is holy, and He intends His Church to be pure, undefiled in faith and in life. When the Church loses its love and its ethic, it loses its power. Paul faced the problem head on in the Corinthian fellowship.

Whatever Happened to Church Discipline?

1 Corinthians 5:1-13

1 It is reported commonly that there is fornication among you, and such fornication as is not so much as named among the Gentiles, that one should have his father's wife.
2 And ye are puffed up, and have not rather mourned, that he that hath done this deed might be taken away from among you.
3 For I verily, as absent in body, but present in spirit, have judged already, as though I were present, concerning him that hath so done this deed,
4 In the name of our Lord Jesus Christ, when ye are gathered together, and my spirit, with the power of our Lord Jesus Christ,
5 To deliver such an one unto Satan for the destruction of the flesh, that the spirit may be saved in the day of the Lord Jesus.
6 Your glorying is not good. Know ye not that a little leaven leaveneth the whole lump?
7 Purge out therefore the old leaven, that ye may be a new lump, as ye are unleavened. For even Christ our passover is sacrificed for us:
8 Therefore let us keep the feast, not with old leaven, neither with the leaven of malice and wickedness; but with the unleavened bread of sincerity and truth.
9 I wrote unto you in an epistle not to company with fornicators:
10 Yet not altogether with the fornicators of this world, or with the covetous, or extortioners, or with idolaters; for then must ye needs go out of the world.
11 But now I have written unto you not to keep company, if any man that is called a brother be a fornicator, or covetous, or an idolater, or a railer, or a drunkard, or an extortioner; with such an one no not to eat.
12 For what have I to do to judge them also that are without? do not ye judge them that are within?
13 But them that are without God judgeth. Therefore put away from among yourselves that wicked person.

J. R. McQuilkin in *Christianity Today* has outlined the problem of incest that Paul faced in the church in regard to church discipline.[23]

It is significant that Paul demanded both unity and purity in the local congregation. Here is where the battle would be won or lost. It is in the local congregation where unity and purity must be achieved and preserved.

It is clear that the Bible teaches church discipline and outlines a pattern to be followed. How should discipline come? McQuilkin writes, "If that discipline or separation is of the wrong person, of the right person for the wrong reason, or of the right person for the right reason but in the wrong way," the Christian or the congregation is guilty of schism. What then is God's pattern?

1. *Who should be disciplined* (5:1)? In cc. 5 and 6, Paul faced a different problem than the divisions spoken of in cc. 1—4. A member of the Corinthian church was living in sin with his stepmother (5:1).

The New Testament teaches that persons who are guilty of overt, unrepented of, moral delinquency (5:1, 11) are to be disciplined by the church. It is important to notice that Paul is not speaking of one who fails in some sin of the spirit or who sins and repents, but "one who sins deliberately and continues without repentance." It is also important to notice that discipline is not subscribed for one who has doubts (Jude 22), but to one who is blatant in his sin, whether it be immorality or heresy (Gal. 1:6-9; 2 John 7-11).

2. *Why should one be disciplined* (3-5)? The primary and only reason for discipline in the church is to save and restore the transgressor to fellowship and his church (5:5; cf. 1 Tim. 1:19-20; 2 Thess. 3:13-15).

a. Discipline in the church is a means of restoration (5). Paul had determined to "deliver this man to Satan" (5, RSV). While he was "absent in body," he would be "present in spirit" at a congregational meeting called to excommunicate the offender. Evidently Paul's authority did not depend on his presence. It was a presence of "knowledge, authority, and power." He had *judged already* on the evidence presented to him (the sin was well known among the members of the church). He did this *in the name of Christ.* He acted as His representative.

The church was to *purge* itself both in the eyes of Christ and the city by excommunicating the offender. That cleansing was for one reason—"that the spirit may be saved in the day of the Lord Jesus" (5).

From earliest times, two different interpretations have been given to the phrase, "to deliver such an one to Satan"

(5): (1) To some it has meant excommunication; that is, separation from the church and its sacraments. (2) For others, it has meant a separation from the fellowship that the offender might be subjected to the person and powers of Satan. Not that the offender's flesh will be destroyed, but that his body be afflicted in order that his soul might be saved "in the day of the Lord Jesus" *(parousia).*

The latter interpretation is probably closer to the understanding of Paul. He was interested both in the health of the church and the offender's salvation. He was willing to risk the second in order to maintain the purity of fellowship. But he was also willing to take the risk in order to bring the offender back into the body of Christ by means of his chastisement. (Evidently Paul and the rest of the apostles were invested with the power to subject a man to Satan; cf. Acts 5:1-11; 13:9-11; 2 Cor. 10:8; 13:10; 1 Tim. 1:20.)

Paul's severe condemnation of the arrogance of the church in the face of immorality in its midst, "your glorying is not good," revealed how he recognized the manner in which evil could rapidly diffuse through the whole fellowship.

b. The challenge, then, is to "cleanse out the old leaven that you may be a new lump" (6, RSV). Here is a strong exhortation to purity. The leaven is said to be old ("evil"). The "old man" is the scriptural metaphor for our corrupt nature. The *new* man is the renewed man in Christ. Leaven is a figurative expression for sin. To say that the Corinthians were *unleaven* was to observe provisionally that they could be pure. The committed man in Christ is the *new* man made possible through "Christ our passover . . . sacrificed for us."

The death of Christ imposes upon us an obligation to purge out the "leaven" of sin, even as the Hebrews were required to purge the "old leaven" (old *lump*) from their houses (Exod. 12:15). Christ's death was a vicarious death for "all iniquity." Paul uses the example of sin in their midst to declare the need of cleansing and renewal in Christ's image.

3. *A current warning* (9-11). Paul, in vv. 9-11, does not speak of total separation from the world ("not altogether," 10), for he realized that such was impossible. He rather meant to separate from a brother in the fellowship who was guilty and unrepentant. He not only included the specific example, but also those who were fornicators, idolaters, railers, drunkards, extortioners, and coveters.

Our Lord ate with the "publicans and sinners," but He did not recognize them as His followers. Hodge concludes that "this is not a command to enforce the sentence of excommunication pronounced by the church, but a denial of social intercourse with the excommunicated." The command is that we not recognize sinful men as Christians.

What is the imperative to every one who confesses Christ as Lord? It is that those who emphasize "purity" must not be weak in love. And those who emphasize "celebration" must follow it with ethical responsibility. It is in biblical balance that spiritual maturity is made possible. McQuilkin writes that unfaithfulness can masquerade as love while it is actually compromise, sentimentality, and self-love. "They are unfaithful though they speak of much love."

Again, "unlove" can masquerade as faithfulness. Discipline can come from unlove under the disguise of faithfulness to the "standards of the church," creating schism for the wrong reasons. "Depart from evil and do good; seek peace and pursue it" (Ps. 34:14, NASB). Here is God's Word for our age in "speaking the truth in love" (Eph. 4:15). We cannot be found at the blessed *parousia* compromised, polluted, dismembered, grotesque, and impotent.

Paul's letter to the Corinthians (c. 5) carried a spirit of authority in severely disciplining the sinner in their midst, in chastening them for allowing it, and calling for a "purging of the lump."

Our prayer is that in these latter days our people will choose the way of the Cross in exercising discipline faithfully and choosing the welfare of another in love.

1 CORINTHIANS 6

Truths That Every Christian Should Know

The whole issue of the previous chapter brought the matter of relations with a secular society to a head. What does a church do when confronted by pagan practices? It cannot withdraw from the world. How shall it relate to a society to which it is inevitably a part?

Chapter 6 divides itself naturally into three divisions, each beginning with "Do ye not know . . . ?" or "Know ye not . . . ?" (2, 9, 19). Paul usually used the expression when he wanted to bring home an important truth—a truth which his readers knew but disregarded.

1 Corinthians 6:1-8

> 1 Dare any of you, having a matter against another, go to law before the unjust, and not before the saints?
> 2 Do ye not know that the saints shall judge the world? and if the world shall be judged by you, are ye unworthy to judge the smallest matters?
> 3 Know ye not that we shall judge angels? how much more things that pertain to this life?
> 4 If then ye have judgments of things pertaining to this life, set them to judge who are least esteemed in the church.
> 5 I speak to your shame. Is it so, that there is not a wise man among you? no, not one that shall be able to judge between his brethren?
> 6 But brother goeth to law with brother, and that before the unbelievers.
> 7 Now therefore there is utterly a fault among you, because ye go to law one with another. Why do ye not rather take wrong? why do ye not rather suffer yourselves to be defrauded?
> 8 Nay, ye do wrong, and defraud, and that your brethren.

1. *Indignities to the church* (1). The first problem dealt with litigations between church members. They were not criminal offenses, but property grievances (7-8). Paul

argues that the disputes should be settled within the Christian community and not taken before the courts. There was no necessity for the practice of taking civil suits before pagan judges. Christians must not be involved in the disgraceful spectacle of Christian suing Christian. The Rabbis said, "It is a statute which binds all Israelites, that if one Israelite has cause against another, it must not be prosecuted before the Gentiles."

"Dare any of you . . . ?" indicates the shocking sense of impropriety with which the apostle viewed the matter. To go before the *unrighteous* was absurd. That Christians should sue Christians without being able to resolve their own differences was beyond Paul's belief.

2. *Privileges which the Christians were ignoring* (2-6). Paul reminded the Corinthians that the saints *(hagioi) would judge the world and angels* (3). He had identified them as "saints" in 1:1; that is, they were members of the community of God and "sanctified" to His service. The pagans were not saints; therefore, they were of the world.

The context and spirit of the passage require that we think eschatologically rather than of the present order. Paul is not speaking of the time when the Christians might become magistrates, nor of the spirit of the Christian which would condemn the world. He is thinking of the future and final judgment at which time the saints will sit with Christ judging the unrighteous. Because Christ will judge, the Christians will judge with him (Eph. 2:6). They are associates of the Son of Man, the appointed Judge of the "living and the dead" (cf. Dan. 7:13; Matt. 16:27; John 5:27; Acts 17:31; etc.).

Thus, if you have "trivial" (2, RSV) matters, Paul said, why bring them before the *unjust?* Can't you, who will judge the world "in that day," settle your own personal disagreements? "Can it be that there is no man among you wise enough to decide between members of the brotherhood?" (RSV). Paul again resorts to a mild taunt in reminding the church of its responsibilities and privileges.

What was Paul really interested in? He was concerned that the breakdown of the *koinonia* (fellowship) not damage the witness of Christ and the church's service to the world. The Corinthians had showed their "dirty linen" to the world. They were taking their quarrels into public courts. Paul did not reprimand them for their problems— they were inevitable—but he did reprimand them for not keeping and settling the issues within the fellowship of Christ.

3. *The privilege and responsibility of standing in judgment upon the world* (2-3). We have previously defined the meaning of that *judgment*. It is important, once again, to notice that the Church is not an exclusive fellowship apart from the many who confess Christ. It is the product of the gospel preached without respect to race or class. The Church is a missionary institution bearing the same commission.

Members of the Corinthian church were guilty of breaking fellowship with other members. The problems of litigation came not because of the legal aspects, but because of their lack of love for one another.

When Paul saw the church's great inheritance in Christ, he was heartsick. They were playing with the trivial when they should have been dealing with universals. They were to sit as judges of men and angels for two reasons:

a. Christ is the Church's exaltation and dominion. This is the continuous message of the Word. In Eph. 2:6 and Heb. 2:5-9, the Word teaches that "all things" are subject to man, the condition being that "all things" are fulfilled in Christ. The Church will judge the world only because Christ is the Head of the Church, and all things are fulfilled in Him.

b. Christ's people are associated with Him in His dominion. Paul later identifies the Christian as a "joint-heir" with Christ (Rom. 8:17), suggesting that if we suffer with Christ, we shall also reign with Him (2 Tim. 2:12).

In Dan. 7:22 it was prophesied that judgment should be reserved to the "saints of the most High" (cf. Matt. 19:38; Luke 22:30; Rev. 2:26ff.). If, then, the saints are to judge with Christ, why should they be so "incompetent" in judging the "trivial" now? (RSV).

If I read Paul rightly, rigidity of judgment seems to be responsible for the Corinthian error. The result was that "worldly wisdom" apart from Christ was incompetent because it refused to be judged by God. And while excommunication was not the sentence as it was in c. 5, yet the church was the less because of its lack of wisdom. It also suggests that a vain, conceited confidence in one's ability to judge others disqualifies a person as a competent arbitrator.

Gordon Poteat, speaking of the incident, wrote, "The occurrence of the disputes is not reprimanded, for it is impossible to avoid the rise of offenses, even within the most ideal church. But when they occur, there are means available for their resolution so long as the members are faithful to their primary obligations to Christ. Confession of sin, forgiveness, and reconciliation are of the essence of the Christian way of life. The church is a laboratory for the practice of these methods" (cf. Gal. 5:25—6:2).[24]

Here is the spirit of holiness—an openness to the "rebukes" of the Holy Spirit in aiding us to conform progressively to the image of God in Christ.

There is one more reason for the apostle's remonstrations. Such problems in the church plunge its fellowship into disrepute in the world—a fellowship which should be grounded in love and forgiveness. Much harm can be done to the body of Christ if different procedures are followed. Many a church bears "years of scars" because its members are not subject to godly compromise and a spirit of compassion.

4. *A cure for the problem* (7-8). The apostle suggests a solution to the issue of personal litigation by suggesting that it is better to suffer *wrong* than to insist on one's own way.

If there is a difference of opinion, then allow for arbitration within the fellowship. If there is no resolution, it is better to *suffer the wrong* than allow the issue to be settled in a pagan court (7-8). This was the "more excellent way." In this we catch a gleam of the "face of the suffering Christ." His spirit becomes the final court of appeal. Better to lose the case than to "dim the splendor of the cause."

The two farmers were both Christians and members of the same Church of the Nazarene in northern California. God had blessed them both with abundant harvests, but one thought the other had defrauded him in a business transaction and threatened to take him to court. In a few weeks, the second came to his Christian brother and said:

"Here is a check for $10,000. I am not guilty, but it is far more important for me to keep your fellowship than it is to win the case. The reputation of our church is at stake, and I do not plan to jeopardize it before the community."

Paul was saying the same thing. Christ's Church is more important than the personal justification of any one person. Sometimes we are called to suffer the wrong for Christ's sake.

Standards of the Kingdom of God

The lines between righteousness and unrighteousness were fuzzy in Corinth. Their life in paganism was so close behind, and they were so integrated into pagan society that it was necessary for Paul to draw sharp lines of demarcation. "Know ye not . . . ?" again awakens the Corinthians to what they should have known but ignored.

1 Corinthians 6:9-20

9 Know ye not that the unrighteous shall not inherit the kingdom of God? Be not deceived: neither fornicators, nor idolaters, nor adulterers, nor effeminate, nor abusers of themselves with mankind,
10 Nor thieves, nor covetous, nor drunkards, nor revilers, nor extortioners, shall inherit the kingdom of God.
11 And such were some of you: but ye are washed, but ye are sancti-

fied, but ye are justified in the name of the Lord Jesus, and by the Spirit of our God.

12 All things are lawful unto me, but all things are not expedient: all things are lawful for me, but I will not be brought under the power of any.

13 Meats for the belly, and the belly for meats: but God shall destroy both it and them. Now the body is not for fornication, but for the Lord; and the Lord for the body.

14 And God hath both raised up the Lord, and will also raise up us by his own power.

15 Know ye not that your bodies are the members of Christ? shall I then take the members of Christ, and make them the members of an harlot? God forbid.

16 What? know ye not that he which is joined to an harlot is one body? for two, saith he, shall be one flesh.

17 But he that is joined unto the Lord is one spirit.

18 Flee fornication. Every sin that a man doeth is without the body; but he that committeth fornication sinneth against his own body.

19 What? know ye not that your body is the temple of the Holy Ghost which is in you, which ye have of God, and ye are not your own?

20 For ye are bought with a price: therefore glorify God in your body, and in your spirit, which are God's.

1. *The unrighteous* (9-10). Paul insists that the Christian believer be distinguished by righteousness of life in "every way." Obviously the apostle was disturbed by the influence of a secular society upon the members of the church. He was transparent in his teaching that the list of vices in vv. 10-11 excluded all participants from the kingdom of God. There is particular emphasis upon homosexuality, which, while condoned in some pagan communities, could not be accepted in the Christian fellowship.

Hodge writes that some professed Christians may be zealous in religious services and in defense of the truth while equally as deficient in outward piety. This arises from looking upon religion as outward service rather than loving obedience to a God of love. To be religious and yet immoral, according to Christianity, is as contradictory as to be good and evil at the same time.

Paul assures the Corinthians that only the righteous can "inherit the kingdom of God." No man who indulges in any known sin can be saved. "Do you confess to be Christians and still do not know this first principle of salvation?"

In a religious culture where "celebration" often does

not carry any moral requirements, the words of Paul come through loud and clear. "Don't fool yourself! There are ethical obligations which follow the grace of our Lord and are concomitant to it." While it is true that we are not saved by works, it is also true that we cannot be saved without ethical commitments in obedience to God. Faith is not only belief but entrance into vital ethical relationships which God makes known in His love and holiness by Jesus Christ.

A famous preacher killed a man in his study on Saturday and preached Sunday morning from Rom. 8:1: "There is therefore now no condemnation to them which are in Christ Jesus." But he forgot to read v. 9: "If anyone does not have the Spirit of Christ, he does not belong to Him" (NASB).

An amoral conception of salvation had infected the church in Corinth; it must not be allowed to infect the Church today. With Paul, however, Christ is the Foundation of the Church, and ethics its superstructure. There is no building when either is missing.

2. *The answer to unrighteousness* (11). "And such were some of you." These words were a climax to a noble sermon. After Paul has listed the acts of the unrighteous, he returns once more to the church, remembering that *some* were once such but now are followers of Christ. And while the apostle did not charge the Corinthians with any of these gross sins, he reminded them of their background and alerted them to continuing obedience.

Though Paul stresses righteousness in conduct, he is never led to say that salvation is any other than by grace. If men are to enter the Kingdom, it is not what they have done but what Christ has done for them. This is mentioned in 1:30, which almost parallels 6:11 with the exception of the added word "redemption."

a. Ye are washed. The construction of the verb *(apelousasthe)* is very unusual but acceptable. Men are called upon to wash away their sins (Acts 22:16). F. F.

Bruce translates the phrase, "you got yourself washed." The Corinthians confirmed the cleansing of their former sins by baptism. As a result, they were declared righteous before God. "Ye have purified yourselves" of the sins of the past. This being *washed* refers to the purging away of sin in repentance, of which water baptism is the sacramental seal (Acts 22:16; cf. *BBC*, 8:364).

b. Ye are sanctified. This does not refer to process or ethical development, or it would have preceded "you are justified." It means that having been *washed,* the Corinthians were claimed by God and made His holy people *(hagios)* "by calling." Neither does it refer to "entire sanctification," but that sanctification initially bestowed by God (see comments on 1:2, 30).

c. Ye are justified. The Corinthians were not only *washed* and *sanctified,* but also declared just in the sight of God. They were accepted as righteous in God's sight— the recipients of His gift of righteousness. They were under the highest obligation not to slip into their former state of pollution and condemnation.

The calling upon Christ's name and in the Spirit of God suggests that Paul had baptism in mind. He was, however, interested in the inner meaning rather than the outward ceremony.

Barrett concludes that because of what God has done, the possibility of a new life is before them. They are of the "unleaven," and now must purge the old leaven and keep the Christian feast in sincerity and truth. They were adulterers, etc., but now are no longer. Their problems show their imperfections and need for full salvation. They must now become holy and righteous morally as they already are by participation in the holiness and righteousness of God.

3. *The principle of Christian liberty* (12-17). Liberty and license cannot live together. "All things are lawful unto me, but not all things are expedient" ("helpful," RSV).

The principle which Paul lays down is still binding on every Christian community.

a. In all things lawful, Paul asserts the freedom of the believer, who may do anything he wishes because of his love for and obedience to God. Augustine's famous saying, "Love God and do as you like," might well have been stated, "Love God and do what He likes."

b. All things are not expedient (12). The apostle quickly points out that while he can do anything under the law of Christian liberty, the antithesis is just as true. He knew that in a pagan society, Christian liberty could become license, whether it be sexual impurity or "gluttony" (13).

The tension is between freedom and responsibility. Paul had previously stated that "all things are yours" (3:21), but he immediately recognized that while some things were "lawful" to the Christian community, they were not helpful.

Baird writes that this is an example of the *absolute* and the *relative* which run through all of Paul's ethical teaching. The basic *absolute* is this: Response in faith to the revelation of God's righteousness in Jesus Christ. This is the ground for serious denial of the claims of gross immorality. The sinner must be put out of the corporate fellowship, since "Christ, our paschal lamb, has been sacrificed" (5:7, RSV). The stark figure of the Cross stands in stern judgment on all the immorality of men.[25]

The principle of the *relative* was on the same ground. "Only those relations could be allowed which were commensurate with fellowship in Christ."

4. *The sanctity of the body* (15, 19). Paul speaks primarily of sexual license and gluttony in vv. 15-20 after he boldly asserts the paradox of liberty and servanthood (see c. 9). It is important, then, that he reaffirm the Corinthians' close and intimate relation to Christ. He does so in v. 13. "Now the body is . . . for the Lord; and the Lord for the body."

The body is designed to be a member of Christ and the "temple of the Holy Spirit" (19).

After meditating on what God has done for us, Paul is not surprised that Christ redeems the *body* with His blood, unites it in "his body," and makes it an instrument of true righteousness unto holiness. The sin of fornication (18) is absolutely incompatible with God's design for the *body*.

a. The body is the temple of the Holy Spirit because the Spirit dwells therein (19). Since it is the dwelling place of God, it must not be profaned. Man's body is a temple because God dwells within it.

Paul's arguments are addressed to those who have accepted the premise that life is "sacramental," that is, consecrated to God's highest purpose. "The body is for the Lord" (13). Thus, Christians have a high rationale for their lives. The body is never an end, but an instrument of God bringing fulfillment to life through Him. When the "immoral man sins against his own body" (18, RSV), he violates the temple of God.

b. The temple is not man's, but God's (19-20). "Ye are not your own, for ye are bought with a price." The body, as the temple of God, belongs to Him. Therefore, it can neither be profaned nor used for selfish reasons without incurring "great and peculiar guilt."

Only here does Paul use the verb *agorazo* (bought) to speak of Christian redemption. Since we are bought with the precious blood of Christ, it is imperative that we glorify God in our body. No wonder Paul reaches a climax in Rom. 12:1: "that ye present your bodies a living sacrifice."

It is nearly incomprehensible to realize that redemption makes us His and not *our own*. That changes our whole perspective on life. It means that God is responsible for our salvation, our spiritual culture, and our final destiny. What more can we ask?

c. A true appraisal of the body is important to Christian development (19-20). It must be confessed that a true scriptural appraisal of the body has not always been realized in Christian preaching. Sermons are addressed "to disembodied intellects" or "disincarnate souls," forgetting the close relation between the soul and the body. (In Christian psychology they are one.) Man is a psychophysical being.

The history of the church has been one of false modesty and prudery in the face of perpetual and pressing personal and social problems. Paul was more realistic. He presented a positive application of the principles of spiritual health and a challenge to a consecration of bodily powers to the "creative purposes of God."

We need to liberate men's minds from believing that all the gospel has to say is *no!* We need to recognize that not suppression but creative expression and fulfillment is God's purpose for the body. At the same time, there are biblical guidelines which help in treating the body as God's temple. It must be treated with nobility.

1 CORINTHIANS 7

The Sanctity of Christian Marriage

Eros has become a universal deity in urban society. The mobility of population, suburban living, leisure time, and changing principles of morality have uprooted "ancient ethical mores." As someone has put it: "The pain of urban monotony is to be remedied by the elixir of sexual excitement."

The church, as every institution, has suffered from the cultural and moral changes in society. One part of the church community has entered the arena talking about sex with candor; others have followed the medieval taboos in their silence. Apart from one's judgment of Paul in c. 7, two things are evident in the Corinthian problem. (1) The issue of sex had invaded the church; and (2) Paul was prepared to give counsel on the problem.

1 Now concerning the things whereof ye wrote unto me: It is good for a man not to touch a woman.

2 Nevertheless, to avoid fornication, let every man have his own wife, and let every woman have her own husband.

3 Let the husband render unto the wife due benevolence: and likewise also the wife unto the husband.

4 The wife hath not power of her own body, but the husband: and likewise also the husband hath not power of his own body, but the wife.

5 Defraud ye not one the other, except it be with consent for a time, that ye may give yourselves to fasting and prayer; and come together again, that Satan tempt you not for your incontinency.

6 But I speak this by permission, and not of commandment.

7 For I would that all men were even as I myself. But every man hath his proper gift of God, one after this manner, and another after that.

8 I say therefore to the unmarried and widows, It is good for them if they abide even as I.

9 But if they cannot contain, let them marry: for it is bettery to marry than to burn.

10 And unto the married I command, yet not I, but the Lord, Let not the wife depart from her husband:

11 But and if she depart, let her remain unmarried, or be reconciled to her husband: and let not the husband put away his wife.

12 But to the rest speak I, not the Lord: If any brother hath a wife that believeth not, and she be pleased to dwell with him, let him not put her away.

13 And the woman which hath an husband that believeth not, and if he be pleased to dwell with her, let her not leave him.

14 For the unbelieving husband is sanctified by the wife, and the unbelieving wife is sanctified by the husband: else were your children unclean; but now are they holy.

15 But if the unbelieving depart, let him depart. A brother or a sister is not under bondage in such cases: but God hath called us to peace.

16 For what knowest thou, O wife, whether thou shalt save thy husband? or how knowest thou, O man, whether thou shalt save thy wife?

1. *Christian principles in sexual behavior* (1-16). One cannot discuss the issues which Paul discusses in c. 7 without recognizing the universal truth which he establishes in 6:13, "The body is for the Lord." Because a Christian is "bought with a price," he is to glorify God in his body. All relative judgments are based on that overriding judgment.

a. Every man must seek that for which he is fit (1-2). While Paul rejects every suggestion that marriage is sinful, he does reveal a personal preference for celibacy (cf. 8). "It is good for a man not to touch a woman." Later he urges others to remain as they are (11, 27).

The word "good" *(kalon)* means "expedient" or "profitable" rather than that which is antithetical to moral evil.

Paul is not depreciating marriage, but assenting a personal preference on eschatological principles without violating nature or revelation.

It was a stern and disciplined position, and Paul recognized that each person would have his "specific gift" (7), but contended that celibacy for some was better than marriage (38).

In declaring this preference, Paul admits that what he says is "not of commandment" (6), but only "by permission." And yet he continues in v. 40, "I think I have the Spirit of God." Apart from his apocalyptic reason there is the possibility of giving undivided devotion to the Lord through celibacy (32-34).

While Paul's viewpoint mirrors the asceticism of his own time and does not say much to our day, it does say that every man should seek that for which he is "fit" (7).

Barclay writes that Paul is actually saying two things: (1) "Remember where you are living [for] . . . temptation is on every street corner." (2) "Remember your own physical constitution and the healthy instincts which nature has given you."

Again, Paul is not depreciating the holy estate of marriage, but pointing out the peculiar fitness that some people have for celibacy and the profits it personally incurs. It has only been in recent years that many Christian young people have looked upon celibacy not as a stigma, but as an opportunity to serve the Lord without the usual family distractions.

b. The marriage vow is a sacred and holy bond (3-9). There is no question that Paul teaches the principle of monogamy—and that for life! He was concerned about the prevalent adultery in Corinth. The word from "Chloe's people" did not increase his confidence.

Paul was speaking to a specific need of his culture— and to ours. He clearly forbids extramarital sex, though he is not opposed to sex within the marriage bond. Phillips translates v. 5, "Do not cheat each other of normal sexual intercourse" (cf. 3-4). It is important to notice that Paul sees in sexual relations values beyond reproduction, and gives a position to women that is equal to men.

Marriage is a partnership. "The husband should give to his wife her conjugal rights, and likewise the wife to her husband" (3, RSV). The husband cannot act independent of his wife, nor the wife of her husband. They must always act together as a Christian couple.

Neither husband nor wife can be used as a means to an end. Paul sees a spiritual unity in the Christian marriage which is the proper fulfillment of all desires.

The only justifiable reason for abstinence is for fasting and prayer (5). But this is a temporary separation, and one should be careful lest Satan take advantage of the situation (5b-9).

c. *Divorce is unthinkable for the Christian* (10-16). Paul is very straightforward in writing to the Corinthians that divorce is not allowed in the Christian community. He feels so strongly about the matter that in v. 10 he leaves his "personal preference" and speaks properly of revelation. "I give instructions, not I, but the Lord, that the wife should not leave her husband" (NASB).

Jesus, too, spoke just as clearly in Mark 10:9: "What therefore God hath joined together, let not man put asunder." (Paul does not even take into consideration the exception clause in Matt. 5:32, "on the ground of unchastity." He simply repeats the absolute command of Jesus: "There must be no divorce at all."

The highest expression of marriage is that of mutual love and obligation. When a couple has made their vows, they must stand by them at all costs. However, if tensions become unbearable, the first step toward divorce should be taken by the pagan rather than the Christian (13). This is the "high road" for the Christian husband or wife when the partner flaunts his spiritual and moral incompatibility. But there is an adequate reason. It may be that "the unbelieving husband . . . [will be] sanctified by the wife,

and the unbelieving wife . . . sanctified by the husband"
(14).

Conversion is always a possibility through the "consecrated life" of the spouse. A life of patience, forbearance, and love may provide the motive for a union that is complete both physically and spiritually. Any pastor can give illustration after illustration of both Christian men and women who have won their partner to Christ through loving example rather than temperamental debate. John Short writes superlatively:

> To frame a vow, and to give public adherence to it, is like tying oneself to a stake that is driven into the swirling, spuming stream of time and circumstance. It is meant to prevent us from being swept off our feet and carried away. Fewer marriages would come to shipwreck if people would seek the grace that is fully offered them in Christ. We are invited not only to be patient, to be forbearing, or to endure: We can also pray. It was a wise writer in the Hebrew tradition who penned these words: "Except the Lord build the house, they labor in vain that build it" (Psm. 127:1). Let Christ have his place in the home, and his presence will sanctify the marriage relationship: his grace will enable those who seek and accept it to stand by their vows.[26]

The one exception that Paul makes is in v. 15. A brother or sister is free, or not under bondage, when the unbeliever divorces the believer. It is Paul's wish that they remain unmarried in such a case (11).

Being a Christian Where You Are

After establishing a great principle and relating it to Christian marriage, Paul inserts a paragraph (17-24) which again supports the principle that the "body is the Lord's."

1 Corinthians 7:17-24

> 17 But as God hath distributed to every man, as the Lord hath called every one, so let him walk. And so ordain I in all churches.
> 18 Is any man called being circumcised? let him not become uncircumcised. Is any called in uncircumcision? let him not be circumcised.

19 Circumcision is nothing, and uncircumcision is nothing, but the keeping of the commandments of God.

20 Let every man abide in the same calling wherein he was called.

21 Art thou called being a servant? care not for it: but if thou mayest be made free, use it rather.

22 For he that is called in the Lord, being a servant, is the Lord's freeman: likewise also he that is called, being free, is Christ's servant.

23 Ye are bought with a price; be not ye the servants of men.

24 Brethren, let every man, wherein he is called, therein abide with God.

When the Corinthians became Christians, they were zealous to break away from their former life, their vocation, and their social and cultural relations. Paul saw this as a danger. He insisted that the function of Christianity is not "to give a man a new life but to make his old life new."

1. *We ought not to be anxious to change our social status in which we were saved* (17-20). It is very difficult to appreciate the ferment in the minds of converts in the beginning days of the gospel message. It is not surprising that Christians were disposed to break their ties of every sort. They knew no different. In fact, it seemed the virtuous thing to do. The change was too rapid for many who broke tradition, civil law, and social mores under the guise of the new law of liberty.

This was an evil which called for counsel. Paul calls for every man to lead the life assigned to him by the Lord (17, 20). "This is my rule in all the churches," he says. This coheres with v. 14, when Paul does not favor the separation of a couple because of differences in religion. "God has called us to peace" (NASB).

The first application of the principle was to circumcision. Paul takes the position that a circumcised Jew should not obliterate the mark when he became a Christian, but wear it as though it mattered not. The same was true of a pagan who was not circumcised. The important matter was not circumcision, but "the commandments of God" (19). Whether a convert was circumcised or not, he was to remain as he was. It was not an issue—nor was it to be made an issue.

If I read Paul rightly, he is saying once again that we ought to live by absolutes rather than particulars, relating the particular to the absolute. Why get uptight about an incidental issue when obedience to God is the absolute?

2. *This does not exclude the possibility of a man bettering his lot in life* (21-22). The force of Paul's argument is to "remain" as they are, but not to allow their social standing to disturb them. Paul could just as well have spoken, "Let not your being a slave give you any concern; but if you can become free, choose freedom rather than slavery."

So Paul speaks paradoxically in the face of the coming *parousia*. His expectation was that all earthly distinctions would soon be obliterated—so why worry? On the other hand, he encourages all who can naturally better their lot and still preserve their witness to do so.

3. *The most important principle is to follow the commandments of God* (23-24). The apostle consistently returns to his major premise. Since we were bought with a price, we are His and not the slaves of men (1 Pet. 1:18-19). The Christian can have only one master and cannot be the slave of another. When he is redeemed by the "precious blood of Christ," he belongs to the Lord and is inwardly free regardless of what the external relations might be. The Corinthian Christians were not to be men-pleasers, but God-pleasers because of their obligation to Him.

In v. 24 Paul reiterates what he had previously written. External relations are really of no account. Every man ought to be content with the station that God has assigned him. "Brethren, let every man remain with God in that condition in which he was called" (NASB). Even if a man is a *slave,* he is a *freedman* before the Lord. In God is the Christian's security and happiness. "To live near to God is, therefore, the apostle's prescription both for peace and holiness."

Advice to the Unmarried

1 Corinthians 7:25-38

25 Now concerning virgins I have no commandment of the Lord: yet I give my judgment, as one that hath obtained mercy of the Lord to be faithful.

26 I suppose therefore that this is good for the present distress, I say, that it is good for a man so to be.

27 Art thou bound unto a wife? seek not to be loosed. Art thou loosed from a wife? seek not a wife.

28 But and if thou marry, thou hast not sinned; and if a virgin marry, she hath not sinned. Nevertheless such shall have trouble in the flesh: but I spare you.

29 But this I say, brethren, the time is short: it remaineth, that both they that have wives be as though they had none;

30 And they that weep, as though they wept not; and they that rejoice, as though they rejoiced not; and they that buy, as though they possessed not;

31 And they that use this world, as not abusing it: for the fashion of this world passeth away.

32 But I would have you without carefulness. He that is unmarried careth for the things that belong to the Lord, how he may please the Lord:

33 But he that is married careth for the things that are of the world, how he may please his wife.

34 There is difference also between a wife and a virgin. The unmarried woman careth for the things of the Lord, that she may be holy both in body and in spirit: but she that is married careth for the things of the world, how she may please her husband.

35 And this I speak for your own profit; not that I may cast a snare upon you, but for that which is comely, and that ye may attend upon the Lord without distraction.

36 But if any man think that he behaveth himself uncomely toward his virgin, if she pass the flower of her age, and need so require, let him do what he will, he sinneth not: let them marry.

37 Nevertheless he that standeth stedfast in his heart, having no necessity, but hath power over his own will, and hath so decreed in his heart that he will keep his virgin, doeth well.

38 So then he that given her in marriage doeth well; but he that giveth her not in marriage doeth better.

In vv. 25-28 and 36-38, the ascetic cultural environment enters into the picture as well as the idea of celibate marriage, which may be suggested in v. 36. F. F. Bruce writes that the question was probably one as to whether a "betrothed girl should proceed to marriage in the normal way or remained unmarried—in a state of permanent betrothal . . . the decision . . . would involve others—her fiancee, naturally, and also her father who was responsible for giving her in marriage."[27]

Paul's feeling in the matter is transparent. Since the end time is near, it would be better for a person to remain as he is (26). Hodge writes that Paul is probably speaking of the virgins *(parthenoi)* rather than both sexes, though some commentators believe that he is speaking of the latter.

Verses 36-38 either are speaking of the position expressed by Bruce or of celibate marriage, which Barclay seems to feel is indigenous to the passage. It is true that in the Early Church there were those who lived together but tried not to consummate their relation. Theirs was a shared spiritual partnership but not a physical one. Paul, on this hypothesis, would say, "If any man think that he behaveth himself uncomely toward his virgin . . . let him do what he will, he sinneth not: let them marry."

More than one church council forbade the practice and looked upon it as an aberration of the Christian ethic. Looking upon the passage generally, what does Paul say to this generation as he did to his? Barclay suggests three principles of guidance.

1. *Self-discipline and continence are not to be despised* (25-28, 37). While Paul's counsels are an "interim ethic" in the light of the soon coming of the Lord, his ground rules are authentic expressions of Christian behavior.

Any means that a person has to keep balance between desire and asceticism is a Christian virtue. One must return repeatedly to Paul's absolute that "the body is the Lord's." Because it is, disciplined control of the basic drives of personality are acceptable and necessary. The natural drives of man are part of his constituent nature and will always be, regardless of his religious confession. The call of God is to use them for His glory and not for personal and selfish gratification.

2. *Don't make an unnatural thing of your religion.* Barclay writes that this was the fault of both monks and hermits. They believed that they must separate themselves from normal life and enter into an unnatural existence to please

God. Nowhere in the Scriptures does this seem to be taught. Christianity was never meant to cancel ordinary life; "it was meant to glorify it."[28]

3. *Don't make an agony of your religion.* How many times has the idea been expressed either by word or attitude that the Christian faith is burdensome and dreary, as if what was "left behind" was so much more joyful than the Christian way. No man should be haunted rather than helped by his religion. It is the most natural thing in all the world to follow Jesus. The great thing about the evangelical faith of the last few years is that our young people have found a new joy in the Lord and have learned to express it without apology. *It is the way to live!*

Jesus Is Coming Soon

The teaching of the soon coming of the *eschaton* (the end) is a sort of parenthesis in Paul's counsels concerning marriage but not unrelated. Though we know now that his timing was off, he was not wrong in his expectations. Let us not confuse the immediacy of Christ's coming with the fact of His coming.

1. *The age is coming to a close* (26-35). In the face of the impending distress, Paul thought it well to look upon his counsels as an interim ethic. (Luke 21:23; 2 Cor. 6:4; 10:12; 1 Thess. 3:7). He was not looking at the problems they were involved in as much as what was hanging over them in the future. The Scriptures clearly indicate that the last days will be accompanied by persecution and calamity.

2. *Marriage in the present circumstances will prove a burden* (26 ff.). While this is not ground for divorce, it is ground for remaining as one is (29-31). There were three reasons why Paul wished the early Christians to remain celibate: *(a)* The increased suffering that marriage might bring (29); *(b)* The transitory nature of things (31); *(c)* The comparative freedom from care in order to give themselves to the things of Christ (32-33).

Even the most important things must be laid aside if

they are threatening a man's loyalty as he looks forward to Christ's coming. He must please only Christ.

Paul did not minimize marriage in the Christian community. He saw it in comparison with Christ's love for the Church and man's noblest expression—"the loveliest relation on earth." But in this context the imperative was that the "fashion of this world would soon pass away" (31). Regardless of how important, everything else must take second place to the life that was to come rather than the life that is.

Counsels on Remarriage

Paul closes his counsels on marriage by giving instructions on remarriage.

1 Corinthians 7:39-40

> 39 The wife is bound by the law as long as her husband liveth; but if her husband be dead, she is at liberty to be married to whom she will; only in the Lord.
> 40 But she is happier if she so abide, after my judgment: and I think also that I have the Spirit of God.

1. *Marriage is for life* (39a). Once again Paul teaches under inspiration that the "wife is bound as long as her husband lives" (NASB; cf. Rom. 7:2). Marriage is a lifelong contract between one man and one woman. No civil or ecclesiastical body can with justice design another rule. There is no higher rule of authority than the Scriptures.

2. *At death, the survivor is free to remarry* (39b). The death of either party leaves the other free to remarry. And while Paul would rather see the widow remain single (40) and believed that she would be happier, he placed his judgment in the category of personal opinion as he had other passages of the same thrust.

3. *But only in the Lord* (39c). Paul lays down one condition, namely, that marriage must be "in the Lord." It must be between Christian and Christian. Plutarch, long ago, said, "Marriage cannot be happy unless husband and wife are of the same religion." Paul teaches that mixed

marriages should not be broken, but prays that they shall never be contracted. In a real sense, marriage is an act of worship. The common love of the two become one in their love for God in Christ.

It is not that Christ is the Answer for all of our problems, but He is "all in all"—the Basis upon which problems can be resolved.

Secularism and the Life of Faith
1 Corinthians 8:1—11:1

1 CORINTHIANS 8

Idolatry is not our heritage. We have worshipped one God for generations. Neither do we eat meat offered to idols. Zeus and Artemis mean very little to us outside of the classroom. Thus, while from one point of view cc. 8—10 are irrelevant, from another point of view they are vitally relevant.

Is a discussion of the relation of rights to responsibilities irrelevant? Is the question of the use or abuse of power of no interest? Are we immune to the comfortable complacency that often settles down upon those of us who enjoy many good things—and that in the face of poverty?

Once again, Paul is speaking ethically of the relation of the universal principle to the particular case. It just could say a great deal to us!

Setting an Example

1 Corinthians 8:1-6

1 Now as touching things offered unto idols, we know that we all have knowledge. Knowledge puffeth up, but charity edifieth.
2 And if any man think that he knoweth any thing, he knoweth nothing yet as he ought to know.
3 But if any man love God, the same is known of him.
4 As concerning therefore the eating of those things that are offered in sacrifice unto idols, we know that an idol is nothing in the world, and that there is none other God but one.
5 For though there be that are called gods, whether in heaven or in earth, (as there be gods many, and lords many,)

6 But to us there is but one God, the Father, of whom are all things, and we in him; and one Lord Jesus Christ, by whom are all things, and we by him.

A very important aspect of Christian teaching is our responsibility to our brother or sister in Christ. What a tragedy it is when we allow a divergence of opinion to break fellowship, and our example to cause another to stumble! Paul begins a new phase of his correspondence with the words: "Now touching things offered to idols" (1).

The temptation to conform to the patterns of the world was an acute problem in the Corinthian church. The idolatry of the Greeks and Romans pervaded their whole life. The Christians were used to stopping at the pagan shrines and paying their homage. It was now difficult to stop customs so engrained in their consciousness.

All of their neighbors followed the customs, and to them the Christians looked eccentric and odd. It was easy, therefore, to worship the "one God," and still pay homage to pagan gods for the sake of "image." After all, even a pagan knew that the idol was a symbol only—and perhaps they worshipped the same God after all.

Most of the Greeks were highly cynical about gods. The mystery cults arose primarily because of the loss of confidence in the gods of Mount Olympus. But after all had been said, idolatry still remained a problem—it failed to acknowledge the "transcendent Lord." It still admitted a form of magic that gods could be placated and manipulated. Idolatry was still self-deceptive. Baird suggests that while the temples to Aphrodite are long gone, "temples enshrining the splendid creations of man's hand and mind are erected on every corner of the modern metropolis."

In addition, the Corinthians ate certain portions of meat left after the offerings were made to the idols. Evidently the issue was raised in a letter, and Paul's response is an effort to clarify the matter. It was inevitable that a Christian would be offered meat of this character as an entree at a dinner or a banquet. Could a Christian attend such a party with pagan friends? If or when he attended, should he eat meat which was a part of the initial sacrifice?

Paul suggests that the line between the church and the world must be clearly drawn, and begins his argument to that end.

1. *The contrast between knowledge and love* (1-3). Evidently Paul is reflecting one of the parties of the Corinthian church when he says, "All of us possess knowledge."

a. Knowledge in itself produces arrogance. Some of the Corinthian Christians had assumed a superior position because of professed insights of a different nature from their brethren. The result was a pride which belied the true meaning of *knowledge.* Paul reminds them that *knowledge* is not everything, and that it is only *love* that edifies.

Those whose *knowledge* enabled them to eat meat offered to idols with a good conscience ought to exercise *love* grounded in self-control for the sake of the "weak."

b. True knowledge begins in humility (2). Knowledge should make men humble rather than arrogant, and the only knowledge that leads anywhere results in love. The more comprehensive the knowledge, the more humble the student becomes.

c. True knowledge comes as a result of a relationship with God in Christ. Verse 3 has its antecedents in Hebrew literature: "But if any man loves God, the same is known of him" (cf. Ps. 1:6; Jer. 1:5; Amos 3:2). That knowledge that he speaks of is a "knowledge by communion" which always results in love and humility. How can a man *know* God and remain *puffed up?*

d. Love builds a man up in the faith (1). Paul continues to say, as he will in c. 13, that love is the constructive constituent of the world's building. For the Christian it is *agape* rather than *eros.* Paul pleads for that love revealed in Jesus Christ which will yield true knowledge of God in communion.

2. *Paul's real feeling in the matter* (4-6). These verses are a

confession of faith on the part of the apostle. He is frank to admit that eating sacrificial meat means nothing to him. After all, an *idol* is nothing (4). It has no "real existence" (RSV). This does not mean that an idol is powerless, since Paul calls them "demons" (10:20). But it does mean that there is only one God, revealed as Father in Jesus Christ.

a. God is the Father of whom are all things (6). The word *Father* suggests a Supreme Being, the "triune Jehovah." He is the Ground and the Source of the whole universe. He created all things by the "word of his power." He is our end—and for that end we were created and redeemed. Paul is Christianizing the ancient Hebrew *Shema* (Deut. 6:4). We are to love that one God *(heis theos)* without exception.

b. Jesus Christ is Lord of all (6b). The faith that Paul had in Jesus as Lord was bound up with his faith in God —"a moral and spiritual unity" which revealed in time what God the Father was to all eternity. The Eternal Word found expression in the Personal Word, Jesus Christ.

The other *gods* and *lords* are real enough in the minds of their followers; but for those who worship the *one God* through the *one Lord,* they are only called *gods* and *lords.*

The suggestion in v. 6 is very clear. Paul accepted the faith that those with knowledge were not bound to idols. At the same time, their knowledge was to produce a spirit of love toward the "weaker brother."

Christian Attitudes: The Strong Toward the Weak

What then should be the Christian's attitude toward the "weaker brother"? After preparing the way, Paul now champions the role of the latter.

1 Corinthians 8:7-13

> 7 Howbeit there is not in every man that knowledge: for some with conscience of the idol unto this hour eat it as a thing offered unto an idol; and their conscience being weak is defiled.
> 8 But meat commendeth us not to God: for neither, if we eat, are we the better; neither, if we eat not, are we the worse.
> 9 But take heed lest by any means this liberty of yours become a stumblingblock to them that are weak.

> 10 For if any man see thee which hast knowledge sit at meat in the idol's temple, shall not the conscience of him which is weak be emboldened to eat those things which are offered to idols;
> 11 And through thy knowledge shall the weak brother perish, for whom Christ died?
> 12 But when ye sin so against the brethren, and wound their weak conscience, ye sin against Christ.
> 13 Wherefore, if meat make my brother to offend, I will eat no flesh while the world standeth, lest I make my brother to offend.

1. *Meat does not commend us to God* (8). It is admitted by Paul that meat makes us no better nor worse. F. F. Bruce quotes Jeremias, "Food will not bring us before God's judgment seat (Rom. 14:10-12) because it is an 'indifferent thing.'" We are no *worse* or *better* because we ate. It makes no difference to God.

2. *Only our love commends us to Christ* (9-10). Even Paul recognized his right *(exousia)* to eat, but he would not allow that *liberty* to become "a stumbling block to them that are weak" (9). That is, the weak, by the example of the strong, would sin against their conscience. This placed a tremendous responsibility upon those who had *knowledge,* but not a burden in a Christian context.

Many persons will ask, "Are my judgments to be continually conditioned where I cannot ethically behave as I think fit?" It is a good question, but it does not take into consideration a second factor. What the Christian *does* must not depend upon personal desire, but upon Christ's glory.

Shall my knowledge cause my weak brother to perish? If the "word of the cross" is the heart of the gospel, shall I place my own desire before the best interests of another?

Do I recognize that when I "sin so against the brethren, . . . [I] sin against Christ" (12)? The real heart of the plea, then, is not the value or the disvalue of sacrificial meat. It means nothing. But the consideration and love that I hold toward my brethren means everything. An absence of such amounts to sin because I place my brethren in spiritual jeopardy (cf. Matt. 25:40, 45; Mark 9:37, 41; Acts 9:4).

Christ died for every member of the Corinthian

church. Compared to His sacrifice, it was nothing to give up a small indulgence. The mind of Christ was a "cross-bearing mind, and His law is love."

3. *An eloquent postscript* (13). Paul closes his argument and plea with his oft-quoted climax: "Wherefore, if meat make my brother to offend, I will eat no flesh while the world standeth, lest I make my brother to offend."

As was said in the beginning, sacrificial meat means nothing to us, but there are a good many things in our secular society that do! Others are watching our lives critically. Alan Redpath remarked, "One step to the cross would be made easier for another because the Lord Jesus is revealed in your life the more clearly now that you are taking a stand."

Christian fellowship carries great responsibilities. Every decision must be made in the light of our relation to our Christian brethren. "Have you thought about that in terms of your entertainment, of what you eat and drink, of where you go and what you watch?" Alan Redpath concludes:

> Perhaps I should add that as far as I am concerned, there is no room in my life at all for the movies, television, social drinking or anything else of that character. But my reason for abstention is not based upon a legalistic argument which only serves to create a vacuum in the life of the one submitting to it, but rather upon love to the Lord Jesus Christ which involves total consecration of time, money and everything that I am to Him, and also my concern for my brethren in Christ, and especially for the young convert, before whom I would ever seek to be an example for His sake.

Paul, the apostle of Christian freedom, proclaims his own determination in the light of Christian love. Wesley Harmon paraphrases v. 13, "As long as the other fellow is around, love, not knowledge, will determine the limits of my liberty." We are troubled in our secular society by many idols, and Paul's arguments speak to us in a peculiarly contemporary way:

a. What is safe for one man may be quite unsafe for another.

b. Each action ought to be judged from the viewpoint of love first and knowledge second when the "other fellow" is around.

c. No man has the right to demand any right which may be the ruination of someone else.

d. Paul's omission of Acts 15 (the Council of Jerusalem) in his discussion teaches us that there are some problems that cannot be solved by quoting church rules.

1 CORINTHIANS 9

The Magnificent Obsession

"A fanatic," said Winston Churchill, "is the man who. will not change his mind or change his subject." In a most healthy sense, Paul was such a fanatic. So obsessed was he for the gospel that he would not allow even his lawful prerogatives to interfere with his preaching.

1 Corinthians 9:1-18

1 Am I not an apostle? am I not free? have I not seen Jesus Christ our Lord? are not ye my work in the Lord?
2 If I be not an apostle unto others, yet doubtless I am to you: for the seal of mine apostleship are ye in the Lord.
3 Mine answer to them that do examine me is this,
4 Have we not power to eat and to drink?
5 Have we not power to lead about a sister, a wife, as well as other apostles, and as the brethren of the Lord, and Cephas?
6 Or I only and Barnabas, have not we power to forbear working?
7 Who goeth a warfare any time at his own charges? who planteth a vineyard, and eateth not of the fruit thereof? or who feedeth a flock, and eateth not of the milk of the flock?
8 Say I these things as a man? or saith not the law the same also?
9 For it is written in the law of Moses, Thou shalt not muzzle the mouth of the ox that treadeth out the corn. Doth God take care for oxen?
10 Or saith he it altogether for our sakes? For our sakes, no doubt, this is written: that he that ploweth should plow in hope; and that he that thresheth in hope should be partaker of his hope.
11 If we have sown unto you spiritual things, is it a great thing if we shall reap your carnal things?

12 If others be partakers of this power over you, are not we rather? Nevertheless we have not used this power; but suffer all things, lest we should hinder the gospel of Christ.

13 Do ye not know that they which minister about holy things live of the things of the temple? and they which wait at the altar are partakers with the altar?

14 Even so hath the Lord ordained that they which preach the gospel should live of the gospel.

15 But I have used none of these things: neither have I written these things, that it should be so done unto me: for it were better for me to die, than that any man should make my glorying void.

16 For though I preach the gospel, I have nothing to glory of: for necessity is laid upon me; yea, woe is unto me, if I preach not the gospel!

17 For if I do this thing willingly, I have a reward: but if against my will, a dispensation of the gospel is committed unto me.

18 What is my reward then? Verily that, when I preach the gospel, I may make the gospel of Christ without charge, that I abuse not my power in the gospel.

1. *Paul had every legitimate claim to be a Christian minister* (1-14). He carried authentic credentials both as an apostle and as a minister. And yet, he was so obsessed by the love and conviction for the gospel, he would not allow even his rights to enter the picture and perhaps confound the issue.

a. As an apostle. He had seen Jesus our Lord on the road to Damascus (1-5). That work was authenticated in the winning of men to the Master—they were his "seal of . . . apostleship . . . in the Lord."

(1) That he was an apostle was substantiated by the risen Christ appearing unto him (Gal. 1:16). Both his call and authority came directly from the living Lord. His understanding of apostleship included an ordination that was not from man to man, but from God to man.

The passage was written with deep and moving emotion. He was overwhelmingly in love with his job. He could do no other (16). The passage is an autobiographical flash from a man "whose passion is as deep as his vision is high and wide."

The doubts that were cast at Paul concerning his claim to apostleship followed him all through his life. The underhanded subversive movements of Corinth clearly reinforced the issue at hand.

It is not surprising that there were doubts after Paul declared his freedom from any human tribunal (4:3 ff.). There were those who declared that if he were really an apostle, he would use his rights rather than forego them. Hence the four indignant questions in v. 1 are countered with an implied *yes!*

Paul first establishes his argument. He has seen Jesus our Lord (cf. 15:8 ff.; Gal. 1:15 ff.). He claims to be a witness of the Resurrection in his Damascus road experience (cf. Acts 22:14 ff.; 26:15 ff.). The claim to apostleship was always accompanied by evidence of that person seeing the risen Lord (Acts 1:22 ff.). But this was known to Paul alone.

(2) Paul appeals for confirmation in his work (cf. Rom. 15:15-21): "For the seal of mine apostleship are ye in the Lord" (2). It was a confident answer to those who would desire to "check him out" (3).

While the second evidence of apostleship has been confused with error, there was no question in Corinth. His message carried such a character in the changed lives of men that it superseded the necessity of any other evidence.

(3) Paul uses the evidence of apostleship to support his right to support (4). "Do we not have the right to our food and drink?" (RSV). "Power" in v. 4 means "right." The "right" that he speaks of is explained in vv. 4-17. The right is in abstaining from manual labor and in turn finding support in the church.

Paul is really not as concerned for his "right" as he is to show the Corinthians that as he has foregone some "rights" for personal reasons, they could forego some "rights" for the sake of the *weaker brethren.* Paul has exercised his freedom by foregoing his "rights."

(4) Paul uses his apostleship to support the right to a normal homelife (5). Verse 5 is an amplification of v. 4. "To lead about" expresses the itinerant nature of the apostle's work. Evidently other apostles with their wives were supported by the church.

Paul contends that all apostles and, by inference, all

Christian ministers have a right to support in the ministry. But Paul is also saying that one mark of Christian liberty is to renounce this for the gospel if he so desires.

The apostle vindicates his apostleship, therefore, by pointing out what was absolutely legitimate, but to which he said no for the Lord's sake. What finally counts for anyone is not orthodoxy but the brand of the Cross upon his heart and life. It had cost Paul something to follow Jesus. This was the only true orthodoxy.

b. As a minister. The circle of Paul's rights are enlarged to include all the Christian ministry (6-14).

(1) The minister's right to refrain from working for a living (6). Evidently both Barnabas and Paul followed the rabbinical pattern of carrying a trade while they ministered (4:12; 1 Thess. 2:9; 2 Thess. 3:7 ff.; Acts 18:3; 20:34). Paul's insistence on making his living through tentmaking while in Corinth for three years may have been resented by the Corinthian church. And while Paul was noble in his gesture, it formed an example for which the Christian Church has sometimes been regretful.

He is not saying that the ministry should not be supported adequately when giving full time to service. He is establishing his personal freedom through self-discipline as an example to an indulgent church.

(2) The minister's right to have his expenses paid by the church (7-11). Paul's right for support was not questioned. It was confirmed through human analogy (7) and divine law. Does a soldier fight at his own expense? Does a farmer not eat of his own fruit? Does a shepherd not drink of the "milk of the flock"? The servants of God are not inferior in their rights.

The principle is expressed in v. 9 (cf. Deut. 25:4; 1 Tim. 5:18). God is as interested in His ministers as He is in the "plowman" or the "thresher" (10, RSV). Thus, if the ministry sows in spiritual benefits, is it unreasonable that they should "reap . . . material benefits" (11, RSV)? On every principle of "commutative justice" the minister has the right of support.

(3) The minister's right to equal consideration (12). Though Paul refused to claim the right *(exousia),* he clearly declares an equivalent right among all the ministers to the prerogatives spoken of in vv. 4-11. The argument was directed particularly to the Corinthians. They had supported other teachers, and there was no reason why they should not support Paul or his co-laborers.

c. Paul's conduct was dictated by what was needful rather than what was lawful (12*b*-14). He was more interested in avoiding any cause which would give the enemies of the gospel a ground for criticism.

(1) The abiding principle (12*c*). Always before the apostle's eyes was a standard of conduct that would cause neither offence nor ground of criticism for the *message of the cross.* Paul *suffered all things.* He endured all privations for the sake of Christ. Under the circumstances, and surrounded by enemies, Paul would do nothing to give a single person cause to question the purity of his motives. He was willing to suffer anything rather than give his opponents the slightest pretext for their opposition to him.

(2) The abiding privilege (14). The whole overview of this passage is privilege rather than duty. "In the same way, the Lord commanded that those who proclaim the gospel should get their living by the gospel" (RSV). The "magnificent obsession" of Paul was to preach the gospel. His vision of the risen Lord was the supreme motivating force. His call was clear and abiding. He was willing to do anything to carry out his commission. His was a superlative privilege.

Paul had detailed with deep feeling and some indignation his reasons for not exercising his "rights." Who among us has not shared his feelings? How we long to be free from the necessity of depending on others in order to preach the gospel for its own sake. He considered himself a *slave* to Christ that *he might win the more* (19). "Inclination and duty find triumphant confidence in preaching the message of deliverance that is the very heart of the Gospel." It is Paul's master motive. It must be ours as well!

2. *Paul's basic motivation in his conduct was to keep himself on "shouting ground"* (15-18).

a. Paul did not want any back pay. "But I have made no use of any of these rights, nor am I writing this to secure any such provision. For I would rather die than have anyone deprive me of my ground for boasting" (15, RSV). The word "boast" or "exult" suggests a "shouting ground." Here is where the glory came upon him. Here is where Paul felt the Lord's presence in a very real and personal way.

b. Paul wanted more than a weekly paycheck (16). Only a God-called man can understand the words of v. 16. *Necessity* rather than duty was the motif of Paul. "Necessity is laid upon me; yea, woe is unto me, if I preach not the gospel!" He would boast only in an area where he was free to do or not to do. He was free to accept remuneration or refuse it. His refusal was the ground for "shouting." His exultation (boasting) was the proof of his integrity which he could appeal to with confidence.

His preaching was out of necessity. His reward was preaching itself. He had no choice but to preach. He was driven by divine compulsion as Jeremiah (Jer. 20:9). But he relinquished his "right" to support in order to exult in the great calling that was his.

Paul was a man with a "magnificent obsession." The gospel of Christ was entrusted to him. He could do no other than preach—and so he did until the angel of the Lord called him home on the Appian Way outside of Rome.

Openness Is Next to Holiness

Can you recall one person whom you regard as a saint? That person was probably the most open-minded individual that you have known—in him was understanding and help. Personal holiness is important to sainthood. But so is openness. In fact, they are like love and marriage—twin-born.

> 19 For though I be free from all men, yet have I made myself servant unto all, that I might gain the more.
> 20 And unto the Jews I became as a Jew, that I might gain the Jews; to them that are under the law, as under the law, that I might gain them that are under the law;
> 21 To them that are without law, as without law, (being not without law to God, but under the law to Christ,) that I might gain them that are without law.
> 22 To the weak became I as weak, that I might gain the weak: I am made all things to all men, that I might by all means save some.
> 23 And this I do for the gospel's sake, that I might be partaker thereof with you.

1. In holiness there is *freedom from bondage to others* (19*a*). While the apostle was yielding in matters of indifference, he was unyielding in matters of principle. He was "free from all men." He was under no obligation to conform to their conduct or opinions. His acceptance of the "yoke of Christ" had brought this freedom.

He was free from man's sin and guilt. He was free from evil habits. He was free from carnal fear. He was free of the ceremonial law and the standards of ethical particularism. No wonder you can feel the excitement of Paul's exultation, "I am free!"

2. In holiness there is *openness to others in their bondage* (19*b*-22). Though Paul was free from all men, he had made himself "a servant of all." The superlative motive is found in vv. 19 and 22—"that I might win the more" (RSV). Such language reflects the spirit of Jesus in Paul (cf. Mark 10:45; Luke 22:27). It also prompted the paradox with which Luther begins his *Liberty of a Christian Man*. "A Christian man is a most free lord of all, subject to none. A Christian man is a most dutiful servant of all, subject to all."

a. Notice the volitional accommodation in "yet have I made" (19*b*). Here again is an expression of his liberty. It was like a breath of fresh air. I am *free,* but I have become a *slave (doulos)* for one unquestionable reason—"that I might win the more." What more can be said?

(1) Accommodation to the Jews (20*a*). Paul used

his national identity to relate to his religious and cultural group. He knew their language. He was one with them. He insisted on Timothy's circumcision (Acts 16:3), and had taken a vow before his trip to Jerusalem (Acts 18:18). Upon hearing that some suspicious Nazarites were paying their fees at the Temple in Jerusalem, he acted in their behalf (Acts 21:26). It was not a return to legalism ("though not being myself under the law"), but an identification with those under the law that he might "win those under the law" (RSV).

(2) Accommodation to the Gentiles (21). "To those outside the law I became as one outside the law" (21, RSV). It was not suggested that the Gentiles were without law, but were apart from the Jewish law and a "law unto themselves" (Rom. 2:14). Paul related to their way of thinking while still "under the law to Christ" *(ennomos Christou)* which is parallel to Gal. 6:2 where to walk "by the Spirit" amounted to fulfilling the "law of Christ." While Paul was not under the Jewish law, except by choice, he was under the moral law which encompassed all men. Thus, when in Jerusalem he conformed to Jewish law; but when in Antioch, he accommodated his spirit to the Gentiles in order to win him to Christ at his level of interest. No wonder he rebuked Peter for acting like a Jew among Gentiles in Antioch (Gal. 2:11-21).

Here was true greatness. Paul knew that the gospel would not reach the Gentile if the Christian message was burdened by Jewish custom (law). Therefore, he related to the Gentile as he also related to the Jew.

(3) Accommodation to the *weak* (22). Paul's practice in 8:13 is now made a universal policy rather than a particular example. It was more than an "indifference."

He was speaking to the *weak* of chapter 8 in order that no stumbling block be placed in their way. To *win* them was of more importance than his own personal convictions. His personal restriction was an expression of that wonderful liberty that he had discovered in Christ.

Paul holds himself up as an example to the church. He

accommodated himself to their prejudices that he might win them over to better views. Within the "law of Christ" he was conciliatory to all men. "I am made all things to all men, that I might by all means save some" (22).

Paul did not expect to win all men, but he would do anything within the "law of Christ" to win some! He was never careless about his own discipline and the self-discipline of the community (10:1-22). Verse 23 is the transition which leads us to the personal conclusion of the passage. Paul's accommodation is carefully defined in the freedom of self-discipline.

The Conditions of Christian Existence

The conditions of the Christian life, says Paul, are very much like a footrace. One cannot run as he wills, but always within the rules of the contest if he is to gain the prize.

1 Corinthians 9:24-27

> 24 Know ye not that they which run in a race run all, but one receiveth the prize? So run, that ye may obtain.
> 25 And every man that striveth for the mastery is temperate in all things. Now they do it to obtain a corruptible crown; but we an incorruptible.
> 26 I therefore so run, not as uncertainly; so fight I, not as one that beateth the air:
> 27 But I keep under my body, and bring it into subjection: lest that by any means, when I have preached to others, I myself should be a castaway.

Under the metaphor of a runner (24) and later a boxer (26), Paul makes a final plea for self-discipline. We must always think of how our conduct will appear, not for the sake of mere respectability, but for the sake of others.

1. *A Christian must be temperate in all things* (25). Verses 24-27 are packed with figures of speech from the athletic contests which Paul had observed more than once. As usual, he mixes his metaphors (a gloriously bad habit), and beginning with a race where there was only one winner, he quickly shifts to the vigorous training of all Christians for the race in which there should be no losers (25).

In either case, a contestant must be temperate in all things, even foregoing the lawful indulgences for the sake of the prize.

A runner or a boxer can close his training after a contest, but not so a Christian. He must continue his rigid abstinence as an ongoing necessity for one reason—that he might win an *incorruptible* rather than a *corruptible* crown (25).

2. *A Christian must be definite in his aim* (26-27). At this point Paul shifts from the second to the first person. He is still remembering the problem of "meat offered to idols." His aim is to be a pastoral example to his people. Having seen a good deal of "roadwork" in his missionary journeys, he was not used to shadowboxing. His opponent was his own body. His heart cry was to be so personally consistent that when he preached to others, he should not be a "castaway."

Out of the jumble of figures of speech comes one clear picture—the earnestness and integrity of Paul. It is a warning and challenge to every follower of Christ. Even though he had given himself to the demands of the gospel, he still remembered the possibility of weakness. The "strong" must take care!

It is to that end that the apostle "buffets" (NASB) his body and makes it his "slave" (NASB). He took no chances that his own carelessness and lack of purpose would make him a "has-been."

And so, there are two conditions to a successful Christian race. The first is faith in the message of the Cross. The second is faithfulness to the demands of that Lordship until the race is finished. God help us to hold fast our faith and to be faithful to the implications of the lordship of Christ! It is in that fidelity that one discovers that an incorruptible crown is reserved for every servant of the Master.

It must have been in a moment of inspiration that Thomas O. Chisholm wrote:

> *Oh, perfect life of Christ, my Lord!*
> *I want to be like Jesus.*
> *My recompense and my reward,*
> *That I may be like Jesus.*
> *His Spirit fill my hung'ring soul,*
> *His power all my life control;*
> *My deepest pray'r, my highest goal,*
> *That I may be like Jesus.*

Wasn't this the spirit that John Wesley was talking about when he spoke of "perfect love"?

1 CORINTHIANS 10

Scriptural Warnings and Divine Promise

The Israelites through self-indulgence lost the Promised Land. They had presumed on their privileges and fell into idolatry. It could have been different! Paul expresses his fear for the Corinthians by using the history of Israel as an example.

1 Corinthians 10:1-14

1 Moreoever, brethren, I would not that ye should be ignorant, how that all our fathers were under the cloud, and all passed through the sea;

2 And were all baptized unto Moses in the cloud and in the sea;

3 And did all eat the same spiritual meat;

4 And did all drink the same spiritual drink: for they drank of that spiritual Rock that followed them: and that Rock was Christ.

5 But with many of them God was not well pleased: for they were overthrown in the wilderness.

6 Now these things were our examples, to the intent we should not lust after evil things, as they also lusted.

7 Neither be ye idolaters, as were some of them; as it is written, The people sat down to eat and drink, and rose up to play.

8 Neither let us commit fornication, as some of them committed, and fell in one day three and twenty thousand.

9 Neither let us tempt Christ, as some of them also tempted, and were destroyed of serpents.

10 Neither murmur ye, as some of them also murmured, and were destroyed of the destroyer.

11 Now all these things happened unto them for ensamples: and they were written for our admonition, upon whom the ends of the world are come.

12 Wherefore let him that thinketh he standeth take heed lest he fall.

13 There hath no temptation taken you but such as is common to man: but God is faithful, who will not suffer you to be tempted above that ye are able; but will with the temptation also make a way to escape, that ye may be able to bear it.

14 Wherefore, my dearly beloved, flee from idolatry.

1. *Take warning from the history of Israel* (1-4). The opening illustration is taken from the record of incidents occurring during the Exodus from Egypt under the leadership of Moses. (The passage indicates the pattern of typological use of the Old Testament in the instruction of converts.)

Paul reminds the strong (spiritual) that their forefathers had extraordinary advantages which seemed to secure their success.

a. They were under the providence *(cloud)* of God (1) and had known deliverance by passing "through the sea."

b. They had pledged their confidence in the leadership of Moses (2) by following him "in the cloud and in the sea."

c. They had eaten of the same "supernatural" food and drank of the "supernatural" drink (3). And the rock from which they drank was not the material rock but "that spiritual rock . . . and that rock was Christ." It was Paul's confidence that the rock was really a manifestation of the Messiah. There was not a thing they could do for themselves, and yet the providence of God kept them from tragedy in the wilderness.

Paul is attempting to show the Corinthians their privileges in Christ. He was saying to the church: All of us are under His guiding hand. We have been delivered from the bondage of sin by the blood of Christ at Calvary and baptized into His body. All of us have been sustained by His spiritual food and the river of life from His throne. The deepest ties we share are in community.

We have experienced the forgiveness of sins and

cleansing through His grace. We have fed on His Word and have been sustained by His grace. We have done nothing to deserve it at all.

2. *See how the Israelites were laid low through ingratitude* (5). While the Israelites were partakers of divine favor, yet there was no corresponding realization of the responsibility that ought to accompany such privilege. They were guilty of ingratitude which John Short calls the "meanest sin in the world." In rapid succession, Paul summarizes a series of disasters in the wilderness which came as a result of their disobedience.

3. *These warnings are for the strong* (6-12). How could a people who were so blessed ever fail God? The answer is that their disobedience and ingratitude occasioned their fall. God was not well pleased.

Paul defines four areas that will spell tragedy for the Christian as they did for the Israelites.

a. Lust (6). We must not confine lust to its narrower meaning of immorality, though fornication is included within its broader understanding. Num. 11:4-34 explains the full scope of the Israelites' desire. God provided His people with what they needed, but they desired a "change of diet" which was not in the will of Jehovah. God knew what was best for them, but they followed their own way which is the heart of sin. God gave them what they wanted rather than what He wanted for them.

David, reflecting on the incident, said, "He gave them their request; but sent leanness into their soul" (Ps. 106: 15).

It all started in the Garden of Eden when Adam and Eve said, "We know what is best for us" (Gen. 3:6). The heart of sin is self-idolatry. God always meets a man on the level of his own desire. If he hungers and thirsts after righteousness, He will fill with His Spirit. If we resort to our "own thing," He will allow it but give us "leanness of soul." Alan Redpath observes that if we take our own way, "the mark of spiritual authority vanishes, the ring of integrity departs; the one thing that distinguishes a Christian, a man of God, from other people, leaves us."

The Israelites who sinned by insisting on their own way *(lust)* were buried in *Kileroth-hattaavah* (graves of craving). Their desires for the "flesh-pots of Egypt" were more important than the leadings of Jehovah.

b. Idolatry (7). Paul quotes from Exod. 32:6 as an example of idolatry among the Israelites. Bruce suggests that this "may have been an apt summary of what happened at the idol feasts which some Corinthian Christians were happy to attend."

The Israelites were not planning to change their God but to have some token of His presence. The Corinthians had fallen into such a depth of infatuation as to believe that their God could be delighted with the feasting and play of idol worship in the Temple. While they did not frequent the pagan temples to prostrate themselves before the idol, they did not keep their distance from the tokens of idolatry.

Paul intimates that God will have no part of idolatry, and that the tokens of idolatry are polluting.

It is not out of order to suggest that Paul feared for the "strong" who played with the tokens of idolatry and opened the doors to later involvement.

So Paul seems to be remembering the extreme case in 8:10 of a Christian showing his superior wisdom by sitting at a merchants' banquet in an idol temple. While idolatrous worship did not take place at the banquet, the apostle intimates the danger that the "enlightened" Corinthian was tempted not to accept. The lesson to the Christian Church is obvious.

c. Immorality (8). The apostasy of idolatry was closely associated with immorality *(fornication)*, in which 24,000 Israelites lost their lives under divine judgment (Numbers 25).

Their standard which gradually disintegrated finally ended with illicit relations with the women of Moab. It is apparent likewise that the pagan customs of the Corinthians were still a strong temptation to the church. It had occasioned the command of Paul to the Thessalonians, "This is the will of God, even your sanctification, that ye should abstain from fornication" (1 Thess. 4:3).

d. *Unbelief* (9-10). "Neither let us tempt Christ . . . Neither murmur ye." The story is found in Numbers 21, where the Israelites became weary of the journey and had gone sour on the whole project of the Exodus.

Many a man trades on the mercy of God. He is tempted to believe that the goodness of God will keep him safe regardless of his disobedience. He forgets that the holiness of God demands fidelity.

Murmuring and grumbling is almost a theme song in the Book of Numbers. God in the end sent the plagues to destroy the unfaithful (Num. 14:12, 37; 16:41-49; 21; etc.).

How often do we find Christians living in sourness instead of radiance, in criticism rather than confidence, in pessimism rather than godly optimism. The temptation is always there!

Paul uses the Old Testament as an example for admonition and example (11). He insists on the need of vigilance: "Let him that thinketh he standeth take heed lest he fall." Barclay observes that "again and again a fortress has been stormed because its defenders thought it could not be" (see Rev. 3:3). "Life is a chancy business; we must be ever on the watch."[30]

4. *Recognition of the nature of temptation and the promise of God* (13). The record of the wilderness travels ought to have been a sufficient warning to the Corinthians who were inclined to be overconfident. There were two observations about temptation which seems to be indigenous to the verse.

a. The universality of temptation (13a). Paul is quite sure that the temptations suffered by the Corinthians were not unique to them, but were common to all men. The purpose of temptation was not to promote failure, but to test character (Deut. 8:2). John Short says, "To be fiercely tried and tempted is part of the price he must pay if he would win the fight for true manhood." And William James concludes that no one has ever graduated from the school of life until he is well tempted.

Even Jesus was not immune to temptation. It was the threshold of His moral and spiritual development—the understanding of what His purpose was in life and who He was. Was He to take the easier and more spectacular course, the difficult way of the Cross?

Temptation is of the very stuff of life. It meets every man at some stage in life's way.

b. The promise of God in the face of temptation (13*b*). God is faithful and will not allow a temptation more severe than a man is able to bear. God does not say that He will remove the temptation, but He promises a resource so that a Christian need not fall. Temptation will always be graded to the fibre of a man's life. And God will not allow temptation to continue a moment's notice beyond the ability of a person to "take it."

Alan Redpath observes that "temptation will be sent along the particular line that God knows you need in order that He might draw you to himself, but the way of escape is guaranteed." He "will with the temptation also make a way to escape."

5. *A means to defeat temptation* (14). Sometimes it is wiser to run than it is to fight. The warning against idolatry is repeated. In Paul's mind, the real peril to the Corinthian church was idolatry in all of its forms.

Anything or anyone that takes God's place in a person's affection is an idol. It is the ground of the Hebrew and Christian thought on this issue and led Cowper to write:

> *The dearest idol I have known,*
> *Whate'er that idol be,*
> *Help me to tear it from the throne,*
> *And worship only Thee.*

Rules for Christian Discernment

It is not easy to discern in given situations what the will of the Lord might be. We cannot thrive without fence posts and directional signals. The principles of Christian conduct are for our edification. Following them in the Word will give honor to the name of the Lord and assure personal Christian development. Breaking them can only bring tragedy.

1 Corinthians 10:15-33

> 15 I speak as to wise men; judge ye what I say.
> 16 The cup of blessing which we bless, is it not the communion of the blood of Christ? The bread which we break, is it not the communion of the body of Christ?
> 17 For we being many are one bread, and one body: for we are all partakers of the altar?
> 19 What say I then? that the idol is any thing, or that which is offered in sacrifice to idols is any thing?
> 20 But I say, that the things which the Gentiles sacrifice, they sacrifice to devils, and not to God: and I would not that ye should have fellowship with devils.
> 21 Ye cannot drink the cup of the Lord, and the cup of devils: ye cannot be partakers of the Lord's table, and of the table of devils.
> 22 Do we provoke the Lord to jealousy? are we stronger than he?
> 23 All things are lawful for me, but all things are not expedient: all things are lawful for me, but all things edify not.
> 24 Let no man seek his own, but every man another's wealth.
> 25 Whatsoever is sold in the shambles, that eat, asking no question for conscience sake:
> 26 For the earth is the Lord's, and the fulness thereof.
> 27 If any of them that believe not bid you to a feast, and ye be disposed to go; whatsoever is set before you, eat, asking no question for conscience sake.
> 28 But if any man say unto you, This is offered in sacrifice unto idols, eat not for his sake that shewed it, and for conscience sake: for the earth is the Lord's, and the fulness thereof:
> 29 Conscience, I say, not thine own, but of the other: for why is my liberty judged of another man's conscience?
> 30 For if I by grace be a partaker, why am I evil spoken of for that for which I give thanks?
> 31 Whether therefore ye eat, or drink, or whatsoever ye do, do all to the glory of God.
> 32 Give none offence, neither to the Jews, nor to the Gentiles, nor to the church of God:
> 33 Even as I please all men in all things, not seeking mine own profit, but the profit of many, that they may be saved.

1. *Identification with the world may lead to tragedy* (15-22). By "identification" we are not speaking of Christian involvement. A follower of Christ finds himself in the

world, but "not of the world" (John 17:16). It is in the world that he finds his area of service, but he does not indulge in practices that will "provoke the Lord to jealousy."

The context of the passage leads to the conclusions already dealt with in c. 8. To eat of food offered to idols was a matter of Christian conscience, but to eat the same food with idolaters as a part of an idol feast was something else. From *idolatry*, Christians must *flee* (14). They should not see how close they can come to idolatry, but how far they can keep from it.

It is difficult to apply the principle to contemporary issues. Some practices may be questionable, while others are wrong under similar conditions. Matters of moral indifference may take on a different color when practiced with the godless and in places associated with evil. They may so identify a Christian with the enemies of Christ as to ruin the Christian's influence and grieve the Saviour.

a. An argument from the sanctity of the Lord's table (16-17). Turning from the Old Testament as an example, Paul comes closer home with an analogy based on the Corinthian experience.

The Corinthian church was, of course, familiar with the "cup of blessing" and the "bread" which was a sign of personal identification with Christ. (The passage is not intended to give a complete understanding of the Lord's Supper as Paul will later give in 11:17-22.)

As we have seen previously, Paul takes us back to the Cross as our starting point. He must always begin there! He knows that the issue can only be settled in our identification with the cross of Calvary. He reminds us that our new life is a participation, a communion *(koinonia)* in the blood of Christ.

Bruce points out that neither the blood nor the body is spoken of in any material sense, but that the communicants "partake jointly of the life in Christ, yet not in such a way as to be immunized against divine judgment, regardless of their subsequent behavior."

Communion, then, identifies the communicant with

Christ alone, and the Corinthian Christians could not belong to two Lords.

b. An argument from the foolishness of idol worship (18-22). While it was true that idol deities were nonexistent, yet behind them were the demons. They were not divine beings to whom worship was due, yet they were used by evil spiritual powers to prevent men and women from the true worship of the one true God. Even if Paul were speaking figuratively, demons would represent lust, cruelty, and ignorance with which idol worship was identified.

While idol worship placed the Christian in dangerous contact with demons, to join in the celebration of sacrificial meals destroyed the Christian's contact with Christ. "You cannot drink the cup of the Lord and the cup of demons; you cannot partake of the table of the Lord and the table of demons" (NASB).

Christians have their own sacrificial feast (the cup of blessing and the bread) which is a means of sharing in the blood and body of Christ. It is in the Eucharist that Christ makes available the spiritual benefits "which he secured in principle for the whole human race as a result of his death."

Because of the sanctity of the Eucharist, a Christian cannot join in the Lord's Supper and at the same time continue a practice which puts him in touch with evil spirits (eating meat offered to idols in the temple) who are hostile to Christ.

As Paul puts it (22), we are not stronger than He is, and since the practice provokes the Lord to "jealousy," we shall be the worse for it. The practice can only end in tragedy. The Corinthians could not serve two Lords—neither can we!

2. *Discrimination in personal judgment is a necessary Christian ethic* (23-33). Paul concludes his long discussion of the use of meat offered to idols by stating the great comprehensive principle which must be applied to all Christians in matters of conscience: Consider what is

expedient and what edifies—doing all to the glory of God!

a. The grace of freedom ("All things are lawful," 23*a*). Notice the change of person in Paul's speech. He has been writing to persuade the strong-minded and "enlightened" to waive their claims in the interest of those who are sensitive in conscience. Now he writes of himself—"all things are lawful for me."

Paul has discovered a new freedom in Christ Jesus. He will not allow that freedom to be trammeled by narrow-mindedness or Jewish prejudice. "For why should my liberty be determined by another man's scruples? If I partake with thankfulness, why am I denounced because of that for which I give thanks" (29-30, RSV).

The apostle's conscience was not troubling him. He was in good spiritual health. He now identifies himself with an "enlightened" guest in the home of a pagan.

b. The law of love ("but all things are not expedient," 23*b*-30). In c. 6 Paul insisted that liberty must be guarded as a personal defense; now he insists that liberty must be limited for the sake of others.

(1) Not all things are "helpful." It is not everything, even though lawful, that edifies. All things do not build Christian character; neither do they always help those influenced by my example; neither do they always build the Christian community.

To attend a banquet in a pagan temple is of no spiritual benefit to either self, neighbor, or community. While participation need not harm one spiritually, it can bring great harm to another because of *his* conscience. Therefore, Paul concludes in a great ethical climax: "Let no man seek his own, but every man another's wealth [good]."

(2) An illustration of Christian expediency (25-30). Paul advises Christians to purchase food offered for sale in the market ("shambles") without raising any questions as to whether it had been used in the worship of idols. They are to ask "no questions for conscience sake." The meat is purchased for food, not as a sacrifice, and all that

the earth produces is the Lord's, to be graciously supplied for man's use. It is a gift of God. However, when another person with a sensitive conscience is involved, the picture changes.

Supposing an unbeliever invites a Christian to dinner, and he is disposed to go. He is to "eat whatever is set before" him "without raising any question on the ground of conscience" (NASB).

However, if someone says to him, "This is offered in sacrifice in the temple" (whether it be the host or another), he should not eat it in deference to that person whose conscience will not allow him to eat what the guest is eating. The judgment is not made for the sake of his own conscience, but for the sake of the neighbor who would be misled and injured by his eating.

Charles Erdman suggests that the course should be followed for two reasons: *(a)* Only harm can come from eating such food and exposing his freedom to the condemnation of another's conscience; and *(b)* "An assertion of liberty in the face of conscientous condemnation would result in positive harm" to that one who knew a blessing was given to meat offered to idols.[31]

c. Some concluding principles (31-33). What does all this mean? Are we to be constantly restricted by the weak because of their conscience? It is a sensitive question, and Paul does not attempt to answer it to the satisfaction of all of his readers. However, he does posit a superlative law of love within the framework of personal responsibility. A man limits his liberty because of his concern for others.

The strong do not undermine the weak by ridiculing their position, even though "the weaker brother can be somewhat of a nuisance at times." However, there may be times, on the issue of priority, when a weaker brother must be disregarded. Paul never carried his principle of expediency to the place of abrogating his liberty in Christ.

God expects every Christian to use his wisdom in seeking the good of his neighbor within the ethical hierarchical principle of "the greatest good for the greatest number." John Short says:

> To put the matter into a metaphor, let this pyramid be placed firmly on its base; never attempt to balance it precariously on its apex. For the rest, we must seek the full salvation of our fellowmen, however weak, and lead them gently into the fulness of the liberty that we ourselves seek to enjoy as followers of Jesus Christ.[32]

1 CORINTHIANS 11

A Remarkable Request

1 Corinthians 11:1

> 1 Be ye followers of me, even as I also am of Christ.

It is astonishing that Paul felt able to say, "Follow me as I follow Christ"—yet not so remarkable when we examine his life. He can fairly claim that he incarnates in his own life and spirit, as far as possible, the life and the spirit of the Saviour. While the Corinthians might question his arguments, they could not question his life. The first verse of c. 11 provides a conclusion for the whole message of c. 10.

Paul had no wish to dominate the Corinthian Christians, but to point them to their Lord. He was probably the first consistent Christian they had ever seen. Moffatt remarked:

> It is an acknowledged fact that Christian faith depends often upon belief in some guide or spiritual counsellor who stands more effectively than anything for the reality of religion. Struggling aspirations may be reinforced, vague doubts may be resolved, and loyalty to the cause may be revived and purified, as men are able to see their cherished end in the personality of one to whom they have good cause to pay grateful homage.[33]

Most of us do not wish to live so dangerously. Yet

Paul, though an apostle, was no superman, but a bond-slave of Jesus Christ. That made the difference!

What was the driving force which gave an authentic expression to his request? The motif in 11:1 has already been presented in c. 4 and can be summarized in three statements: (1) Paul was willing to be exposed for the sake of Christ (4:9-10); (2) He was indifferent to the externals of life (4:11-13); and (3) He exhibited a self-giving concern for the needs of others (4:14-21).

I talked to a number of those who returned from the World Congress on Evangelism in Lausanne, Switzerland, in 1974. They were unanimous in suggesting that after the first three days, there was a spirit of unity in Christ which transcended race, denominations, national boundaries, and individual differences. One layman observed, "I came home to discipline myself to a simpler life-style. I have too much with so many having too little."

He expressed the spirit of Paul. The apostle did not condemn possessions but exhibited a spirit of indifference to them. He enjoyed good things but did not make them primal in his loyalties.

Tradition says that after Thomas Aquinas closed his writings of the unfinished *Summa Theologica,* the angel of the Lord appeared to him and said, "Thomas, you have written well of Me; what can I give to you?"

And Thomas replied, "More of Thee, Lord; only more of Thee."

Paul was ever ready to instruct and guide by example (4:17). It was a love that came to others because he loved Christ more than all his possessions.

He reiterates in 11:1 what he had previously said in 4:16. He saw that Christ had not pleased himself (Rom. 15:3), but made himself the "servant of all" (cf. Mark 10:45; Luke 22:27; Phil. 2:7; and 2 Cor. 8:9). It is instructive to compare the qualities that Paul recommends to the church with the spirit of Jesus in the Gospels.

There are few of us who have the audacity to say, "Follow me as I follow Christ." But the example that Paul gave in Christ is a superlative model to all those who claim to be followers of Him.

Some Concluding Remarks on Secularism

Can Paul speak to us today? Any casual observer of the church and culture will know that society is plagued by secularism. "Secularism," wrote Leroy E. Loemker, "is our failure to let God be God in our lives. Its nature is neither to affirm nor deny religious faith, but to live indifferently to it."[34]

Baird points out that just at the moment that "the world was getting superficially interested in religion the church was becoming conformed to the world." Will Herberg writes that "every aspect of contemporary religious life reflects this paradox—pervasive secularism and mounting religiosity."[35]

It is this paradox that led Bonhoeffer to speak of secular Christianity. The German martyr was not speaking of a "cheap grace," but a life-spending commitment in *this* world where "one learns to believe."[36]

No wonder man is plagued by a plethora of gods. While he worships society, culture, sex, peers, and the nation, the "God of radical monotheism is remote and rejected."

The evangelical tradition (and the holiness movement within it) must reject the "success cults" with their "cadillacs and steaks" if it is to recover the heart of the message of the Cross.

Paul speaks to us when he says, "Shun the worship of idols" (1 Cor. 10:14); and, "You cannot drink of the cup of the Lord and the cup of demons" (1 Cor. 10:21). Any other loyalty is self-worship and, as someone has said, "This sort of egocentrism is the essence of sin."

Baird concludes that

so long as the church measures her success by the standards of the world, so long as it confuses activity with service, so long as it mistakes organization for divine commission, the believer will not know whether he has come to the church of the living God or to the shrine of human achievement. . . . In the latter meat is offered to idols. That is, man is called to partake of things not essentially wrong in themselves but potentially blocks to the brother.[37]

Bonhoeffer elaborates as follows:

It is the Christocentric principle which is basic to all our ethical action in the secular society. Christ has come to us in the flesh to show that God works in the world for the redemption of man. In the world the church must remain to do his work. Christ has come to set us free—free to make decisions, free from the bondage of the overscrupulous, yet under obligation to decide, under demand to make responsible decisions even over the trivial, even about meat offered to idols. All our actions, no matter how small, stand under the call of God. The character of that demand is revealed in Christ, who emptied himself to take on the form of a servant, becoming obedient unto death. In that death we see the love of God—a love which demands our obedience, which drives us into the world to express that love. This is the love that judges all our actions when they fall short of the glory of God. Nothing judges us so severely as the cross of Christ. Nothing so demands our discipline as the demand of the suffering servant of God. Yet, the Cross which judges us is the Cross which redeems us; the love which compels us is the love that forgives us. The Cross is the symbol of the intersection of God's judgment and God's mercy; before it we confess.[38]

"For us there is one God, the Father,
    from whom are all things
    and for whom we exist,
And one Lord, Jesus Christ,
    through whom are all things
    and through whom we exist" (1 Cor. 8:6,
        RSV).

Public Worship and the Life of Faith
1 Corinthians 11:2—14:40

The Corinthian church was troubled by issues involved in worship. This was due, in part, to the backgrounds of the participants. The Jews were used to simple services, while the converted pagans could not forget the emotional content of the mystery religions. Both longed for emotional satisfactions grounded in their former contexts.

It is no wonder that liturgical issues arose as well as the problems of dress and propriety in worship.

The Veiling of Women

1 Corinthians 11:2-16

> 2 Now I praise you, brethren, that ye remember me in all things, and keep the ordinances, as I delivered them to you.
> 3 But I would have you know, that the head of every man is Christ; and the head of the woman is the man; and the head of Christ is God.
> 4 Every man praying or prophesying, having his head covered, dishonoureth his head.
> 5 But every woman that prayeth or prophesieth with her head uncovered dishonoureth her head: for that is even all one as if she were shaven.
> 6 For if the woman be not covered, let her also be shorn: but if it be a shame for a woman to be shorn or shaven, let her be covered.
> 7 For a man indeed ought not to cover his head, forasmuch as he is the image and glory of God: but the woman is the glory of the man.
> 8 For the man is not of the woman; but the woman of the man.
> 9 Neither was the man created for the woman; but the woman for the man.
> 10 For this cause ought the woman to have power on her head because of the angels.
> 11 Nevertheless neither is the man without the woman, neither the woman without the man, in the Lord.
> 12 For as the woman is of the man, even so is the man also by the woman; but all things of God.
> 13 Judge in yourselves: is it comely that a woman pray unto God uncovered?

14 Doth not even nature itself teach you, that, if a man have long hair, it is a shame unto him?
15 But if a woman have long hair, it is a glory to her: for her hair is given her for a covering.
16 But if any man seem to be contentious, we have no such custom, neither the churches of God.

Some of the problems were cultural, such as, What role does a woman play in the life of worship? Paul will come back to this issue in 14:34-36. His attention was brought to the problem by the conduct of certain women members of the congregation who were not wearing veils (covering their heads). The issue illustrates the perennial problem of the relationship between culture and Christian morality.

1. *A word of praise* (2). Is this a hint of Paul's celebrated irony? No doubt Paul was aware of certain problems in the churches of Asia Minor, Macedonia, and Greece, and accepted the assurances of their loyalty to the traditions as he had delivered them. The apostle makes courteous acknowledgment but immediately maintains that he does so with some limitations (cf. Barclay and Baird for historical and cultural context).

2. *A graded scale of authority* (3-16). It is possible that Paul may someday be recognized as the great emancipator of women. His teachings on liberty and equality in Christ lend themselves to principles equivalent to present practices.

However, the timing was not right for that kind of a decision, and Paul teaches in principle what he was unable to do in the particular case because of accepted custom.

The problem arose no doubt because of the practice of some women appearing in worship with their heads uncovered. They had taken the truth expressed in 2 Cor. 5:7 literally. They felt themselves to be under a new dignity in Christ which transcended certain accepted customs. Women were certainly active in worship (5), but to pray and prophesy without the veil was an increase upon Jewish custom which Paul was not quite ready for.

It does not appear that Paul was as much concerned about the custom as he was an "attitude of mind." Must women assert their right within this context? Paul argues that by the Scriptures, nature, and custom, women are subordinate (not inferior) to men in the chain of authority.

a. A basic theological principle (3-10). The verse indicates a position upon which the practical instructions are based. Margaret E. Thrall suggests that it is a diagram of divine-human relations.[39] Every man has Christ for his head; and a woman's head is man, as Christ's head is God.

God
Christ
Man
Woman

The obedience of Christ to the Father-God is emphasized in John's Gospel and in 1 Cor. 15:24-28. Paul's belief that all men ought to be obedient to Christ is grounded in the creation story as reflected in 8:6. Man was brought into existence to glorify God by living out God's will. Women should obey men (7-9) because men are of the "image and glory of God" (Gen. 1:27). In turn, women are the glory of men (Gen. 2:22). Man was not created to meet the needs of woman, but woman of man (cf. Gen. 2:18; 1 Tim. 2:13).

One can only find the teachings of Paul palatable when he recognizes that the apostle was thinking of the family. The insistence on the independence of women threatened the cohesiveness of family relations—as it does today!

It was decorous for a man to worship with an uncovered head (7) and a woman to worship with a *veil*. If she removed her *veil*, indicating her proposed independence, why not go all the way and *shave* her head (5-6)? Paul knew the absurdity of the suggestion, it being a sign of slavery or mourning. In other words, Paul is suggesting that a woman's emancipation from and equality with men was not a raising but a lowering of her status. It was a violation of the divine order of things.

In v. 10, the angels are invoked as defenders of the divine order imposed by God in creation. It is highly suggestive that the veil *(exousia)* was a symbol of authority given to a woman to serve in worship. If so, the wearing of the veil was far more than an act of subordination; it was rather a symbol of privilege.

b. The end of the argument (11-16). Verses 11 and 12 seem to indicate that Paul thought he had gone too far in his argument for the subordination of women from the Scriptures, nature, and social convention. If so, he once again states the interdependence of men and women and their total dependence upon God. Nothing must detract from this basic faith. In the new creation there is neither male nor female—they are all one in Christ Jesus (Gal. 3:28).

The covering of the head is neither here nor there with the Lord, but Christians should give no unusual offence (10:32) in the accepted cultural mores of their day.

A number of years later, the pagans were looking for scandalous rumors about Christian worship. Bruce observes that "unnecessary breaches of customary propriety would be regarded as confirmation of such rumors. It was far better to give the lie to them by scrupulous maintenance of social decorum."[40] Though the application of the principle is relative, the principle itself is valid when the reputation of the "believing community" is at stake.

c. Some conclusions about a sensitive matter. While not many of us would insist on the particular illustration and view the particular as the "mind of Christ," the principles from which Paul worked are both contemporary and valid. (1) There is a graded order in nature which pervades all of the created order; (2) There is a mutual interdependence between man and woman established for their good; and (3) There is an absolute dependence upon God.

There is always dialectical tension in truth between the absolute and the particular, or between principle and example. In this, the poles of the paradox contribute to understanding rather than undermine understanding. Paul rather consistently uses this method in religious language to enforce what he declares to be truth. The paradox between the subordination of women and the application of the law of liberty is an example of his method.

The Lord's Supper

It is important to emphasize frequently the manner in which Paul treats the questions which were referred to him by the Corinthian church. The first is the habit of interpreting all matters (regardless of how insignificant) in the light of their underlying and abiding principles. The second is his ability to take a delicate or distasteful matter and "state some truth in terms of such striking beauty as to make it appear like a precious jewel embedded in a clod of earth."

Thus, when Paul turns to a review of the serious abuses in the practice of the Lord's Supper, he speaks to the principle of the matter and then records in exquisite language the institution of the Supper.

These verses (17-24) mark a change in Paul's address to the Corinthian church. There is an emotional deepening that shows the difference Paul attributes to former matters and the issue at hand. He is not dealing with a transient aspect of church life, but the central symbolism of the gospel. Someone has expressed it thus: "He shakes off from his feet the clogging, hampering mud of meretricious controversy and spreads his wings for a flight to the great sunlit heights of God's deepest and highest revelations to mankind."

1 Corinthians 11:17-34

17 Now in this that I declare unto you I praise you not, that ye come together not for the better, but for the worse.
18 For first of all, when ye come together in the church, I hear that there be divisions among you; and I partly believe it.
19 For there must be also heresies among you, that they which are approved may be made manifest among you.
20 When ye come together therefore into one place, this is not to eat the Lord's supper.

21 For in eating every one taketh before other his own supper: and one is hungry, and another is drunken.

22 What? have ye not houses to eat and to drink in? or despise ye the church of God, and shame them that have not? What shall I say to you? shall I praise you in this? I praise you not.

23 For I have received of the Lord that which also I delivered unto you, That the Lord Jesus the same night in which he was betrayed took bread:

24 And when he had given thanks, he brake it, and said, Take, eat: this is my body, which is broken for you: this do in remembrance of me.

25 After the same manner also he took the cup, when he had supped, saying, This cup is the new testament in my blood: this do ye, as oft as ye drink it, in remembrance of me.

26 For as often as ye eat this bread, and drink this cup, ye do shew the Lord's death till he come.

27 Wherefore whosoever shall eat this bread, and drink this cup of the Lord, unworthily, shall be guilty of the body and blood of the Lord.

28 But let a man examine himself, and so let him eat of that bread, and drink of that cup.

29 For he that eateth and drinketh unworthily, eateth and drinketh damnation to himself, not discerning the Lord's body.

30 For this cause many are weak and sickly among you, and many sleep.

31 For if we would judge ourselves, we should not be judged.

32 But when we are judged, we are chastened of the Lord, that we should not be condemned with the world.

33 Wherefore, my brethren, when ye come together to eat, tarry one for another.

34 And if any man hunger, let him eat at home; that ye come not together unto condemnation. And the rest will I set in order when I come.

1. *The offenses* (17-22). Paul is grieved by the divisions and heresies in the church (18-19). It was the object of the "common meal" to develop a united and robust fellowship among the members of the church. Why not? Were they not all of the body of Christ? While Paul is not offended by the order of events described, he is concerned about certain social aspects of the common meal.

Partisanship had invaded the practice of fellowship, which in turn had a bad effect on the sacred rite accompanying the meal. In fact, it was "not for the better, but for the worse." The divisions neutralized the good and promoted wrong attitudes in the congregation.

As Moffatt puts it, "God's living church has parts, but no parties." John Short tells the story of a high-caste Brahman who accepted Christianity and was cut off from family, inheritance, and friends. This he was willing to accept for Christ's sake, but the crisis came when he sat down at the Lord's table with an outcaste Hindu Christian brother. His stomach turned upside down. If this is what happened in the Corinthian church, the spirit had to be disciplined and exorcised. Fellowship was at stake. Paul was incensed at the fragmenting of the body of Christ.

Paul was also disturbed about the practices accompanying the common meal. According to the custom, each person brought provisions commensurate with his resources. The rich brought much while the poor brought little. Evidently each would eat of their own provisions, with some becoming drunken and others remaining hungry. The contrast is between too much and too little. Paul was so righteously indignant that he declared, "I praise you not." While he is restrained in his language ("I partly believed it," 18), he intimates even a divine purpose in order that those who were loyal to Christ might be recognized (19).

Paul reminds them, however, that such revelry makes it impossible to observe the beauty and reality of the Lord's Supper, whether it was observed prior to, during, or after the common meal. "What, do you not have houses to eat and drink in? Or do you despise the church of God and humiliate those who have nothing?" (22, RSV).

2. *The institution* (23-26). The drama of the Lord's Supper makes God's action vital in the life of the church. It is so important that Paul reminds them of what Jesus said and did, and what he meant by commanding that it be a regular part of worship. (In all probability this is the earliest of the accounts, since Mark was written some 10 years later.)

a. The authority given to the Lord's Supper (23a). Paul claimed that the account of the original institution was received from the Lord himself and that Paul, in turn, delivered it to the church. Hodge observes that "the sin of many in the fellowship of the church was therefore one of irreverent disobedience, without the excuse of ignorance."

Paul refuses to accept the ordinance as based on tradition or having come by human instruction, but rather through divine revelation (cf. Gal. 1:1, 12; 1 John 1:5). The institution was more than an authentication of tradition by revelation. The context here and in other references assures the reader that the "words of institution" were communicated immediately by Christ to the apostle. It also shows the profound importance that the Lord attributed to the sacrament.

b. The elements of the Lord's Supper (23*b*-25). Jesus took bread (unleavened) and after giving thanks, He said, "Take, eat: this is my body, which is broken for you." Obviously, the bread cannot be applied literally to the body of Christ, since He was in the Upper Room when He originally uttered the words.

The bread speaks to us of our Lord's incarnation. "He took bread . . . this is my body." It brings to vivid memory that "the Word was made flesh, and dwelt among us." He came not as an angel but as a man. It also speaks to us of the Lord's redemption—"which is broken for you." The thought is not the breaking of the body but the self-giving Sacrifice in behalf of all of us. It is a symbol of the giving of himself. Thus, it was the sacrificial character of the death of Christ that redemption takes on meaning.

Jesus also took the cup (25) and represented it as "the new testament in my blood" (cf. Luke 22:20). In Matthew and Mark the corresponding expression is "this is my blood of the new testament." In either case, Paul is speaking of the "blood of the covenant" by which the covenant was ratified and its blessings secured (Exod. 24:8). The covenant is called "new" in contrast to the Mosaic covenant. And so God in Christ promised to confer all the promised blessings to those who receive the cup and embrace the covenant of grace and bind themselves in obedience to the Lord's will. In receiving the cup, the communicant receives the earnest of that pledge.

Every time the fruit of the vine touches the lips of the

communicant, it is a sacred symbol of the application of the blood of Christ, in faith, for the remission of sins in reconciliation to God.

The cup represents the faith that Jesus is the Son of God; that He loved us and gave himself for us; and that His blood cleanses from all sin. In the sacrament we receive the benefits accruing from His death. It is a pledge of obedience in grateful love for what He has done for all mankind.

c. The motive of the Lord's Supper (26). Jesus Christ, who cared very little for rites, established two ordinances which cover the whole ground of Christian experience: (1) The rite of initiation through baptism, and (2) the rite of commemoration through the Lord's Supper. The first is experienced once in a lifetime; the second is repeated with frequency.

The primitive form of the Lord's Supper contains a reference to the past, to the present, and to the future:

(1) It is a memorial to the past. Remembrance *(anamnesis)* is the activity of calling to mind. By receiving the bread and the cup, we recall Christ's sufferings for us. "Of me" is emphatic in the original Greek and stresses the Christ-centered nature of the service.

MacClaren points out that in this sublime moment "a greater than Moses is here." In "remember me" (TLB), Christ is insisting that we give Him His place at "the very apex and shining summit of all religious aspiration."

(2) It is a memorial to the present. The Christian life is not only the memory of a past experience, but the living out of Christ's presence in our lives today. It is not only "Christ for us," but "Christ in us."

In the Lord's Supper, Christ is very near to us and we feed upon Him. This is no mysticism but the very fact and condition of Christian existence. We are Christian insofar as we live in Him, walk after Him, and obey His commandments. It is through loving communion that remembrance takes on the clothes of the present.

(3) It is a memorial to the future (26). The im-

portant word is "show" *(katangello),* meaning to "announce" or "proclaim." It is an activity directed toward men rather than God. The Lord's Supper is an "acted sermon," an acted proclamation of His death and its meaning. "Till he come" reminds us of the eschatological aspect of the Eucharist.

In the original words of the institution, Jesus said, "Till I drink it new with you in my Father's kingdom" (Matt. 26:29). In the Corinthian context there is the provision for the perpetuation of the sacrament until the Lord returns. In this the Cross and the crown are linked together in an indissoluble bond.

We move from the agony and death of Gethsemane and Calvary to Christ's table in His kingdom. The prophecy promises the "oil of joy for mourning" and the full promise of His blessing.

> The future is unlike the prophetic past in that "we shall go no more out," there shall be no sequences of sorrow, and struggle, and distance and ignorance; but like it in that we shall feast on Christ, for through eternity the glorified Jesus will be the bread of our spirits, and the fact of His past sacrifice the foundation of our hopes.[41]

3. *The warning and instruction* (27-34). In the closing verses of the chapter, Paul reminds the Corinthian Christians of the solemnity of the Lord's Supper and their conduct in the light of that solemn act of remembrance.

"Wherefore" *(hōste)* in v. 27 stresses consequence. It is because of the meaningfulness of the sacrament that Christians must observe the rite with care. In one sense, all partake unworthily; but in another, we can come worthily—that is, in faith, with that which is fitting to the believer. To attend the sacrifice with carelessness or with a casual attitude is to come unworthily. The worthy approach demands two things: self-examination, and concern for others.

a. Self-examination (28-31). The responsibility for worthiness lies with the communicant himself. No one knows his heart as he does. If we judge ourselves now, we shall be blameless at the judgment seat of Christ (31). If we allow the Holy Spirit to search our hearts now, we shall not be judged.

"Examine" *(dokimazetō)* is often used of the testing of metals. Damnation is better translated "condemnation" *(krima)*. Paul does not mean that a careless communicant incurs eternal damnation but a judgment appropriate to his act. He who treats the symbols of Christ's body and blood irreverently is guilty of irreverence toward the Lord himself.

It is because of those who have participated unworthily that many are sick and many have died (30). Paul looked upon the prevailing sickness among many Corinthian Christians as a judgment of God because of their irreverence in celebrating the Lord's Supper. It is not without reason that some of their suffering was psychosomatic with its concomitant results. Paul viewed the chastening as a judgment of the Lord (32).

b. Concern for others (33-34). Arising out of the discussion, Paul gives the conclusion of the matter. He urges them to "tarry one for another." The disgraceful scramble of v. 21 must cease. The rich must wait for the poor, and the poor must find fellowship with the more affluent, if the "agape meal" is to mean anything at all. The apostle believed very firmly in the ability of the gospel to bring all to a common level.

The scripture may indicate that it is now Paul's motive to separate the common meal from the Lord's Supper. "If anyone is hungry, let him eat at home" (RSV). If so, the Lord's Supper stands out alone and apart from the common meal, and the church has gained from the procedure. On the other hand, it may have lost the element of fellowship which is implied by eating together. We will have to admit that by enacting them together, there is a sacredness which the church has lost in its semisecular activities.

Out of Paul's great love for the community comes a depth of passion which is now exhausted. He has high hopes for this church and is not forgetful of the things he can commend as well as that which he must condemn. He concludes with a plea and a promise. "Wait for one another" to establish true fellowship. And if you have more questions, "I will give directions when I come" (RSV).

1 CORINTHIANS 12

Spiritual Gifts

Paul treats the *charismata* with caution and tact. He includes a list of gifts and places them in a certain order of value. In the meantime he will say something important about their origin, the channels of expression, and the relationship of the whole to the lordship of Christ.

The ancient prophets clearly predicted that the Messianic period would be attended by a remarkable effusion of the Holy Spirit (Ezek. 36:25-27; cf. Joel 2:28-32; John 14; Mark 16:17-18; Acts 1:5). It was not to be confined to one class of people, but was to express itself in a wonderful diversity of supernatural endowments.

Under these extraordinary circumstances it was unavoidable that disorders should arise and the gifts be abused. Some would be dissatisfied with their gifts; others would falsely claim gifts not their own; and many would be jealous of others who were now highly favored. A few would make a display of their powers for personal interest.

Paul devotes cc. 12—14 of First Corinthians to the correction of these evils. Bruce remarks succinctly that the argument of 12:1—14:40 might be summed up in one sentence: "The primary token of the indwelling Spirit, the indispensable evidence that one is truly 'spiritual,' is not *glossolalia* (tongues), but love."

1 Corinthians 12:1-11

1 Now concerning spiritual gifts, brethren, I would not have you ignorant.

2 Ye know that ye were Gentiles, carried away unto these dumb idols, even as ye were led.

3 Wherefore I give you to understand, that no man speaking by the Spirit of God calleth Jesus accursed: and that no man can say that Jesus is the Lord, but by the Holy Ghost.

4 Now there are diversities of gifts, but the same Spirit.

5 And there are differences of administrations, but the same Lord.

6 And there are diversities of operations, but it is the same God which worketh all in all.

7 But the manifestation of the Spirit is given to every man to profit withal.

8 For to one is given by the Spirit the word of wisdom; to another the word of knowledge by the same Spirit;

9 To another faith by the same Spirit; to another the gifts of healing by the same Spirit;

10 To another the working of miracles; to another prophecy; to another discerning of spirits; to another divers kinds of tongues; to another the interpretation of tongues:

11 But all these worketh that one and the selfsame Spirit, dividing to every man severally as he will.

1. *The variety of gifts* (1-11). The word *pneumatikōn* is of indeterminate gender. It could denote either "spiritual men" or "spiritual things." Usually it is held to denote spiritual things or gifts.

a. Paul begins by stating some basic principles. He argues first that emotional excess is not a sign of superior piety. He points out that they were "carried away" ("swept off," NEB) "wherever [they] might be led" (Williams). They were swayed by a blind, unintelligent impulse. Now that they were under the influence of the Spirit of God, their life was to be entirely different—a discipline about which their former life gave no information. Again, Paul certainly teaches that emotional excess is not a sign of superior piety nor proof of the possession of spiritual gifts.

Some remarkable things were happening in the Apostolic Church, but Paul was determined that hysterical excitement, self-delusion, and utter mistakenness would not delude the Corinthians from the "genuine article."

Secondly, the confession "Jesus is Lord" is the true criterion of the Spirit's presence (3). This fascinating passage gives two battle cries, the other being "Jesus be cursed" (RSV). While there are several suggestions as to the manner in which the latter slogan was used, Paul was probably speaking of tongues with its emotional abandon, its intellectual poverty, and its "nonsensical syllables" which could even add up to a curse of Christ. Barclay suggests that it might have been used by the Jews as an anathema against the Christians, or used by the Christians when, under persecution, they were forced to curse Christ or die.

The great battle cry of the early Christian and his purest creed was "Jesus is Lord." The word *kurios* is a wonderful word. It is the name given to Jehovah in the Greek version of the Old Testament (LXX). To say, "Jesus is Lord," in the sense that Paul was using it, was to acknowledge Him as truly God. And as the name Jesus was the name of the historical Person, one has the full appellation, "truly God and truly man."

While it is true that anyone can say, "Jesus is Lord," he is not talking authentically apart from the agency of the Spirit of God. All spiritual gifts must be brought to the touchstone of the Christian confession.

b. Paul continues by describing the variety of gifts (4-11).

(1) The gifts are diverse, but their Source is one. The gifts are not divided into three sections (gifts, manifestations, operations), but are presented under three aspects. From the perspective of the Spirit, they are gifts; in relation to the Lord, they are ministrations; and in relation to God, they are operations. Their Source is the one God (6). The Spirit is the Giver; the Lord Jesus is the Authority through which the gifts are exercised; and it is God the Father who exalted Jesus as Lord and sent the Holy Spirit "which worketh all in all" (6). The doctrine of the Trinity is fundamental to an understanding of this passage.

(2) The gifts are given for the "common good" (7). In Paul's mind, every gift is given to benefit both the individual and the community. A spiritual man was not going to use his gift for his own purposes, but for the good of the whole.

The special gifts that the apostle speaks of tell us something about the character and work of the Early Church. It would be well if we would interpret his concept to include all that members of the body of Christ do, and give them a sanctity as implied in his later discussion of the "body of Christ."

(3) The gifts are listed in order to show the diverse character of the Church and the need for unity under the lordship of Christ (8-11). It is important to observe that after each gift or series of gifts, Paul is careful to observe that they are all of the same Spirit (8-9, 11). *This speaks to us!* In a day when so much emphasis is given to the charismatic character of the Spirit-filled life, the Source of that life must without exception rest with confidence in the Spirit of God.

Usually the gifts are classified in three groups: the teaching gifts (8), the supernatural gifts (9-10), and the gifts of special communication (10*b*).

(a) The teaching gifts include "the word of wisdom" and "the word of knowledge." The former *(sophia)* is the knowledge of God himself. Communion with God probably speaks better of that wisdom which comes not so much by thought but through a spiritual relationship—an I-Thou relation. Blessed is the man who knows God because he lives close to Him.

The word of knowledge *(gnōsis)* is the gift of communication of knowledge, as the gift of wisdom is a quality of maturity and insight. The latter seems to be the more practical—the application of wisdom to the given affairs of life.

The church needed both. It needed those who discerned the wisdom of God and those who could apply that wisdom to the practical affairs of life.

(b) The supernatural gifts include "faith," "healing," and "miracles." Faith is not the "saving faith" of Rom. 3:27, but a special endowment for a special service (cf. 13:2*b*). It is a marvelous gift that really produces

results—a faith that can "move mountains." Barclay says it is the gift that turns visions into deeds.

> *O God, when the heart is the warmest,*
> *And the head is the clearest,*
>   *Give me to act;*
> *To turn the purposes Thou formest*
>   *Into fact!*

In the Early Church (and hopefully for today's Church), it was the faith to cure the sick and cast out demons in His name. The gift of healing was closely related to faith and not apart from it. The healing power of Christ was for the whole man—body, soul, and spirit. Jesus healed both the sick and the mentally deranged. Pain to Him was terribly real. When opportunity was given, Jesus stepped in to heal the whole personality.

The working of miracles (*dynameis,* mighty works) compares with the events recorded in Acts 2:22, 43 and was a sign of the new age to come (cf. Gal. 3:5; Heb. 2:4). It is demonstrated in the raising of Lazarus, the death of Ananias, the miracle of Dorcas, and the smiting of Elymas with blindness.

The foregoing gifts of power represent a supernatural endowment. Jesus said, "He that believeth on me, the works that I do shall he do also; and greater works than these shall he do; because I go to my Father" (John 14:12). They are "overcoming gifts" in the face of failure, the gifts of openness in the face of closure.

(c) The gifts of special communication include "prophecy," "discernment," "tongues," and "the interpretation of tongues."

The nature of prophecy was not quite clear in the Early Church. The word as used here means "forthtelling." Although this aspect was not absent, the declaration of the Word of God more clearly defines the function. Men were gifted to make the gospel relevant in any situation. God was interested in men who could bring rebuke and warning as well as advice and guidance in their prophetic function as preachers.

The gift of discernment was given to supplement and correct the gift of prophecy. In a society with its tensions and aberrations, it was important to have those in the body of Christ who could discern between what was genuine and what was false.

Lastly, Paul lists divers kinds of tongues and the interpretation of tongues (10). Bruce suggests that these gifts included those intelligible to some hearers (2:6 ff.) and those which could not be understood unless someone present could exercise the ninth gift of the series, the interpretation of tongues (cf. the list in v. 28).

The matter caused a great deal of perplexity in the church at Corinth as it always has in the history of Christian fellowships. The gift of tongues was a highly coveted gift which Paul did not question, but he was fully aware that it had its dangers in the areas of hysteria, ecstasy, and self-hypnotism which were not for the common good.

The Corinthians seemed particularly susceptible to this emotional experience and ranked it above the other gifts, though Paul always listed it last. John Short observes that Paul applied his "sanctified common sense" to the situation so that the church might be saved from confusion and lack of discipline. (See the BBC for an exegesis of the passage.) No two authors agree. E. Stanley Jones looked upon it as exclusively apostolic. In any case, Paul in c. 14 will correct the perversion of the gift through positive instructions as to its use.

However we may interpret the gifts, they are given by one and the same Spirit of God (11) who has alloted them not as we see fit, but as He *wills*. The list is not exhaustive nor exclusive. They are directed toward the ongoing of the fellowship. The whole passage excludes any expression of selfishness in their demonstration. They always give praise to their Source—the Holy Spirit of God— and when exercised properly, will build up the body of Christ in unity and love.

The Body of Christ—Diversity in Unity

Verses 12-31 constitute one of the most beautiful passages in the Holy Scriptures concerning the Church—the body of Christ (cf. Rom. 12:4-5; Eph. 4:14-16; Col. 3:14). It was apparent that the Corinthians were unaware of the true character of the Church, or else in their carnalmindedness they refused to admit its unity. To see its unity is to "ring a new note of passionate concern for Christ in His World."

Before His ascension Christ was in the world. The Church is now His body, carrying out His task in the power of the Holy Spirit.

> *He has no hands but our hands*
> *To do His work today;*
> *He has no feet but our feet*
> *To lead men in His way;*
> *He has no voice but our voice*
> *To tell men how He died;*
> *He has no help but our help*
> *To lead them to His side.*

1 Corinthians 12:12-31

12 For as the body is one, and hath many members, and all the members of that one body, being many, are one body: so also is Christ.

13 For by one Spirit are we all baptized into one body, whether we be Jews or Gentiles, whether we be bond or free; and have been all made to drink into one Spirit.

14 For the body is not one member, but many.

15 If the foot shall say, Because I am not the hand, I am not of the body; is it therefore not of the body?

16 And if the ear shall say, Because I am not the eye, I am not of the body; is it therefore not of the body?

17 If the whole body were an eye, where were the hearing? If the whole were hearing, where were the smelling?

18 But now hath God set the members every one of them in the body, as it hath pleased him.

19 And if they were all one member, where were the body?

20 But now are they many members, yet but one body.

21 And the eye cannot say unto the hand, I have no need of thee: nor again the head to the feet, I have no need of you.

22 Nay, much more those members of the body, which seem to be more feeble, are necessary:

23 And those members of the body, which we think to be less honourable, upon these we bestow more abundant honour; and our uncomely parts have more abundant comeliness.

24 For our comely parts have no need: but God hath tempered the body together, having given more abundant honour to that part which lacked:
25 That there should be no schism in the body; but that the members should have the same care one for another.
26 And whether one member suffer, all the members suffer with it; or one member be honoured, all the members rejoice with it.
27 Now ye are the body of Christ, and members in particular.
28 And God hath set some in the church, first apostles, secondarily prophets, thirdly teachers, after that miracles, then gifts of healings, helps, governments, diversities of tongues.
29 Are all apostles? are all prophets? are all teachers? are all workers of miracles?
30 Have all the gifts of healing? do all speak with tongues? do all interpret?
31 But covet earnestly the best gifts: and yet shew I unto you a more excellent way.

1. Paul was determined that the witness of the church should not be nullified by either division or divisiveness, so he reinforces his argument by showing the "mystical unity of the body" which is animated by the Spirit of Christ (12-13). He further defines the body as a universal expression of Christ, the Head, transcending all distinctions of race and class.

It is obvious that the Corinthians, as well as most fellowships, needed to be reminded of "that word." Both *Jews* and *Greeks* were members of that church. "God reckons little of nationality or race or status in the fulfillment of his purposes." The church was more than international—it was supranational. It provided the authentic unity in faith, program, and spirit in a world which was distraught and fractured. Paul gives a beautiful description of that essential unity of which Christ is the Head.

2. *Jealousy is absent when there is unity in the body* (14-20). The lovely metaphor leaves no question as to its meaning: "We need each other." There is no spiritual isolation in the community. The body is composed of many members, not just one.

The foot cannot say, "Because I am not the hand, I am not of the body" (15). The ear cannot stand apart from the eye. If the whole body were one of its members, what is the use of its balance? But God has organized the body "as it hath pleased him," because it consists of many in the one. Jealousy is impossible, for every member of the body has its place and function. To eliminate even one of the members makes the body function less perfectly.

3. *Pride is absent when there is unity in the body* (21-24). The eye cannot say to the hand, "I don't need you," nor the head to the feet, "I have no need of you."

Paul is warning those who had taken "unwarranted airs" because of personal pride. There were those with very little self-esteem. The schism between the prideful and those who felt they did not count destroyed the self-image of the latter. The former were more concerned with self than with Christ. Again, they had forgotten that every part was vital to the effective functioning of the body.

If vv. 14-20 warned against jealousy and demonstrated how we need each other, vv. 21-24 warn against pride and show how we must respect each other.

4. *Unity provides for both sympathy and identification within the body* (25-27). It is only natural, by definition, that the members of the body should "have the same care one for another." When one suffers, all suffer together. When one is honored, all rejoice with him. "We stand in each other's moccasins." It is that empathetic identity that makes the Church ideally what it was created to be.

In reiteration, every Christian is a necessary part of the community. Every Christian needs the help of every other Christian. Respect is to be shown to the less gifted as well as the highly gifted. And every Christian is involved in the success or failure of his fellow members.

What is true to the metaphor is applicable to the Church. "You" *(humeis)* is emphatic. There is no question in Paul's mind. *You are the body. Now act like it!*

5. *Unity demands a mutuality of interdependence within the body* (28-30). The Church is Christ's body; and men and women who make up that body have a distinctive contribution to make for the benefit of the whole.

Within that unity Paul lists eight kinds of members

with special functions. Some of them he has already mentioned, some of them are new. At the head of the list and in order of importance he places the apostles; those who had either been with Jesus or were a witness of His resurrection (Acts 1:22).

They are divided by importance into two classes. *First,* apostles, prophets, and teachers. *Second,* miracles, gifts of healings, helps, governments, diversities of tongues (cf. Eph. 4:11).

Following the apostles are the prophets (cf. 14:1) who declare the mind of God in the Spirit, and teachers who are gifted to instruct their fellow members in Christian faith and practice (Rom. 12:9—13:14). The balance are listed earlier with the exception of "helpers" (who are those directed to help the poor, the widows, the orphans and strangers) and the administrators ("governments") or helmsmen of the Church to pilot the organization in its life and action. Once again "speakers in various kinds of tongues" (RSV) come last, as they do in vv. 8-10.

Paul emphatically teaches the responsibility of mutual interdependence by asking seven questions in vv. 29-30 in descending order of value, each introduced by the Greek negative *mē,* implying that the answer is *no!* Bruce supports Paul's position that it is preposterous to assume that all have or need one and the same gift or a monopoly on all the gifts. "Once more he (Paul) inculcates the principle of diversity in unity, and incidentally explodes any tendency to claim that all spiritual persons should manifest *glossolalia.* "

6. *A final plea and promise* (31). If a member of the church desires any gifts, let him "covet earnestly the best gifts" (or the greater ones). Phillips says, "You should set your hearts on the best spiritual gifts" (cf. 14:1). And while apostleship was not now open to them, Paul is suggesting that the members cultivate an appetite for teaching and prophecy (preaching), particularly the latter (14:1).

Paul was pleased when a church was richly endowed

with spiritual gifts and was using them for sharing Christ. Blessed are those members who are cultivating the endowments that are theirs by the Spirit's will! Christ deserves the best that we can give Him. The "ongoingness" of the church is guaranteed if we use our gifts, not for our sake, but for His.

That plea is concluded in a promise, "Yet shew I unto you a more excellent way," which is the open door to the "Hymn of Love" in c. 13. Paul thus moves from the selective work of the Holy Spirit in the endowment of gifts to the universal call to love. It is the heart of the Corinthian letter and the resolution of the Corinthian problem.

1 CORINTHIANS 13

A Hymn in Praise of Love

1 Corinthians 13:1-13

> 1 Though I speak with the tongues of men and of angels, and have not charity, I am become as sounding brass, or a tinkling cymbal.
> 2 And though I have the gift of prophecy, and understand all mysteries, and all knowledge; and though I have all faith, so that I could remove mountains, and have not charity, I am nothing.
> 3 And though I bestow all my goods to feed the poor, and though I give my body to be burned, and have not charity, it profiteth me nothing.
> 4 Charity suffereth long, and is kind; charity envieth not; charity vaunteth not itself, is not puffed up,
> 5 Doth not behave itself unseemly, seeketh not her own, is not easily provoked, thinketh no evil;
> 6 Rejoiceth not in iniquity, but rejoiceth in the truth;
> 7 Beareth all things, believeth all things, hopeth all things, endureth all things.
> 8 Charity never faileth: but whether there be prophecies, they shall fail; whether there be tongues, they shall cease; whether there be knowledge, it shall vanish away.
> 9 For we know in part, and we prophesy in part.
> 10 But when that which is perfect is come, then that which is in part shall be done away.
> 11 When I was a child, I spake as a child, I understood as a child, I thought as a child: but when I became a man, I put away childish things.
> 12 For now we see through a glass, darkly; but then face to face: now I know in part; but then shall I know even as also I am known.
> 13 And now abideth faith, hope, charity, these three; but the greatest of these is charity.

How can any expositor unwrap the beauty of this great chapter other than by quoting it? Paul's "more excellent way" is the way of love which he proceeds to unfold with "singular beauty and power." Von Harnack speaks of this chapter as "the greatest, strongest, deepest thing that Paul ever wrote," and we with openheartedness give an "Amen."

In c. 13, Paul is not digressing from his argument in 12—14. Though the chapter is an interpolation within the discussion of spiritual gifts, it is really central to the progression of Paul's thought. While love is more of a grace than a gift, it is that quality of life which must penetrate the whole if the gifts have any meaning at all. It is love that fructifies the gifts and deepens the devotion to Christ, the Head of the Church. Love is the result of the supernatural power of the Holy Spirit (Gal. 5:22) which enables a Christian to behave as a member of the body of Christ.

The theme of this magnificent chapter is that the gifts of the Spirit are valueless apart from love and are limited in scope and time, while love is permanent and universal.

While the KJV renders *agape* "charity," most other versions make the English equivalent to be "love." *Agape,* as defining love, was not so used prior to the writing of the New Testament, but the Christians gave it this distinctive meaning and made it theirs in much the same way that they attributed *Kurios* (Lord) to Christ. It is a singularly Christian word. It denotes a quality displayed in the Cross, a love which asked for no compensation. It represents a giving which asks not for possession. Christ's giving was one of self-giving *agape.* He sought nothing for himself. Paul sees this quality as the savior and preserver of community.

1. *The necessity of love* (1-3). Love is superior to any of the gifts listed in 12:8 ff. Supposing I am versed in all the mysteries and all the knowledge of God and am able to declare the truth with superlative finesse, and have no love, my message would be "nothing."

Supposing I have absolute faith and can do mighty

works of healing and other miracles, without love it would be useless.

Supposing that I am the greatest philanthropist in the world and give all I have to feed the poor—even so far as to give my life for the Lord; if it is not done in the spirit of love, it really would make no difference.

2. *The spirit of love* (4-6). "Love is patient and kind. Love is not envious or boastful. It does not put on airs. It is not rude. It does not insist on its rights. It does not become angry. It is not resentful. It is not happy over injustice, it is only happy with truth" (Goodspeed). But self-seeking is the very spirit the Corinthians displayed at the Lord's table and in their pride in spiritual possessions. Baird points out that the Corinthians had gone their own way, resentful of their brethren, "happy in the midst of the errors" and eager to "dote on the evils of others."

3. *The permanence of love* (7-10). In contrast to the carnal spirit of the Corinthians, love will "bear anything,"'is always eager to "believe" the best, and "put the most favorable construction to ambiguous actions." Love hopes against hope and is always willing to give a second chance and forgive "seventy times seven" (Matt. 18:22). All the gifts of the Spirit will pass away in this dispensation, but love will never pass away. Inspired preaching will come to an end; speaking in tongues will end. Even knowledge will pass away—but love will never "die out" (Goodspeed).

Though our "knowledge is imperfect and our prophecy is imperfect, when the perfect *[teleion]* comes, the imperfect will pass away" (ASV). The perfect is the *eschaton*—that one to come! The glorious promise of the New Age is the promise of vv. 8-13.

4. *The insight of love* (11-12). Paul illustrates the permanence of love in two ways. First, he shows that the gifts of the Spirit are instrumental. They belong to "this time." In the "fulness of time" they will lose their purpose and "come to an end." He may well have also been chiding them for their babbling. They must give up their childish-

ness (cf. 14:20). The things to which they have attached great importance must be put away, and they must learn to evaluate what is permanent.

The second illustration is a serious comparison with a common experience. "For now we are looking at a dim reflection in a mirror, but then I shall know as fully as God knows me" (Goodspeed).

The Corinthian bronze and silver mirrors were treasured by rich and poor alike. However, the poor could afford to purchase only those of inferior quality. Regardless of how highly they were polished, though, they could give only an imperfect image. So it is with our knowledge of God. Nature has dimly revealed Him, the Scriptures have pointed us to Him, and trust in Christ has identified us with Him. But we still see in a mirror dimly. The mystery is on man's side, not God's. The wonder is that we see at all. But what we see is true to God's purpose. God in Christ has revealed himself adequately for our redemption.

But there will be a day! After leaving his metaphors, Paul looks forward to the blessed *parousia* (coming of Christ). In that day we shall see Him face-to-face. "Now my knowledge is imperfect, but then I shall know as fully as God knows me" (Goodspeed).

We know God now only as He is reflected in the face of Jesus Christ; but He knows us perfectly (Gal. 4:9). Then, "we shall know him as we are known." The change from "know" to "understand" *(epiginoskein)* denotes the knowledge of God which comes from the unimpeded vision of God. It is only then that our knowledge of Him shall be equivalent to His knowledge of us.

But for now, while we see dimly, we *do* see! While our understanding of God is distorted, it is our faith and hope that there will be a day which will bring us face-to-face with our Heavenly Father. It is in "that day" when the expectations seen obscurely here will be fully realized and understood. What more can be said?

5. *The rank of love* (13). "So faith, hope and love abide,

these three; but the greatest of these is love" (RSV). Love is greatest because "he first loved us" (1 John 4:19). Faith and hope are our response to His love (Rom. 5:1-5; Phil. 1:9-10; Col. 1:4-5; 1 Thess. 1:3; 5:8; 2 Thess. 1:3-4). When faith gives place to transparent vision (2 Cor. 5:7) and hope is "swallowed up in realization" (cf. Rom. 8:24), love remains unchanged. Therefore "the greatest of these is love."

John Short beautifully expresses what Paul must have had in mind when he suggested that "love completes and crowns every human relationship." International relations must be cemented with love if there is to be mutual cooperation, justice, peace, and security. Married life is soon shipwrecked if love does not burn with a steady flame. Parenthood is a tragedy unless the family circle is bridged in a continuing love. The relationship between the Master and His disciples was incomplete until it was crowned by His love.

While the gifts of the Spirit are selective, the grace of love is for all men. We cannot yield to the temptation that our life counts for nothing. Love brings the indispensable ingredient that makes all things possible. "Let the lamps of love shine," for the love of Jesus Christ is "the great central sun from whose energy we draw our light." In heaven itself there will be no night at all—physical, mental, or spiritual—for His love will be the light of all (Rev. 22:5).

No wonder Paul said, "the greatest . . . is love"!

> O Love that wilt not let me go,
>   I rest my weary soul in Thee.
> I give Thee back the life I owe,
> That in Thine ocean depths its flow
>   May richer, fuller be.
>
> O Light that followest all my way,
>   I yield my flick'ring torch to Thee.
> My heart restores its borrowed ray,
> That in Thy sunshine's blaze its day
>   May brighter, fairer be.

O joy that seekest me through pain,
  I cannot close my heart to Thee.
I trace the rainbow through the rain,
And feel the promise is not vain
  That morn shall tearless be.

O Cross that liftest up my head,
  I dare not ask to fly from Thee,
I lay in dust life's glory dead,
And from the ground there blossoms red
  Life that shall endless be.

—GEORGE MATHESON

1 CORINTHIANS 14

A Comparison of Gifts

Having made love the criterion of judgment and value, and making it crystal clear that the supreme fruit of the Spirit is available to every member of the community, Paul now turns to the delicate task of evaluating prophecy and tongues.

The whole passage is marked by a refreshing wisdom, deep insight, and rewarding tactfulness. Here was the "gentle touch."

The Corinthian Christians held the gift of tongues in high esteem, but Paul placed little value on it. He compared tongues to prophecy (preaching) at the former's disadvantage.

1 Corinthians 14:1-25

1 Follow after charity, and desire spiritual gifts, but rather that ye may prophesy.
2 For he that speaketh in an unknown tongue speaketh not unto men, but unto God: for no man understandeth him; howbeit in the spirit he speaketh mysteries.
3 But he that prophesieth speaketh unto men to edification, and exhortation, and comfort.
4 He that speaketh in an unknown tongue edifieth himself; but he that prophesieth edifieth the church.

5 I would that ye all spake with tongues, but rather that ye prophesied: for greater is he that prophesieth than he that speaketh with tongues, except he interpret, that the church may receive edifying.

6 Now, brethren, if I come unto you speaking with tongues, what shall I profit you, except I shall speak to you either by revelation, or by knowledge, or by prophesying, or by doctrine?

7 And even things without life giving sound, whether pipe or harp, except they give a distinction in the sounds, how shall it be known what is piped or harped?

8 For if the trumpet give an uncertain sound, who shall prepare himself to the battle?

9 So likewise ye, except ye utter by the tongue words easy to be understood, how shall it be known what is spoken? for ye shall speak into the air.

10 There are, it may be, so many kinds of voices in the world, and none of them is without signification.

11 Therefore if I know not the meaning of the voice, I shall be unto him that speaketh a barbarian, and he that speaketh shall be a barbarian unto me.

12 Even so ye, forasmuch as ye are zealous of spiritual gifts, seek that ye may excel to the edifying of the church.

13 Wherefore let him that speaketh in an unknown tongue pray that he may interpret.

14 For if I pray in an unknown tongue, my spirit prayeth, but my understanding is unfruitful.

15 What is it then? I will pray with the spirit, and I will pray with the understanding also: I will sing with the spirit, and I will sing with the understanding also.

16 Else when thou shalt bless with the spirit, how shall he that occupieth the room of the unlearned say Amen at thy giving of thanks, seeing he understandeth not what thou sayest?

17 For thou verily givest thanks well, but the other is not edified.

18 I thank my God, I speak with tongues more than ye all:

19 Yet in the church I had rather speak five words with my understanding, that by my voice I might teach others also, than ten thousand words in an unknown tongue.

20 Brethren, be not children in understanding: howbeit in malice be ye children, but in understanding be men.

21 In the law it is written, With men of other tongues and other lips will I speak unto this people; and yet for all that will they not hear me, saith the Lord.

22 Wherefore tongues are for a sign, not to them that believe, but to them that believe not: but prophesying serveth not for them that believe not, but for them which believe.

23 If therefore the whole church be come together into one place, and all speak with tongues, and there come in those that are unlearned, or unbelievers, will they not say that ye are mad?

24 But if all prophesy, and there come in one that believeth not, or one unlearned, he is convinced of all, he is judged of all:

25 And thus are the secrets of his heart made manifest; and so falling down on his face he will worship God, and report that God is in you of a truth.

1. *Love always comes first* (1*a*). The final verse of c. 13 is confirmed in the first verse of c. 14. The answer to the Co-

rinthian issue and to all church problems is to act in love. The superlative virtue of love is not only first, but encompasses all the others. Here is where the Christian and the Christian community must always begin.

2. *Prophecy is preferable to tongues* (1b-12). There are at least two reasons that Paul gives to show why love would draw one to prophecy rather than tongues. The first is a "consideration for fellow Christians" (1-19). The second is a desire for the "conversion of unbelievers" (20-25). Either reason is sufficient to make prophecy superior to tongues.

a. The apostle begins by observing that he that speaks in tongues speaks not to men, but to God (2). No one understands him because he is uttering "mysteries in the Spirit" (RSV). On the other hand, he who prophesies speaks words that build up, encourage, and comfort. Tongues may in some way help the speaker, but they cannot help the church. Only he who witnesses to the Word helps (edifies) the fellowship.

b. Although Paul did not prohibit the speaking in tongues, he points continually to the need for clarity in communication. He is pointing toward a proper sense of values. As with asceticism and libertarianism, he goes as far as he can but finally draws the line. And while tongues must be interpreted (3) if the gift is to achieve its purpose, prophesying under the power of the Spirit cannot fail to communicate with clarity. For that reason, he who prophesies is greater than he who speaks in tongues.

Today, as well as then, the spoken word must stand on all fours to move the hearts and minds of men. When the Saviour is lifted up, preaching and participation in the sacraments are, as they have always been, the "twin focuses of the great ellipse of the gospel." Paul is very anxious that other gifts shall not encroach on this important aspect of the Church. Preaching established the Church; preaching must sustain the Church.

c. To illustrate the uselessness of uninterpreted

tongues, Paul draws two analogies. The first is from musical instruments (7-8) and the other from human languages (9). Melody and harmony are dependent upon consistency of tone and tempo. Only then can music be understood. So it is with languages. Each language has a structure of its own, and if this is not followed, "how shall it be known what is spoken?" Paul says it is just so much speaking "into the air." No ideas are conveyed.

If one, then, is to consider the gifts in the corresponding scale of values, utility and usefulness must come before personal edification (7-12). Preaching through revelation, knowledge, prophecy, and doctrine (6) build up the church; tongues uninterpreted can only build up the ego. The strengthening of the church can develop if information is communicated with clarity. Speaking in tongues, then, must mediate revelation, knowledge, prophecy, and teaching if the love of God is to be revealed through Christ to the world.

The true test of ecclesiastical speech is intelligibility and clarity. Emotional speech must have clear interpretation if it is to relate to worship. On that ground, Paul concludes that he will pray with both the spirit and the mind; he will also sing with both the spirit and the mind (14-15).

The whole passage clearly indicates that (1) the gospel message is more important than the speaking in tongues (2-4); that (2) clarity is to be coveted while confusion is to be avoided (6-11); and that (3) the good of the fellowship is more important than personal fulfillment. In fact, personal fulfillment can be found only in the fellowship of believers communicating the gospel with clarity and understanding.

3. *Intelligence and understanding are necessary to edification* (13-25). After Paul confesses his own gift (18), he clinches his argument by stating that in the church he would "rather speak five words with my understanding than ten thousand words in an unknown tongue." It is not

God who needs our worship, but we who need to worship Him.

A second basis for the superiority of prophecy lies in its usefulness as a witness to unbelievers. Tongues will evoke the derision of pagan witnesses (20-25). The Old Testament shows that men will not listen to speech in strange tongues (cf. Isa. 28:11-12). Thus Paul concludes that pagan witnesses will call the church mad if they hear tongues in worship (23). However, if the unbeliever hears the prophetic note, he is convinced and will fall down and worship God. Though prophecy is a sign to the believer, it is also a sign to the unbelievers who are thus led to believe.

In applying the principles discussed to the conditions of our day, Erdman suggests that "one would not feel impelled to desire the gifts of either prophecy or of tongues, but seek a clearer understanding of the relative importance of emotion and reason to Christian life and service."

Most churches need an outpouring and moving of the Holy Spirit in their midst in order that the participants may know something of the full joy and hope of God's presence. On the other hand, if we are serious about winning men to Christ, the appeal must be made to the intellect as well. There should be no longing (coveting) for the gift of tongues (14:1), but for new visions of Christ and His grace with messages so clear and simple that the heart of both the unlearned and learned can understand and obey.

Directions for Worship

Paul concludes this chapter of his letter to the Corinthians with certain practical directions grounded in the principles he has discussed.

1 Corinthians 14:26-40

> 26 How is it then, brethren? when ye come together, every one of you hath a psalm, hath a doctrine, hath a tongue, hath a revelation, hath an interpretation. Let all things be done unto edifying.

27 If any man speak in an unknown tongue, let it be by two, or at the most by three, and that by course; and let one interpret.

28 But if there be no interpreter, let him keep silence in the church; and let him speak to himself, and to God.

29 Let the prophets speak two or three, and let the other judge.

30 If any thing be revealed to another that sitteth by, let the first hold his peace.

31 For ye may all prophesy one by one, that all may learn, and all may be comforted.

32 And the spirits of the prophets are subject to the prophets.

33 For God is not the author of confusion, but of peace, as in all churches of the saints.

34 Let your women keep silence in the churches: for it is not permitted unto them to speak; but they are commanded to be under obedience, as also saith the law.

35 And if they will learn any thing, let them ask their husbands at home: for it is a shame for women to speak in the church.

36 What? came the word of God out from you? or came it unto you only?

37 If any man think himself to be a prophet, or spiritual, let him acknowledge that the things that I write unto you are the commandments of the Lord.

38 But if any man be ignorant, let him be ignorant.

39 Wherefore, brethren, covet to prophesy, and forbid not to speak with tongues.

40 Let all things be done decently and in order.

1. *Edification and orderliness* (26-28). Counsel was necessary because of the rich profusion of gifts in the Corinthian church. Everyone desired to exercise his gift. As a result, all would speak at once. What was designed as an instrument of warmth and orderliness turned out to be a "scene of wild confusion." And the worst disorder came from those attempting to speak in tongues. Paul starts and closes with his fundamental principle for the use of gifts: "Let all things be done unto edifying" (26).

Five elements in worship are mentioned. They are still significant as a model. "When you come together, each one has a hymn, a lesson, a revelation, a tongue, or an interpretation" (26, RSV). Prayer was previously mentioned in vv. 14-15. The note of praise is struck at the outset, for at the core of worship is adoration toward and awe of God. Praise, rightly directed, can sweep a congregation into the presence of God.

This is followed by a "lesson." The order is unimportant, but the presence of the teaching function in worship is of supreme importance. The praiseful person is open to instruction, and through it the church is able to pass on its heritage from one generation to another. The presence of the lesson preserves the heritage and makes possible its renewal. A revelation is an inspired and prophetic insight. It can come through witness or through the declaration of the Word. Paul is interested that all the elements of worship be brought to the fellowship where they can stand the clear evaluation of the congregation. He is afraid of personal, subjective activities apart from the congregation.

Speaking in a tongue is permitted, but is limited at three points: *(a)* Persons shall always speak in turn; *(b)* The number in any one service is to be limited to three; and *(c)* No one should exercise the gift without an interpreter. The restrictions, for all intents and purposes, would eliminate any excess and perhaps the use altogether of the gift in worship. Far better to let the expression run in private and personal devotions (28). The heart of the passage is not speaking in tongues, but the insistence by the apostle that God is not a God of confusion, and that all is to be done for the good of the church. Anything that does not contribute to this ideal is to be eliminated.

2. *The exercise of prophecy* (29-33*a*). Similar restraints are ordered with reference to the preferred gift of prophecy. This gift, too, is subject to certain controls. There is to be no prophesying under a moment of emotion (32-33). The prophet's rational mind is to be in control so he can "speak or refrain from speaking at will," whichever is more expedient. Paul sees no reason why one should not be content with quietness until the speaker's turn came. His conclusion is not ambiguous: "For God is not the author of confusion, but of peace, as in all churches of the saints" (33, RSV).

3. *The role of women* (33*b*-36). Married women were not to exercise the gift of prophecy in public worship without a head covering. Paul argues from the same ground he used previously: The headship of the husband and the

dependence of the wife (cf. exposition on 11:2-16 and 1 Tim. 2:11-12). It is not that women were not to pray and prophesy in public, but rather to restrain the practice with dignity for the sake of order.

In other places Paul speaks with obvious gratitude for the service of devoted Christian women. He owed a great deal to Lydia, Prisca, and others. The Christian Church will always owe a debt of gratitude to women who have approached greatness in both the home and the church. They have exercised their strength and poise in many a storm. Paul is not down-playing their role, but defending their dignity and integrity in a difficult situation.

4. *The nature of the spiritual* (37-40). Paul states that "if anyone thinks he is a prophet, or spiritual," as many Corinthians did (for example, 2:15; 12:1 ff.), he should prove the authenticity of his claim. Certainly, he does not do this by speaking in tongues, but by acknowledging that "what I am writing to you is a command of the Lord" (37, RSV). His ruling was not personal but carried the stamp of God. Gifted men of the Spirit would recognize that authority.

Prophecy is "heartily encouraged" (39); speaking in tongues is permitted but certainly not encouraged. While a gift of the Spirit, tongues is the least helpful, the least benevolent, and the greatest contributor to confusion in worship.

Bruce concludes that "Paul's concern is to direct the Corinthians' zeal into more profitable channels." There are two principles, Bruce points out, which have "permanent and universal validity for church life. Every activity should build up the church, and *all things should be done decently* (*euschemonōs,* 'in a seemly manner') *and in order.*"

The apostle, as usual, has spoken with wisdom and tolerance. He is the model of the "man in Christ," the greathearted follower of the Saviour. In love, he yearns for a like response from this great church. Upon the foundation of love, the building can be raised despite every difficulty and problem.

Paul has completed his argument. He started with fragmented saints; he concludes with a prayer for unity in love.

> *O Love, how cheering is Thy ray!*
> *All pain before Thy presence flies;*
> *Care, anguish, sorrow, melt away,*
> *Where'er Thy healing beams arise.*
> *O Father, nothing may I see,*
> *Nothing desire, or seek, but Thee.*
>
> —P. Gerhardt

The Resurrection of the Dead
and the Life of Faith
1 Corinthians 15:1-58

1 CORINTHIANS 15

The fifteenth chapter of First Corinthians is one of the greatest of the New Testament. It is also one of the most difficult, as it argues for the "resurrection of the body."

It is important to remember that the Corinthians were not denying the resurrection of Jesus Christ. That they were willing and ready to affirm. But they were not ready to acknowledge the relationship of bodily resurrection to the resurrection of their Lord. Their reasons are obscure, but Paul's superlative declarations are clear. The argument begins with a reminder of the fundamentals of the Christian faith—chiefly the resurrection of Jesus Christ and the witness who attested to the event.

The Resurrection of Jesus

1 Corinthians 15:1-11

1 Moreover, brethren, I declare unto you the gospel which I preached unto you, which also ye have received, and wherein ye stand;
2 By which also ye are saved, if ye keep in memory what I preached unto you, unless ye have believed in vain.
3 For I delivered unto you first of all that which I also received, how that Christ died for our sins according to the scriptures;
4 And that he was buried, and that he rose again the third day according to the scriptures:
5 And that he was seen of Cephas, then of the twelve:
6 After that he was seen of about five hundred brethren at once; of whom the greater part remain unto this present, but some are fallen asleep.

7 After that, he was seen of James; then of all the apostles.

8 And last of all he was seen of me also, as of one born out of due time.

9 For I am the least of the apostles, that am not meet to be called an apostle, because I persecuted the church of God.

10 But by the grace of God I am what I am: and his grace which was bestowed upon me was not in vain; but I laboured more abundantly than they all: yet not I, but the grace of God which was with me.

11 Therefore whether it were I or they, so we preach, and so ye believed.

We turn to this glorious passage of urgent and heart-stirring beauty in which the apostle declares the gospel of the Resurrection.

1. *The apostolic gospel* (1-4). Once again Paul affirms that he did not receive the gospel from men, but from Jesus Christ (cf. Gal. 1:11 ff.). It was certainly no human testimony that caused him to receive it (3). Neither was this true of his converts. They too had received the gospel (1). It was through the preaching of the "good news" and their glad acceptance of it that their salvation was realized.

a. The gospel is a message of grace to be received (1). Paul's words ring with a tone of certainty. He had preached in the assurance of the Spirit. His converts received the gospel gladly and embraced it as truth. They then professed it in faith. Of this, Paul was certain.

b. The gospel is the foundation for a continuing relationship in Christ (1c). It was the faith wherein they could stand (cf. Rom. 5:2; 11:20). The collateral function of the Good News was to give a man poise and stability. Moffatt translates Job 4:4, "Your words have kept men on their feet." Paul knew that the heart of the Saviour was breaking over the vacillation of His people. It was never Christ's intention that the gospel should lead to failure. Paul knew that consistent adherence to faith in Christ would result in stability.

c. The gospel contains the ground of salvation (2). It is interesting to note that the passage is in the present tense rather than in the past tense, so that it is proper to translate v. 2 as "in which you are being saved." Here is the glorious paradox of an act which was both complete and continuous. Through the preaching of the gospel "I have been saved," "I am being saved," and "I will be saved." Christ has made possible our salvation, He is leading us onward by His Spirit, and He will open up the full treasure of salvation in the days to come. Barclay suggests that "there are many things in this life which we can exhaust, but the meaning of salvation is something which a man can never exhaust." The full life in Christ is limitless in its possibilities.

d. The gospel relates the things that count (3-4). The Holy Week account reveals the experiences of Christ which form the important fabric of the gospel: (1) He died for our sins; (2) He was buried; (3) He rose again; and (4) He appeared unto His followers. An early creedal formula may echo in Paul's words.

To be a Christian was a serious matter, and the resurrection of the Lord was the authentication of their faith. It was also the ground of Paul's whole argument related to the other great truths, particularly the resurrection of the body. Here Paul affirms the reality of Christ's death in order to declare the reality of Christ's resurrection. The event was neither falsehood nor delusion, but the glorious truth of the Christian faith.

The passage clearly vindicates the historicity of the Resurrection. It is placed in sequence with Christ's death and His later appearances. The message stresses "the events of God's revelatory action in Christ." The Resurrection is an event to be placed beside the other events. It is a unique act of God in history. It is a "sacred event" vindicated in the subsequent appearances and in the acceptance of the gospel—the heart of which is the resurrection of Jesus Christ. No wonder Matthew Bridges would write:

Crown Him the Lord of Life!
Who triumphed o'er the grave;
Who rose victorious to the strife
For those He came to save.

> *His glories now we sing*
> *Who died and rose on high,*
> *Who died eternal life to bring,*
> *And lives that death may die.*

2. *Testimonies to the risen Lord* (5-8). Paul is not content to leave the event of the Resurrection to his word, even though he had received the gospel as revelation and had seen Jesus on the road to Damascus. He adds competent and sufficient testimony from those who also had seen the risen Lord.

Peter was well known and respected in Corinth. It would only be natural that Paul should appeal to the senior apostle for evidence: "He was seen of Cephas." Apart from Mary Magdela, it was Peter to whom the risen Christ first appeared. Peter who had denied him! Peter who had forsaken him! Could it be that this was the time that pardon was granted?

The appearance to the disciples in the absence of Thomas is next mentioned by Paul. It was there that Jesus ate with them to assure them that He was no disembodied spirit (Matt. 28:16; Luke 24:34 ff.).

Jesus then appeared to about 500 followers at once, probably on the mountain where He commissioned them to carry the gospel to the "ends of the earth."

After that, Christ was seen by James, His own brother who "had not believed on him." The final observation includes all the apostles, including Thomas whose skepticism was annihilated in his seeing for himself the risen Christ—"My Lord and my God!" (John 20:28). To tradition Paul added this evidence of those who actually saw him. His illustrations were vividly pertinent.

3. *The confident personal testimony of Paul* (8-11). With a curious mixture of pride and humility, he remembers his persecution of the church of God and his vision of Jesus on the road to Damascus. Paul was not unmindful that he was the "least of the apostles," but aware that his call was just as authentic and telling as anyone's.

His witness was the more authentic because he had changed from persecutor to defender, from "hunter" to preacher. Indeed, he surpassed all others in fervor and labors. There was only one reason: He had seen the risen Lord!

All of the witnesses were instruments. Their evidence was not to outweigh the motive: That others might believe. The testimony of the Resurrection is a united one, and the event central to the gospel and to Christian belief.

The Certainty of the Resurrection of Believers

While most of the Corinthian Christians believed in the resurrection of Jesus Christ, some denied the resurrection of the dead. Paul argues very forcefully that the acceptance of the resurrection of Christ is inconsistent with the denial of the resurrection of the dead.

1 Corinthians 15:12-34

12 Now if Christ be preached that he rose from the dead, how say some among you that there is no resurrection of the dead?

13 But if there be no resurrection of the dead, then is Christ not risen:

14 And if Christ be not risen, then is our preaching vain, and your faith is also vain.

15 Yea, and we are found false witnesses of God; because we have testified of God that he raised up Christ: whom he raised not up, if so be that the dead rise not.

16 For if the dead rise not, then is not Christ raised:

17 And if Christ be not raised, your faith is vain; ye are yet in your sins.

18 Then they also which are fallen asleep in Christ are perished.

19 If in this life only we have hope in Christ, we are of all men most miserable.

20 But now is Christ risen from the dead, and become the firstfruits of them that slept.

21 For since by man came death, by man came also the resurrection of the dead.

22 For as in Adam all die, even so in Christ shall all be made alive.

23 But every man in his own order: Christ the firstfruits; afterward they that are Christ's at his coming.

24 Then cometh the end, when he shall have delivered up the kingdom to God, even the Father; when he shall have put down all rule and all authority and power.

25 For he must reign, till he hath put all enemies under his feet.

26 The last enemy that shall be destroyed is death.

27 For he hath put all things under his feet. But when he saith all things are put under him, it is manifest that he is excepted, which did put all things under him.

28 And when all things shall be subdued unto him, then shall the Son

also himself be subject unto him that put all things under him, that God may be all in all.

29 Else what shall they do which are baptized for the dead, if the dead rise not at all? why are they then baptized for the dead?

30 And why stand we in jeopardy every hour?

31 I protest by your rejoicing which I have in Christ Jesus our Lord, I die daily.

32 If after the manner of men I have fought with beasts at Ephesus, what advantageth it me, if the dead rise not? let us eat and drink; for to morrow we die.

33 Be not deceived: evil communications corrupt good manners.

34 Awake to righteousness, and sin not; for some have not the knowledge of God: I speak this to your shame.

1. *Christ was raised from the dead* (12-19). Paul begins by attacking the major premise of his opponents: "Dead men do not rise again." The apostle answers that such a position wrecks the whole system of Christian faith because it also denies the resurrection of Christ. The consequences of such a denial are fatal.

a. The denial makes both preaching and faith vain, for it empties them of their content (14). The resurrection of Christ was the heart of the Good News. Otherwise, the gospel is a sham.

b. The denial makes false witnesses of all those who preach Christ (15). The apostles, including Paul, were misrepresenting the Christian conception of God if Christ is not risen.

In Christ we have all that we need to form our estimate of the Father. God shines forth in the face of the Saviour. If our ideas of God are founded in Christ, and at the same time we give false testimony concerning Him, how can we with assurance represent God to men? The consequences for the Corinthians were serious, for if Christ be not raised, their faith was vain, and they were yet in their sins (17).

c. The denial seals the fate of the dead (18). They fell asleep trusting in Christ and "confident of a blessed immortality." As Barclay says, "If Jesus had died, never to rise again, it would have proved that death could take the loveliest and the best life that ever lived and finally break it."

Spring has arrived in our community after a long winter. The grass long dead is now green. The birds have returned from the south. The dogwoods in their red and white dress are in full bloom. This says to me again, Death cannot hold life in its bondage. Life springs forth because it is stronger than death. The Resurrection is the final proof that life will have its day.

d. The denial condemns all living Christians (19). If their hope is only in this life, it is a false hope of present salvation and of any future expectations—"we are of all men most to be pitied." The Christian hope rests inexorably in a risen Christ; and if Christ is not risen, then "hopes were dupes indeed."

What a fool Paul was if the Christ who appeared to him was illusory! He had "suffered the loss of all things" for the sake of Christ (Phil. 3:8). Was his hope of Christ's return *(parousia)* false? Was his striving for an imperishable wreath a mockery (9:25)? Paul never for a moment entertained such a thought. The denial of the Resurrection was "out of bounds" and out of thought. Its affirmation was the core of his faith and message.

2. *An assurance of the resurrection of believers* (20-28). With a tremendously confident surge, Paul turns to the positive side of his argument. "But now is Christ risen from the dead"! There is no question. He has in faith accepted the revelaton, assessed the witnesses, shared his personal experience, and confronted the denials directed toward bodily resurrection.

It is a great thing to be possessed of such a faith. It colors our whole life. Forgiveness is real; sin is vanquished (21); and death is defeated. Those who for 2,000 years have believed in Him are safe in His keeping. They are more fully alive than ever before because they share the resurrection life and power of their risen Lord.

a. Jesus is the Guarantor of the resurrection of His followers (20). As the matter actually stands, Christ has become the Representative of the race—"the firstfruits of them that slept" and of all who have died in Christ.

Paul does not mean that Jesus simply preceded His followers in resurrection, but rather that as the first sheaf of the harvest is presented to God as the earnest of the harvest, so the resurrection of Christ is the earnest of the resurrection of His people to come.

Paul applies the principle of racial solidarity to sin and its consequences through Adam, and then turns to the gospel which declares that faith in Christ shall make all alive. Death is not a necessity of finiteness but a consequence of sin. Christ delivers man from death and sin by the victory of the Resurrection.

b. The divinely arranged order (23). When Paul says "each in his own order," he is using a striking military term. It is as though the "Great Captain" comes first, followed in phalanx by the great company of His followers, and then those that sleep in Him.

Christ comes first as the Earnest of the Resurrection, followed by the resurrection of His followers at the Advent. Then comes the end when "he shall have delivered up the kingdom to God" (24).

c. The final victory (24-28). The drama moves on to reveal Christ bringing His redeemed Church to the Father (28). He has defeated sin and vanquished death. The day has come when death is destroyed and all things are subjected to Christ. "Death is swallowed up in victory."

Even as all things are in subjection to Christ, He in turn is subordinate to the Father (28). Christ has not ceased to reign, nor is He less than divine. "It affirms no other subjection of the Son than is involved in Sonship." This implies "no inferiority of nature, no extrusion from power, but the free submission of love which is the essence of filial spirit."

3. *The practical application of the doctrine of the Resurrection* (29-34). Charles Erdman notes that there are four

applications of the doctrine that have contemporary significance:

a. Baptism for the dead is not unreasonable (29). There is a wide diversity of opinion as to what is indicated by baptism for the dead. Certainly it does not mean a vicarious baptism either for an unbeliever or a believer who was not baptized before he died. Baptism by proxy is incompatible with the thrust of Christian belief.

It might well speak of an unbeliever who turned to Christ in his loneliness for a loved one and submitted to baptism in anticipation of a blessed reunion. It was a touching evidence of strong human affection and faith in the future life.

Whatever the interpretation, Paul indicates that the practice is pointless if the dead are not raised at all. Paul does not think of life after death apart from the Resurrection.

b. Sacrifice in Christian service is not madness (30-32). Because of the blessed certainty of the future, it is not utter foolishness, Paul says, to put your very existence on the line. If there is no future life, why had he fought with beasts at Ephesus? (He was speaking figuratively, as *kata anthropon,* "humanly speaking," shows.) He was obviously speaking of some mortal peril where his life was at stake, such as in the Demetrius riot in Ephesus (Acts 19:23 ff.). He was ready to "die daily" (31), for he knew that the future was in the hands of the Lord and that the future was guaranteed by the death and resurrection of Jesus Christ.

c. Sensualism is folly (32*b*). If the resurrection from the dead is a delusion, then we may as well take the attitude of "eat, drink, and be merry"; "for to morrow we die." There is nothing left to us but a hedonistic existence which finds its greatest good in the satisfaction of the senses.

This is what the men of Corinth were saying. It is too common in our society today: There is no future, people say, so we will try to get the best out of life now. Paul counters with his all-pervasive hope and the character of his own life. In the light of bodily resurrection and a life in Christ, the folly was apparent.

d. Association with doubters is perilous (33-34). Paul, therefore, warns the Corinthian church of her associations. "Bad company ruins good morals" (RSV). For to keep fellowship with those who have no knowledge of God is both dangerous and foolish.

The Nature of the Resurrection

With the discussion of the *fact* of the resurrection ended, Paul turns to the *manner* of it. He supposes two questions: How are the dead raised up, and with what body do they come (35)? The latter question seemed to trouble the church most. They supposed our future bodies to be akin to our present bodies.

1 Corinthians 15:35-58

35 But some man will say, How are the dead raised up? and with what body do they come?
36 Thou fool, that which thou sowest is not quickened, except it die:
37 And that which thou sowest, thou sowest not that body that shall be, but bare grain, it may chance of wheat, or of some other grain:
38 But God giveth it a body as it hath pleased him, and to every seed his own body.
39 All flesh is not the same flesh: but there is one kind of flesh of men, another flesh of beasts, another of fishes, and another of birds.
40 There are also celestial bodies, and bodies terrestrial: but the glory of the celestial is one, and the glory of the terrestrial is another.
41 There is one glory of the sun, and another glory of the moon, and another glory of the stars: for one star differeth from another star in glory.
42 So also is the resurrection of the dead. It is sown in corruption; it is raised in incorruption:
43 It is sown in dishonour; it is raised in glory: it is sown in weakness; it is raised in power:
44 It is sown a natural body; it is raised a spiritual body. There is a natural body, and there is a spiritual body.
45 And so it is written, The first man Adam was made a living soul; the last Adam was made a quickening spirit.
46 Howbeit that was not first which is spiritual, but that which is natural; and afterward that which is spiritual.
47 The first man is of the earth, earthy: the second man is the Lord from heaven.
48 As is the earthy, such are they also that are earthy: and as is the heavenly, such are they also that are heavenly.

49 And as we have borne the image of the earthy, we shall also bear the image of the heavenly.

50 Now this I say, brethren, that flesh and blood cannot inherit the kingdom of God; neither doth corruption inherit incorruption.

51 Behold, I shew you a mystery; We shall not all sleep, but we shall all be changed,

52 In a moment, in the twinkling of an eye, at the last trump: for the trumpet shall sound, and the dead shall be raised incorruptible, and we shal be changed.

53 For this corruptible must put on incorruption, and this mortal must put on immortality.

54 So when this corruptible shall have put on incorruption, and this mortal shall have put on immortality, then shall be brought to pass the saying that is written, Death is swallowed up in victory.

55 O death, where is thy sting? O grave, where is thy victory?

56 The sting of death is sin; and the strength of sin is the law.

57 But thanks be to God, which giveth us the victory through our Lord Jesus Christ.

58 Therefore, my beloved brethren, be ye stedfast, unmoveable, always abounding in the work of the Lord, forasmuch as ye know that your labour is not in vain in the Lord.

1. *The resurrection body* (35-49). Paul answers the questions posed in v. 35 by the use of analogy. The seed is put into the ground and dies in order that it might live, emerging in a very different form in maturity and beauty. Its planting and growing represents the process of dissolution; difference and yet continuity. In the process, God gives it a body different from the body of the seed, but the same life in which it started.

The argument demonstrates the process, though it does not prove the resurrection. Our earthly bodies will die and be buried and dissolve, but however different the resurrection may be, it is the same life, it is still we who exist. "It is sown in corruption, it is raised in incorruption" (42).

Paul continues to show the great variety of forms in life, both in animal life and celestial bodies. God is able to provide whatever body is necessary for their functioning in His economy. Why, then, should there be any question about the nature of the resurrected body? Thus, while Paul does not describe the resurrection body, it is evident that it is a different body than the one represented on earth. It is more glorious than the human mind can imagine, for the reality represented by the figure is more real than the symbolism of the figure itself.

It is sown in dishonour; it is raised in glory:
It is sown in weakness; it is raised in power:
It is sown a natural body; it is raised a spiritual
*   body"* (43-44).

The scriptural passage is one of the great pardoxes of the Christian faith. Deathless, perfect and immortal in its nature, the "spiritual body" will be determined in some way by the "body of corruption, dishonor and weakness."

The present body is a natural body, the resurrected body is a spiritual body (46). It "bears the image of the heavenly" (49). In the future we shall be all that God has dreamed for His creation from the beginning. Now we are earthbound; then we shall be as God intended us to be: stamped in Christ's image, unrestricted in insight, bodies not limited by disease or weakness, wills and motives totally attuned to the heavenly vision. What a hope for the Christian! As one has expressed it: "In the life to come we will be able to render the perfect worship, the perfect service, the perfect love that in this world can only be a vision and a dream."

2. *Paul's glowing vision of the end times* (50-57). The apostle, with his breadth of insight, has been writing of an event that takes place at the return of Christ. Evidently there were those who were also anxious about those who were alive at Christ's return. Paul's answers are consistent with his former argument that "flesh and blood cannot inherit the kingdom of God; neither doth corruption inherit incorruption" (50). In other words, there must be a radical change, and so he tells them "a mystery." We shall not all die, but we shall be changed. Then Paul takes off on one of his characteristic "flights" as he sees the *parousia* coming in glory upon glory: "In a moment, in the twinkling of an eye . . . the trumpet shall sound, and the dead shall be raised incorruptible."

How can we be anything but victorious? Here is our

heritage! Here is the perfect vision of what is to come! The change will be as instantaneous as the moving of an eyelid. "For the Lord himself shall descend from heaven with a shout, with the voice of the archangel, and with the trump of God: and the dead in Christ shall rise first: then we which are alive and remain shall be caught up together with them in the clouds, to meet the Lord in the air" (1 Thess. 4:16-17).

> *O death, where is thy sting?*
> *O grave, where is thy victory?*
> *The sting of death is sin;*
> *And the strength of sin is the law.*
> *But thanks be to God, which giveth us the victory*
> *through our Lord Jesus Christ* (55-57).

3. *Paul's practical challenge* (58). At the close of the chapter Paul does what he usually does and what ought to be done after a theological discourse. "The sweep of the mind becomes the demand for action." If you have all that glory to come, "my beloved brethren, be steadfast, immovable, always abounding in the work of the Lord, knowing that in the Lord your labor is not in vain" (RSV). What more can an expositor say?

Practical Plans
1 Corinthians 16:1-24

1 CORINTHIANS 16

The lofty thoughts of c. 15 now give way to earthly concerns. The life of the world to come must now give way to the realities of this world. It must always be so. When a man's head is in the clouds, his feet must stand on the ground. Otherwise, his vision can only be mere fancy, devoid of reality. The issue is here and now. We will hold our dream and live in Christ until He calls us to the life to come.

Principles for Christian Giving

1 Corinthians 16:1-12

1 Now concerning the collection for the saints, as I have given order to the churches of Galatia, even so do ye.
2 Upon the first day of the week let every one of you lay by him in store, as God hath prospered him, that there be no gatherings when I come.
3 And when I come, whomsoever ye shall approve by your letters, them will I send to bring your liberality unto Jerusalem.
4 And if it be meet that I go also, they shall go with me.
5 Now I will come unto you, when I shall pass through Macedonia: for I do pass through Macedonia.
6 And it may be that I will abide, yea, and winter with you, that ye may bring me on my journey whithersoever I go.
7 For I will not see you now by the way; but I trust to tarry a while with you, if the Lord permit.
8 But I will tarry at Ephesus until Pentecost.
9 For a great door and effectual is opened unto me, and there are many adversaries.
10 Now if Timotheus come, see that he may be with you without fear: for he worketh the work of the Lord, as I also do.

11 Let no man therefore despise him: but conduct him forth in peace, that he may come unto me: for I look for him with the brethren.
12 As touching our brother Apollos, I greatly desired him to come unto you with the brethren: but his will was not at all to come at this time; but he will come when he shall have convenient time.

Paul's great concern was the gathering of an offering for the poor of Jerusalem. It is fascinating that he should follow the soaring theology of c. 15 with the social concern of c. 16. Perhaps this is a lesson in sequence for all evangelicals (Gal. 2:10; 2 Corinthians 8—9; Rom. 15:26; Acts 24:17). It is clear that all the churches were expected to cooperate.

Barclay points out that in different letters and speeches, Paul uses nine different words to describe this collection. In this passage he looks upon it as an "extra collection" *(logeia)*. It was to be an offering in addition to the tax a man had to pay to the state. Jesus' question was, "What do ye more than others?" (Matt. 5:47). In v. 3 Paul uses the words *charis* which indicates a "free gift freely given" (cf. 2 Cor. 8:4). Paul does not demand a gift, but asks for it from hearts overflowing with love for the Master and their brethren.

In this passage he lays down the necessary principles of Christian giving:

1. *Every member should be involved in giving* (2). Rich and poor, young and old should be a part of the benevolent endeavor. No one is excluded.

2. *The collections should be systematic* (2a). The time set was "the first day of the week," the day of the Resurrection (cf. Acts 20:7). Every Lord's Day each·one was to lay aside an offering.

3. *The collections should be proportionate to a man's resources* (2b). While the idea of the tithe is not mentioned here, it is strongly indicated, being consistent with the urgency of Malachi (3:8-10). The proportionate giving was intended to introduce the idea of system to one's benevolence and to establish equity in the congregation. The one

who had little gave little; the one who had much gave accordingly.

4. *The collections should not be spasmodic* (2c). Paul was concerned that his visit to Corinth not be taken up with raising money rather than with instruction in the faith. If the collections were taken regularly, it would not be necessary that they be taken upon his arrival. We might say that he was not interested in having an evangelist raise his own support, though this is not the issue at the moment.

5. *The collections should appeal to the highest motive.* The resurrection was a reason for the offering. It was a part of the work of the Lord. The hope of the resurrection made it necessary to sustain the saints here and now, not so much for their sake as for the sake of those who gave in love.

6. *The collections should be carefully administered* (3). Paul instructs the church to appoint a finance committee to receive the offering and to take it to Jerusalem. He will, of course, support them if necessary by accompanying them on the journey. Paul was making sure that no suspicion of maldistribution would cloud his service for Christ. The accounts were to be open to all who were interested. No one could say that the apostle was using the funds for his own private interests. This is the touchstone of any church finance.

At the end of this particular section, Paul commends two of his helpers, Timothy and Apollos. Timothy is commended because of his work for the Lord along with Paul (10). Though Apollos was a man of great wisdom, Paul knew that his presence in Corinth might add to the problem rather than solve it. The aggressiveness of the faction that bore his name certainly would be increased by his presence. So Paul says, he will come "when he shall have convenient time" (12).

In the meantime, Paul is sensitive to opportunities to proclaim the gospel and is remaining in Ephesus where a "great door and effectual is opened" but where there are also "many adversaries" (9). The obstacles never deterred him where there was opportunity to preach the gospel and to nourish the church with Christ's teachings.

Final Exhortations and Greetings

The final words of the Epistle are sprinkled with the great imperatives of the gospel: *Watch ye . . . stand fast . . . quit you . . . be strong.* At the same time, let all be done in love. No minister could pass the first two verses without being moved to textual analysis. The whole challenge to the maturing Christian is there.

1 Corinthians 16:13-24

13 Watch ye, stand fast in the faith, quit you like men, be strong.
14 Let all your things be done with charity.
15 I beseech you, brethren, (ye know the house of Stephanas, that it is the firstfruits of Achaia, and that they have addicted themselves to the ministry of the saints,)
16 That ye submit yourselves unto such, and to every one that helpeth with us, and laboureth.
17 I am glad of the coming of Stephanas and Fortunatus and Achaicus: for that which was lacking on your part they have supplied.
18 For they have refreshed my spirit and yours: therefore acknowledge ye them that are such.
19 The churches of Asia salute you. Aquila and Priscilla salute you much in the Lord, with the church that is in their house.
20 All the brethren greet you. Greet ye one another with an holy kiss.
21 The salutation of me Paul with mine own hand.
22 If any man love not the Lord Jesus Christ, let him be Anathema Maranatha.
23 The grace of our Lord Jesus Christ be with you.
24 My love be with you all in Christ Jesus. Amen.

1. *Paul's heaviness of heart is compensated for by the warmth of loyal friends* (13-18). He experiences refreshment at the hands of those who brought news from Corinth. He mentions Stephanas, who, along with his household, was the first Greek convert and who had consistently devoted himself to the service of the church.

2. *Salutations* (19-20). The names mentioned in the Epistles are always fascinating and usually suggest a remarkable story of the workings of God's grace. Greetings are sent from Aquila and Priscilla who move back and

forth across the history of the Early Church. They were two of those wonderful people who make their homes centers of Christian light and love. More and more, Christians are discovering that their homes can be centers of fellowship and love. They can become a means of winning men to Jesus.

The holy kiss (19) was not given promiscuously, neither was it abused, but it was a beautiful expression of the *koinonia* in its best dimension.

3. *Paul's concluding salutation* (21-24). Paul usually wrote through an amanuensis, or secretary, but he always verified the dictation with his own hand in the last few verses. This he did in the Epistle to the Corinthians.

a. Anathema (22*a*). There is here a double motto, one negative and one positive. If Christ be the fullest Expression of God, Paul says, then our want of love for Him is a violation of our whole duty. *Anathema* (accursed) is the strongest negative term that Paul could conceive of. Note also that this is the only time Paul uses *phileo* (to love one as a friend) rather than *agapao* (to love with no thought of personal reward).

b. Maranatha (22*b*). "Our Lord, come!" Paul uses the beautiful Aramaic benediction without translating it into the Greek, as was also done with the Hebrew "Amen," "Hallelujah," and "Hosannah." It was both a warning and a hope. Hodge concludes that "so deeply were the apostles impressed with the divinity of Christ, so fully were they convinced that Jesus was God manifest in the flesh, that the refusal or inability to recognize him as such, seemed to them a mark of reprobation." It was also the eternal hope of every Christian: *Maranatha!*

c. Grace and Love (23-24). Paul concludes with the two great words of the Christian vocabulary which he faithfully uses in all his Epistles: God's *grace* and *my love*. What more could he say? After all the rebukes, the last word is *love*. It must always be the final word!

Quiet, Lord, my forward heart;
  Make me teachable and mild,
Upright, simple, free from art,
  Make me as a weaned child;
From distrust and envy free,
Pleased with all that pleaseth Thee.

—JOHN NEWTON

The Second Epistle of Paul
to the
CORINTHIANS

Topical Outline of Second Corinthians

Preface (1:1-11)
    God's Messenger, God's People, God's Message (1:1-2)
    Thanksgiving for Divine Comfort (1:3-11)

The Apostolic Ministry (1:12—7:16)
    The Testimony of a Good Conscience (1:12-14)
    Faithful, as God Is Faithful (1:15-20)
    The Threefold Action of God in Christian Experience (1:21-22)
    The Art of Godly Leadership (1:23—2:17)
    The Credentials of a Minister (3:1-3)
    The Superiority of the New Covenant (3:4-11)
    The Glorious Hope of the Gospel (3:12-18)
    The Glory of God in Jesus Christ (4:1-6)
    God's Treasure in Earthen Vessels (4:7-18)
    The Realities of the Future (5:1-10)
    Motivated to Serve Both God and Man (5:11-13)
    The Word of Reconciliation (5:14-19)
    The Ministry of Reconciliation (5:20—6:2)
    Proving Our Ministry (6:3-10)
    An Appeal for Holiness (6:11—7:1)
    An Apostle's Heart Exposed (7:2-16)

The Grace of Christian Giving (8:1—9:15)
    The Example of Macedonia (8:1-6)
    The Criteria for Christian Giving (8:7-15)
    Paul's Plan for the Collection (8:16—9:15)

Spiritual Vindication in Christ (10:1—13:14)
    The Process of Victory in a Ministry for Christ (10:1-18)
    Paul's Defense of His Apostolic Authority (11:1-15)
    The Credentials of an Apostle (11:16—12:10)
    The Signs of an Apostle (12:11-19)
    Final Warnings and Appeals from a Concerned Pastor (12:20—13:14)

Introduction

The passionate appeal of the Second Epistle of Paul to the Corinthians is a fascinating profile of a great heart. The author represents himself as a defender of the loftiest ideals and glorious privileges of Christian ministry. On the other hand, his human weakness, sensitivity, arguments, and tears help us to catch a picture of Christian existence in tension with the incomparable glory and power of the gospel.

In this tension, Christ becomes the Center of all meaning, the Heart of all living, the Message itself. While one struggles with the intransigence of the church and Paul's philosophy of leadership, he is always aware of the centrality of Christ throughout the pages of the Epistle. The apostle is convinced that churchmanship must center in Christ, and Christ works through the leadership and traditions of His Church. It is on this premise that Paul appeals to an ethical criterion in Christ for both his converts and himself.

The Occasion

Paul had established the church at Corinth some five years before on his second missionary journey. When First Corinthians was written, he was planning to visit Corinth a second time, remaining in Ephesus possibly until Pentecost and spending the winter of A.D. 55-56 (?) with them.

However, he modified his plan and decided to visit Corinth twice—once on his way to Macedonia and again upon his return from the northern province. After the last visit he planned to sail for Jerusalem with the offerings he had collected (1:15 f.; 1 Cor. 16:1-4).

During his stay in Ephesus, Paul was in constant communication with his friends. He was afraid that his First Epistle was not as effective as he had hoped for in correcting some tendencies in the church, and his heart was heavy. Timothy, evidently, did not carry enough authority to enforce Paul's instructions. It was Timothy's return which caused Paul to conclude that a direct confrontation was the only solution. The second visit was painful to both Paul and his converts alike (13:2; 2:1), causing the opposition to become openly rebellious and one member, in particular, to openly defy Paul's authority. And while a successful reconstruction of history is impossible, Paul may have written a second letter which he regretted because of the severity of its tone. It was a sorrowful and painful rebuke to the wicked conduct and attitudes of certain leaders in the church, and related his changed plans for travel. (There may have been several letters, both before and after First Corinthians was written [cf. BBC and F. F. Bruce].)

Through Titus' influence the church repented with deep contrition, the abuses were corrected, and confidence in Paul's leadership was fully restored.

Paul eventually left Ephesus for Corinth, finally in Macedonia meeting Titus, whose favorable report left Paul's spirit filled with joy. The so-called second letter to the Corinthians was written in response to Titus' report. However, the church at Corinth had neglected to complete the offering for their needy brethren, and there were false prophets left who tried to brand him a "mercenary imposter."

The apostle explains the change in his plans and the reasons for his delayed visit. He pours out his love for the church, accredits his ministry to Christ, and urges the church to complete the "collection" prior to his arrival.

Paul sternly rebukes his opposition, exposes their hypocrisy, and shows the absurdity of their arguments. In the meantime, he vindicates his apostleship in Christ and warns of severe discipline if certain members of the fellowship persist in their hostility and wicked conduct.

The Content

While the Epistle is neither systematically organized nor doctrinal in its essential expression, the great fundamental doctrines of the Christian faith are clearly discernible. One cannot get away from the glory of the exalted Christ, His work of reconciliation, and the demand for holiness of heart and life in Him. Always there is the promise of forgiveness and the expression of hope for the future.

All through the writings there is a picture emerging of Paul the apostle—a truly great soul. He allows us to look into his very heart. We see the vivid expressions of anguish, joy, fear, hope, wounded feelings, and ardent love. His motives are laid bare to our view.

The writing style is broken, involved, and many times obscure. The changes of mood, the interpolations, and the shifts of emphasis are many. It is apparent that the letter was written under great stress. It was the outpouring of the apostle's deep feelings rather than an organized document in which ideas followed each other in ascending sequence. "Ecstatic thanksgiving and cutting irony, self-assertion and self-abnegation, condemnation and warning, authority, paradox, and apology, all meet and cross and seethe; yet out of the swirling eddies rise like rocks, grand Christian principles and inspiring hopes."

In the midst of all this, Paul stands forth in imposing character. He has been touched by God. His motives are pure and his objectives clear. And while his limitations are obvious, his greatness is untainted by conduct or attitude below his high calling in Christ.

Behind it all and through it all there is a Person whom he represents. His one impelling purpose is revealed when he passionately declares,

> The love of Christ controls us, because we are convinced that one has died for all; therefore all have died. And he died for all, that those who live might live no longer for themselves but for him who for their sake died and was raised (5:14-15, RSV).

The Preface
2 Corinthians 1:1-11

2 CORINTHIANS 1

God's Messenger, God's People, God's Message

This Epistle reflects the outpouring of Paul's great soul. That the church at Corinth had received his letter with a good spirit relieved his mind and filled his heart with gratitude. On the other hand, the increasing boldness of false teachers, their heresies, and their unjust charges against Paul filled him with righteous indignation.

Erasmus compares the Epistle to a river which sometimes flows like a gentle stream, other times rushes like a raging torrent, spreads out like a placid lake, and finally loses itself in sand, only to break out in unexpected places.

2 Corinthians 1:1-2

> 1 Paul, an apostle of Jesus Christ by the will of God, and Timothy our brother, unto the church of God which is at Corinth, with all the saints which are in all Achaia:
> 2 Grace be to you and peace from God our Father, and from the Lord Jesus Christ.

While the Epistle is the least methodical of Paul's writings, it reveals the man to us who is laboring as a pastor to his people. The introduction (1-2) gives an authentic insight into the essential character of (1) God's messenger, (2) God's people, and (3) God's message.

1. *God's messenger* (1). Paul begins his letter as he usually opens his correspondence. But there is a special reason, this time, why he should initiate the letter "Paul, an apostle of Jesus Christ by the will of God." It was written to a church, some of whose members were challenging his authority. He had not chosen to preach the gospel; he was called by the "tap on the shoulder" which was arresting and demanding (Acts 9:15). In the first letter he observed that "Christ sent me not to baptize, but to preach the gospel" (1 Cor. 1:17). He was not reluctant, but joyful and full of passion for the task. His debt to Christ was so great he was willing to take up the responsibility, being grateful for the opportunity. He saw in ministry a service to Christ, for he was ordained by the will of God. He was God's messenger.

If God's man is to be of service in Christ's army, he must be God-called. This is both the starting point and the goal of his very existence. He will on occasion feel that changing times have set him aside and that his years have not made him a "significant other." But divine calling will hold him steady, both in the interpretation of his achievements and the end goals of his life.

Gene E. Barlett, in *The Audacity of Preaching*, quotes from a letter in which a minister said:

> All that I can say and feel is, that by the change of times the pulpit has lost its place. It does only part of that whole which used to be done by it alone. Once it was a newspaper, school master, theological treatise, a stimulant to good works. . . . Now these are partitioned out to the different offices, and the pulpit is no more the pulpit of three centuries back, than the authority of a householder is that of Abraham.[1]

This sounds like a contemporary complaint, but actually it is part of a letter written in July, 1861, by none other than the great preacher, Frederick W. Robertson.

Every preacher must wrestle with the thought that "in his day preaching is not what it once was." His search for identity must center in "call." He is a child of God commissioned to proclaim the Word of God in *his day*. Of this, regardless of persecution and criticism, Paul was sure. He was God's man, in God's will—His apostle, His messenger. That confidence freed him from all the doubt and concern about his personal resources for the task. He knew that his sufficiency was from God (3:5). It freed Paul from anxiety about results and affirmed the faithfulness of God in his declaration of the gospel.

Francis Younghusband was sent by the viceroy of India on a mission to Tibet. He describes the difficult task and the spirit in which he faced it:

> I had the greatest possible confidence in the Viceroy who sent me. He had himself selected me for the mission. . . . He knew what he wanted in sending me, and I knew he would support me through thick and thin in getting it. He would not abandon me at the special moment.[2]

This was Paul's faith. He was commissioned by Jesus to witness to His continuity on earth just as the Twelve were commissioned (cf. Acts 1:1-2; Luke 1:2). Whenever he found it necessary to speak authoritatively to the churches, he spoke as an apostle. He was commissioned by Christ.

2. *God's people* (1). Paul spoke to God's people in Corinth and in all of Greece south of Macedonia (Achaia). The letter was to be read aloud to the church, the fellowship of that body of believers which "God has reconciled to himself and called to be his people." They were the Church of God. They were the *hagioi,* the holy ones "in Christ Jesus." Their vocation was to belong wholly to God and to serve Him utterly—with a purity nothing less than Christlikeness. "Paul, however, does not address his readers as *saints* because they have realized in life the full implications of the name, but simply because they authentically belonged to Christ as a body of believers."[3] It was not Paul's church nor a human fellowship. The church at Corinth, with all its difficulties, was God's church in human brotherhood.

This makes the difference! The Church belongs to no one man or group of men. It is God's Church—and being God's fellowship, it is authentic. No wonder that Samuel Stone wrote:

> The Church's one Foundation
> Is Jesus Christ, her Lord.
> She is His new creation
> By water and the Word.
> From heav'n He came and sought her
> To be His holy bride;
> With His own blood He bought her,
> And for her life He died.[4]

3. *God's message* (2). Many times "grace and peace" expressed merely a personal greeting of courtesy. "Grace" was a common Hellenistic greeting, while "peace" was an Oriental expression which was used in the benediction of the priests *(shalom)*. But now Paul fills both terms with a new and fuller meaning.

He expresses a wish and a fervent prayer that both grace and peace may flow "from God our Father, and from the Lord Jesus Christ." In this context grace suggests the constant divine favor that supports the believer in his daily pilgrimage "in Christ," while peace is the right relationship with God and the quiet poise that comes as a result of His grace.

In the light of the issue at hand, grace and peace were needful in the church at Corinth and were twin-born as a necessary contingency to a stable Christian fellowship.

There are at least three main elements in peace.[5] The first is the "reconciliation with God which comes through His grace" expressed in true repentance. The enmity toward God is overcome and through His forgiving love we are restored to fellowship with Him. This sense of unity with God is peace, "peace with God through our Lord Jesus Christ" (Rom. 5:1).

The second element of peace suggests reconciliation with our brother. Jesus made this clear in Matt. 5:23-24 when He said, "If you are offering your gift at the altar, and there remember that your brother has something against you, leave your gift there before the altar and go; first be reconciled to your brother, and then come and offer your gift" (RSV).

Forgiveness promotes healing. It blesses both forgiver and forgiven. It releases the mind from guilt and brings peace to the soul. "There is evidence that cherished resentment is at the root of some forms of neurotic trouble though the cause may not be recognized. It isolates us from others as well as from God."

The third aspect of peace is peace of mind in a transient and tumultuous society. It is a peace that gives calm in the center of a storm. It is the peace of John 14:27, where Jesus says, "Peace I leave with you; my peace I give to you. . . . Let not your hearts be troubled, neither let them be afraid" (RSV). This peace is not found in wealth, fame, or sensual pleasures. We still live at the mercy of the "changes and chances" of life. It does, however, offer an untroubled heart in a troubled world, a security which does not pass away, a grace that is sufficient (12:9). It is a peace that "passeth all understanding" (Phil. 4:7).

Thanksgiving for Divine Comfort

Paul had faced deadly perils in more than one context. The dangers, which he does not define, were aggravated by his anxiety for the welfare and peace of the Corinthian fellowship. The good news which came by the hand of Titus was a great comfort to Paul, and this magnificent theme of comfort pervades cc. 1—9.

2 Corinthians 1:3-11

3 Blessed be God, even the Father of our Lord Jesus Christ, the Father of mercies, and the God of all comfort;

4 Who comforteth us in all our tribulation, that we may be able to comfort them which are in any trouble, by the comfort wherewith we ourselves are comforted of God.

5 For as the sufferings of Christ abound in us, so our consolation also aboundeth by Christ.

6 And whether we be afflicted, it is for your consolation and salvation,

which is effectual in the enduring of the same sufferings which we also suffer: or whether we be comforted, it is for your consolation and salvation.

7 And our hope of you is stedfast, knowing, that as ye are partakers of the sufferings, so shall ye be also of the consolation.

8 For we would not, brethren, have you ignorant of our trouble which came to us in Asia, that we were pressed out of measure, above strength, insomuch that we despaired even of life:

9 But we had the sentence of death in ourselves, that we should not trust in ourselves, but in God which raiseth the dead:

10 Who delivered us from so great a death, and doth deliver: in whom we trust that he will yet deliver us;

11 Ye also helping together by prayer for us, that for the gift bestowed upon us by the means of many persons thanks may be given by many on our behalf.

1. *Affliction and comfort: a sustaining paradox* (3-11). What a remarkable connection between two apparent opposites! Whether we like to admit it or not, divine comfort and human suffering go hand in hand. By the very nature of Christian existence, some suffering must come into every life.

The root meaning of "affliction" (4) and the most contemporary expression of the word *(thlipsis)* is "pressure." Barclay quotes Samuel Rutherford who wrote to one of his friends, "God has called you to Christ's side, and the wind is now in Christ's face in this land; and seeing you are with Him ye cannot expect the lee-side or the sunny side of the brae."[6]

It is in this context that Dietrich Bonhoeffer, the German Christian martyr of World War II, makes such a powerful attack on easy Christianity and "cheap grace" in *The Cost of Discipleship*. It is never easy to be a Christian and grace is always "costly."

But we are not left alone. Paul blesses "the God of all comfort, who comforts us in all our afflictions" (RSV).

a. Affliction as the school of comfort (4). Comfort has lost much of its meaning in modern speech. The comfort of God is no narcotic. The word "Comforter" applied to the Holy Spirit in John 14 and 16 means "Strengthener." The English word has the same root as the verb "to fortify." The comfort of God establishes, restores, quietens one's fears, speaks peace, reassures, and refreshes.

Affliction and comfort are blood brothers. The first profound questions about God and personal religion are often born in affliction. The first authentic confidence in a living God is discovered in comfort. As with Job, God answered him not in prosperity but through the whirlwind where he discovered God as a living Redeemer (Job 38:1; 40:6; 19:25).

But there is reason for comfort as a means as well as an end. Paul says that it is God in Christ who comforts us in order "that we may be able to comfort them which are in any trouble, by the comfort wherewith we ourselves are comforted of God."

Frank Carver, in a beautiful commentary on this passage, observes that "it is because Paul's afflictions are so vitally related to the *sufferings of Christ* that his 'comfort also aboundeth through *[dia]* Christ' (5, ASV) to the Corinthians." He quotes Phillips' translation in v. 4 as, "Indeed, experience shows us that the more we share Christ's suffering the more we are able to give of his encouragement."

> Paul finds the source of mutual comfort in the character of God as revealed in Jesus Christ. He does this by uniting the sufferings of the church—apostle and people —with the sufferings of Christ. . . . This identification of the sufferings of Christ and the Church arises out of the redemptive participation in the life and death of Christ (6:5) which Paul finds at the heart of being "in Christ." . . . For Paul, participation in the afflictions of this age, which may in a sense be styled the Messianic sufferings, is an indispensable part of the ongoing life of the Church (Acts 14:22; Phil. 1:29-30).[7]

The supreme gift of comfort in Christ is its ability to sustain others in their affliction. The men and women who prove to be the greatest support to the kingdom of God are those who have suffered with Christ in His afflictions. It is expressed superlatively in Heb. 2:18, "For because he himself [Christ] has suffered and been tempted, he is able to help those who are tempted" (RSV).

We must not miss the two little words in v. 5, "as . . .

so." The verse suggests that according to the measure we suffer with Christ for men, we are enabled to comfort men through Christ in their suffering. The word "aboundeth" indicates that the comfort in Christ is adequate under any conditions. But we must remember that it is more than human consolation, however rich, but it is that which "aboundeth by Christ." That makes the difference!

b. The steadfastness of hope (7). Through the comfort which is in Christ and by reason of the good news from Corinth, Paul is confirmed in his hope for the fellowship. It is not a new hope but a hope that has remained through the perilous tensions of the past. It is a hope that is "unshaken" (NASB).

This hope does not arise from confidence in human resources, but from the divine comfort that comes from God in Christ. The difference is not superficial. Hope can come from a human source or through a divine sufficiency. Paul's hope, constant in the face of trials, came from God. The fascinating thought of this passage is that suffering and tribulation can unite with comfort and hope in the ministry of Jesus and Paul—and in ours. This was never mere theory with Paul, but a vital life experience.

2. *An utter reliance on God* (8-11). While the apostle does not reveal what the trouble was in Asia, he does share that it was severe enough that he "despaired of life itself" (RSV). As usual, he does not complain, but places this in a spiritual dimension. It was the purpose of God, through the trouble, to show Paul how he could utterly depend upon Him.

Paul came to the point where he had no other recourse but to fall back on the resources of God himself. He had come to the end of himself. To whom could he turn? Only to the "God who raises the dead" (RSV). But what a Resource!

It was not a debilitating dependence that Paul experienced, but a dependence that exulted in strength. He would not use Christ as a crutch, but as a Foundation.

He discovered that it is only in God-dependence that one discovers life-giving resources for action.

The danger of modern affluency is that it fosters independence rather than creative dependence. A man with the "jingle of change" in his pocket tends to stand alone—and alone God will let him stand. Life has a way, however, of bringing everyone sooner or later to that point where he realizes he cannot depend on his own resources. At that point the believer discovers the resources of faith in God.

Paul knew that if God could bring him through his despair in Asia, He could bring him through anything. His cry was the triumphant cry of the Psalmist in 116:8-9, "For Thou hast rescued my soul from death, my eyes from tears, my feet from stumbling. I shall walk before the Lord in the land of the living" (NASB).

a. It is a chord which reverberates throughout the entire letter (2:13-14; 4:7-12, 16; 12:7-10; 13:4). The God who delivered Paul and on whom he had set his hope for future deliverance (10) is the God who raised Jesus from the dead —the God of the resurrection (Rom. 1:4; 8:11; 1 Corinthians 15; Eph. 1:19-20). This is Paul's proclamation (Acts 17:18). This is his testimony.[8] What more can be said?

b. Finally, Paul asks that the prayers of the Corinthians continue "so that many will give thanks on our behalf for the blessing granted us in answer to many prayers" (11, RSV). He was asking for their greatest treasure, the treasure of their prayers.

Paul calls the church to prayer in the face of trouble and in thanksgiving for deliverance. We cannot avoid trouble at times, but we can turn it into blessing through prayer. Paul is convinced that his affliction can be a blessing to the whole church and so involves them in the experience.

His utter dependence upon God was now transforming and redemptive. In the spirit of Paul, Charles Wesley wrote:

O for a thousand tongues to sing
My great Redeemer's praise,
The glories of my God and King,
The triumphs of His grace!

The Apostolic Ministry
2 Corinthians 1:12—7:16

The Testimony of a Good Conscience
2 Corinthians 1:12-14

> 12 For our rejoicing is this, the testimony of our conscience, that in simplicity and godly sincerity, not with fleshly wisdom, but by the grace of God, we have had our conversation in the world, and more abundantly to you-ward.
>
> 13 For we write none other things unto you, than what ye read or acknowledge; and I trust ye shall acknowledge even to the end;
>
> 14 As also ye have acknowledged us in part, that we are your rejoicing, even as ye also are ours in the day of the Lord Jesus.

In this great witness Paul makes it plain that he is a man of integrity and that a good conscience involves three factors.

1. *Simplicity or "holiness"* (12, RSV, NASB; see fn. 3, BBC, 8:508). Paul in good conscience testified that he had behaved with "holiness" and "godly sincerity." In this context, "holiness" stresses the moral purity of Paul's outward behavior. Paul is defending himself against the charge of duplicity. Single-mindedness (simplicity or holiness) is particularly appropriate as an expression of his integrity. His first point is ethical.

The general sense of "holiness" in other contexts is integrity. It is the heart of biblical perfection (Job 1:1). Nothing can be more damaging to a man than to question his ethical integrity. The enemies of Jesus used this weapon (Mark 3:20-25); now Paul's enemies were questioning his change of plans (15 ff.) as double-talk. His answer was that he had behaved both "in the world, and still more toward you, with holiness" (NASB).

2. *Sincerity* (12-13). If holiness stresses moral purity, sincerity stresses "the transparency of his inner motives" (2:17; 1 Cor. 5:8). It is a *godly* sincerity, once again indicating Paul's dependence upon divine resources. His whole life was determined by a thoroughgoing obedience to God's will rather than manipulation or deceit.

Barclay tells the story of an architect who offered to build a house for a Greek philosopher in such a way that no one could see into it. The philosopher replied, "I will double your fee if you build me a house into every room of which everyone can see." Sincerity means transparency of motive over against either the translucent or opaque. Paul was saying, "You can depend upon what I say!" That is the heart of *godly sincerity*.

This transparency of life is not easy to achieve. Our motives tend to be mixed. We may act from a variety of motives, and some may be selfish—even beyond our comprehension of the character of our intention. In the face of the ambiguity, God knows our hearts and can "sift the gold from the dross." Only God can discern our true motives, and we must let Him be the judge. Elsewhere Paul writes to the Corinthians, "I do not even judge myself. I am not aware of anything against myself, but I am not thereby acquitted. It is the Lord who judges me" (1 Cor. 4:3-4, RSV).

This sincerity extended also to Paul's letters, which were written in simplicity and forthrightness (13). It is his hope that the Corinthians will "understand fully" (RSV) even as now they have "understood in part" (RSV). It is this sincerity that Paul prays will come through until they are as proud of him as "on the day of our Lord Jesus" (RSV), when all that is hidden will be brought to light.

3. *Serenity* (12). The abandonment of fleshly wisdom

and the reception of the grace of God gives a deep inner peace. It was no error that "grace" and "peace" are always closely associated in Paul's letters. He was convinced that in a troubled world the Christian could find the "eye of the storm" and stand steadfastly in the midst of turbulence. The observation anticipates Paul's great maxim in 4:8-10, "We are afflicted in every way, but not crushed; perplexed, but not despairing; persecuted, but not forsaken; struck down, but not destroyed; always carrying about in the body the dying of Jesus, that the life of Jesus also may be manifest in our body" (NASB).

Faithful, as God Is Faithful

1 Corinthians 1:15-20

> 15 And in this confidence I was minded to come unto you before, that ye might have a second benefit;
> 16 And to pass by you into Macedonia, and to come again out of Macedonia unto you, and of you to be brought on my way toward Judaea.
> 17 When I therefore was thus minded, did I use lightness? or the things that I purpose, do I purpose according to the flesh, that with me there should be yea yea, and nay nay?
> 18 But as God is true, our word toward you was not yea and nay.
> 19 For the Son of God, Jesus Christ, who was preached among you by us, even by me and Silvanus and Timotheus, was not yea and nay, but in him was yea.
> 20 For all the promises of God in him are yea, and in him Amen, unto the glory of God by us.

Behind this passage is the charge that Paul has acted with duplicity. It is apologetic, but intertwined through the argument are great principles representing guidelines for Christian conduct. Among other things, it illustrates how a Christian can defend himself when maligned. It also reveals to us the humility of the apostle in the face of misrepresentation. We sometimes forget that the apostles were human and subject to the attacks of others. Paul was no exception. He was a strong but sensitive person. His personality shines through in so many ways as one reads between the lines.

He argues in the face of the implied charges that being "in Christ" makes caprice impossible. He had intended to visit Corinth, but the situation was so bitter that he thought it the better part to delay so that he might spare them pain (23).

His enemies promptly accused him of "vacillating" (17, RSV). His reply suggests that he had not acted "according to the flesh" or, as the RSV puts it, "like a worldly man,"—one who said yes one time and no another in unprincipled and selfish ways.

The charge hurt Paul so much that he answered (as again in 23) by placing himself under oath. "As God is true," or "as surely as God is faithful" (18, RSV), our word has not vacillated, he insists, but "in him was yea" (19). And in answering the charge, Paul once again gives us a great principle that pervades his writings: God is faithful, and the word of those who are "in Christ" can also be trusted.

"Forget about me," says Paul, "and remember the promises of God" (20) God keeps all His promises in Jesus Christ. Handley Moule comments here: "In this we have a rich and beautiful illustration of the all-importance of Christ, the omnipotence of Christ, in every part of the Gospel, and in every part of his followers' lives."[9]

Let us stop long enough to take a few of the great promises of God and see what is meant by the "yea" and "Amen" in Jesus. Moule suggests three promises which seem to be all-encompassing.

1. *The promise of pardon.* The freedom and fullness of the pardon is the "impossible possibility." In God's love and sacrifice in Christ there is full forgiveness. "It is not clogged with exacting conditions." Must I be holy and full of adequate works before God will forgive? No! This is the yea and Amen in Jesus Christ. He is willing to take us as we are and pull the shade on the past. He comes not in "reluctant toleration" but abundant mercy. He is the "Father of mercies." He will love freely (Hos. 14:4). He will cast our sins into the "depths of the sea" (Mic. 7:19). He will remember our sins and iniquities "no more" (Heb.

10:17). When we look at ourselves, we can only despair; but when we look at God in Christ, there is pardon from sin.

> Jesus stands there as the gift of God, Jesus the Son. The invisible pardon becomes in Him as it were visible. You may trust it, because the Son of God came and died, and lives. Let us act in humble simplicity on that Yea and that Amen.[10]

2. *The promise of holiness.* Here is the "impossible possibility" through divine grace: a separation of life from sin and an openness to divine power and purity of heart. The promises are magnificently full.

The promises of God are impossible apart from Him who speaks the yea and Amen. "Heaven is a smaller gift than Thou, Lord Jesus Christ!" With fervor John writes, "These things write I unto you, that ye sin not" (1 John 2:1). And he adds, "Whosoever abideth in him sinneth not" (1 John 3:6). Paul writes, "Sin shall not have dominion over you: for ye are not under the law, but under grace" (Rom. 6:14). Again he pens: "The very God of peace sanctify you wholly; and I pray God your whole spirit and soul and body be preserved blameless unto the coming of our Lord Jesus Christ. Faithful is he that calleth you, who also will do it" (1 Thess. 5:23-24).

How can this be? "The secret is not it, but He Himself." "Christ is made unto us sanctification," Paul says in 1 Cor. 1:30, and again he prays "that Christ may dwell in your hearts by faith; . . . that ye may . . . know the love of Christ, which passeth knowledge" (Eph. 3:17, 19). He affirms the promise to the Colossians, "You have come to fulness of life in him" (Col. 2:10, RSV).

3. *The promise of heaven.* The Lord has not left us alone or in ambiguity about the future. The writer to the Hebrews promises, "He has prepared for them a city," and "they desire a better country, that is, a heavenly one" (Heb. 11:16, RSV). Paul climaxes the list of promises

with "We shall always be with the Lord" (1 Thess. 4:17, RSV).

That hope is the light of every Christian believer, whether newborn or mature in Christ—a life beyond death promised in "the resurrection of the body." The promise is that we shall find a home with Him who is the Source of all life—for He is our Yea and Amen. Here is our promise. When Christ overcame death, He opened the kingdom of heaven to all believers.

The promises are not words alone, but promises in Jesus Christ. He will conclude this passage (21-22) by setting the divine seal of the Spirit on all the promises of God.

The Threefold Action of God in Christian Experience

2 Corinthians 1:21-22

> 21 Now he which stablisheth us with you in Christ, and hath anointed us, is God;
> 22 Who hath also sealed us, and given the earnest of the Spirit in our hearts.

In v. 20 the apostle has spoken of Christ as the truth and substance of all the divine promises, and the acknowledgment of that truth by those who are "in Christ." In v. 21 he brings into view the God who is the Author and Preserver of their faith and who promises the salvation of which He has already given a pledge and foretaste.

In vv. 21-22, God, Christ, and the Holy Spirit are united in the divine work which is "confirmed by three decisive, simultaneous acts of the Holy Spirit." Paul has experienced in his own life the establishment of God in Christ which has given authenticity to his witness. Now, his dynamic union with the Saviour makes possible a transfer of his personal qualities of character to the Corinthians who are "therefore able to reproduce the actions of Jesus in their own lives."[11]

The work of the Holy Spirit is thus represented in three metaphorical expressions—"anointed," "sealed," and "given." While they are spoken of in the context of

Paul's experience, they are universally inferred to all men who respond wholeheartedly to God's call and accept His commission (Acts 9:15-18).[12]

1. *Paul was anointed by the Spirit.* The lovely metaphor reflects the anointing of the kings, prophets, and priests for their task in the Old Testament.

In Luke 4:18 Jesus applies to himself the language of Isa. 61:1, "The Spirit of the Lord is upon me, because he has anointed me to preach the gospel to the poor" (cf. Acts 4:27 and 10:38).

Paul and all those who are "in Christ" are anointed by the Holy Spirit—that is, they are consecrated to God and qualified for service. Paul is speaking to all Christians ("us," 21).[13]

The marvel of it is that God through His Spirit is able to empower for Christian living and witness. It is a promise for holiness in action.

2. *Paul was sealed by the Holy Spirit of promise* (22). This was a mark of identification and security (cf. BBC, 8:511 ff.). Paul in all probability associated the seal or stamp with baptism, where God revealed His love and grace and the believer responded in obedience. It was a sign that God had accepted the candidate as His own and placed him under His protection and care.

It was also a seal of authenticity (cf. 1 John 2:20, 27). It was a stamp of the image of the Spirit of Christ. It was a ratification of ownership. The seal is not the agent of change from the old life to the new, but a mark of that change, a guarantee of the "new creation" (5:17, RSV) which seals God's covenant conditionally into an "indissoluble bond."

What a wonderful corollary of the establishment in Christ (1:21). When we come to Christ as His children and open our hearts to His fullness, He not alone anoints but seals—an authentic mark of identity in sonship.

3. *Paul was given the earnest of the Spirit as the first-*

fruits of the future (22). It is a pledge *(arrabōn)* or a part payment given as a promise of the full payment of the "glory to be revealed in us." The pledge is experienced in our hearts now; but in the brightness of that day the "sufferings of this present time" will pass away, and we will see the pledge fulfilled in the fullness of God's redemptive promise.

"We have been born," says Peter, "to an inheritance which is imperishable, undefiled, and unfading" (1 Pet. 1:3-4, RSV). Eternal life is a new quality of life by the Spirit. It is the gift of the Spirit which makes immortality meaningful and the lordship of Christ inspiring in the here and now.

Great and wonderful are His promises. They are guaranteed for believers through the anointing of Christ's Spirit. They are sealed with the promise unto "the day of the Lord" for every faithful believer. And an earnest is given in part; but it is a real token, beyond all our imagination, of what is to come.

> *Of Father, Son and Spirit we*
>   *Extol the threefold care,*
> *Whose love, whose merit and whose power,*
>   *Unite to lift us there.*

The Art of Godly Leadership

2 Corinthians 1:23—2:17

23 Moreover I call God for a record upon my soul, that to spare you I came not as yet unto Corinth.
24 Not for that we have dominion over your faith, but are helpers of your joy: for by faith ye stand.
1 But I determined this with myself, that I would not come again to you in heaviness.
2 For if I make you sorry, who is he then that maketh me glad, but the same which is made sorry by me?
3 And I wrote this same unto you, lest, when I came, I should have sorrow from them of whom I ought to rejoice; having confidence in you all, that my joy is the joy of you all.
4 For out of much affliction and anguish of heart I wrote unto you with many tears; not that ye should be grieved, but that ye might know the love which I have more abundantly unto you.
5 But if any have caused grief, he hath not grieved me, but in part: that I may not overcharge you all.

6 Sufficient to such a man is this punishment, which was inflicted of many.

7 So that contrariwise ye ought rather to forgive him, and comfort him, lest perhaps such a one should be swallowed up with overmuch sorrow.

8 Wherefore I beseech you that ye would confirm your love toward him.

9 For to this end also did I write, that I might know the proof of you, whether ye be obedient in all things.

10 To whom ye forgive any thing, I forgive also: for if I forgave any thing, to whom I forgave it, for your sakes forgave I it in the person of Christ:

11 Lest Satan should get an advantage of us: for we are not ignorant of his devices.

12 Furthermore, when I came to Troas to preach Christ's gospel, and a door was opened unto me of the Lord,

13 I had no rest in my spirit, because I found not Titus my brother: but taking my leave of them, I went from thence into Macedonia.

14 Now thanks be unto God, which always causeth us to triumph in Christ, and maketh manifest the saviour of his knowledge by us in every place.

15 For we are unto God a sweet saviour of Christ, in them that are saved, and in them that perish:

16 To the one we are the saviour of death unto death; and to the other the saviour of life unto life. And who is sufficient for these things?

17 For we are not as many, which corrupt the word of God: but as of sincerity, but as of God, in the sight of God speak we in Christ.

1. *Paul's openness* (1:23—2:4). The apostle digresses long enough to offer an explanation for his alteration of plans (1:17). If he had come to them for the purpose of apostolic discipline, the result could only end in conflict. And if he had taken disciplinary action toward the offender (1 Cor. 5:1), it would mean that the offender would be driven out of the fellowship and irretrievably lost. So he came not because of fickleness or lack of integrity, but to spare them pain.

The explanation lifts the curtain and bares a heart of love. It was a pastor's heart. It was not his intention to "lord it over" their "faith" (RSV), but to be helpers of their joy. Paul recognized that their standing could only be through faith and not through his coercion.

Paul's first visit to Corinth was very profitable, but his second was painful (12:14; 13:1-2). Because of this he decided to return and send Titus to Corinth with his "stern letter."

There was no reason to return until conditions at

Corinth improved. So there was no sadistic pleasure in disciplining the very ones he loved. "His joy could come only through their joy, their growth in faith and love. Should he grieve them by rebuke and discipline, there would be no one to gladden him. His life was linked with theirs in joy and sorrow."[14]

The letter became the lesser evil, even though Paul wrote with "much affliction and anguish of heart" that the church might know the love which he had for them.

Love was in all that Paul wrote. His indignation was kindled by his love. His dreams for his church could only be realized in their responding with like love.

His openness was verified by a call of "God to witness against" (23, RSV) him if he were not telling the truth. There may have been times when his motives were veiled, but not often. Paul took the risk of telling them the whole story that he might eventually grace the situation with his presence. Honesty became a holy expedient.

2 CORINTHIANS 2

2. *Paul's forgiving spirit* (5-11). The insult offered to Paul, probably on his second journey, was not a personal affront, and the apostle did not handle it on personal grounds. He interpreted the insult as an attack on the whole church. Paul was more than pleased that since the insult was directed toward the church, the reproof was given by the church ("of many"). Quickly satisfied, he abruptly turns to forgive and comfort the offender lest he be lost to the fellowship. While conviction of his sin was the first step in his redemption, the restoration to fellowship was the continuing motive.

There was, however, also a danger. Sometimes deep contrition ends in self-torture until a man is overwhelmed. The letter says that Paul recognized the offender might be "swallowed up with much sorrow." Many a forgiven believer finds it harder to forgive himself than to accept God's forgiveness. This man needed the support of the fellowship in love.

A man cannot continually live in blame. He must rediscover his integrity in the fellowship of love. This is Paul's plea.

The passage is an eloquent expression of Christian interpersonal relationships. Paul saw that the motive for administering discipline could never be vengeance, but correction; not punishment, but rehabilitation in the fellowship.

The prize was worth contending for, "the treasure worth guarding." The very unity of the church was at stake. Since that unity could not be imposed from without, the believing community must act in obedience and love. And since *koinonia* demanded a common life of love, the community could do nothing less than what it did. Paul's forgiving spirit prompting the church to forgive made the difference.

Both Paul and the congregation were not unmindful of how Satan could secure an advantage under the circumstances. They were well aware of his wiles. Knowing this, they must act to forestall any attempts on his part to take advantage of the brother reproved.

3. *Paul's Christian faith* (12-17). The apostle's superlative faith in Christ added to his openness, as his forgiving spirit had characterized his godly leadership.

Paul was tempted to remain in Troas, for "a door was opened unto me of the Lord" to evangelize and establish a church. Titus, however, was not there, and he returned to Macedonia. Verse 14 obviously speaks of his meeting with Titus and his great joy because of the meeting. It is one of those typical Pauline outbursts of blessing (he does not tell of the meeting until 7:5-7).

The shift is characteristic of the apostle. He moves with suddenness from his burden to a shout of joy (14-16).

Some have suggested that the unspoken metaphor is

the moving spectacle of a victorious Roman general returning to Rome. The day of celebration was not only the major event of his life, but one of splendor and magnificence for the capital city itself.

Many times, Paul had seen the chariot drawn by white horses passing through the Arch of Triumph and had heard the cry from thousands, *"Io triumphe."* Now he sees Another marching—the Conqueror of death, hell, and the grave. And in a second metaphor, he hears the shouts of the redeemed of all ages as a "sweet smelling savour"— the fragrance of "his knowledge by us." In preaching the gospel, Paul sees the believing community as the fragrance of Christ to God both in those who are saved and in those who perish.

The second metaphor is double-edged. It may speak of censers of the priests in the Roman triumph, but certainly of an offering at the altar of sacrifice as a pleasing fragrance to God (cf. Eph. 5:2; Phil. 4:18). In either case it was a "savour of life" to the victors and a "savour of death" to the captives. "The same act of salvation which has destroyed death for the saved has made death irrevocable for those who persih."[15]

4. *Paul's Christian integrity* (17). The proclamation (14-16) nearly overwhelmed Paul so that he cried, "Who is sufficient for these things?" (16). The answer was confident, "We are!" (17). For we are not the many which corrupt the word of God, but we are men of integrity, "commissioned by God" to "speak in Christ" (RSV).

Godly leadership is always characterized by utter sincerity. The minister must do his work in the sight of God. It is this clear-sighted integrity before God that saves him from self-consciousness, timidity, and doubt. Integrity is a key word in our society. Expediency tends to creep into all the crevices of experience. God help us to discover that transparent motive "in Christ" that will make the gospel indeed good news to men, for His sake and to His glory.

The Credentials of a Minister

Where can you find better credentials for a minister than in the lives and character of his people? His converts prove or disprove the quality of the work accomplished. At least this is what Paul assumes as he writes to the church at Corinth.

2 Corinthians 3:1-3

> 1 Do we begin again to commend ourselves? or need we, as some others, epistles of commendation to you, or letters of commendation from you?
> 2 Ye are our epistle written in our hearts, known and read of all men:
> 3 Forasmuch as ye are manifestly declared to be the epistle of Christ ministered by us, written not with ink, but with the Spirit of the living God; not in tables of stone, but in fleshy tables of the heart.

1. *The true credentials of a minister are not letters of parchment.* Behind the words of 3:1 was the custom of the ancient world of bringing letters of introduction and commendation establishing the bearer's identity and credentials.

The previous verses seem to indicate that Paul was commending himself. Much to the contrary, he did not need letters either to or from the Corinthians to establish his veracity.

He is here delivering an oblique blow to the "peddlers of God's word" (2:17, RSV), false teachers who had come to Corinth with commendatory letters from Jerusalem (cf. Acts 9:2; 22:5; Rom. 16:1).

Vicious attacks forced the apostle to defend his record (4:2; 6:4 ff.). Both he and the Corinthian Christians were the losers unless he could maintain the authenticity of his record.

2. *The true credentials of a minister are letters from Christ* (2-3). Paul is not beginning again to commend himself. There was really no need for that, because the Corinthians themselves were "letters of commendation," letters from

Christ. "You yourselves are our letter of recommendation, written on your hearts, to be known and read by all men" (RSV).

Paul not only suggests that they were an epistle read of all men, but also a letter written by Christ himself, the agent of God in bringing the Good News to man.

He remembers the wonder of leading the Corinthians to Christ—their changed character being proof of his apostolic work. Those who saw the radical change in their lives should recognize that they are truly letters which Christ has published, Paul being the agent through which they were delivered.

a. These letters were not written with ink which was time-bound, but with the "Spirit of the living God," who is timeless. Then Paul, anticipating the next verses (4-11), fortifies his argument by the contrast between tables of stone (the old covenant) and fleshly tablets of the heart (lit. "hearts of flesh") upon which the terms of the new covenant were written (cf. Jer. 31:33; Ezek. 11:19; 36:26).

Every child of God in Christ is or ought to be a "translation of the gospel," "known and read of all men." He cannot hide his light behind a "bushel" but must put it on a "lampstand" until it "gives light to all who are in the house" (Matt. 5:15, RSV).

b. Paul was confident that the "saints" *(hagioi)* were so changed by the gospel that they were his best proof for vindication—and he was right! "This letter is no literal epistle; the Corinthian church is its content; Christ is its author; Paul is its courier; indeed, it is written on his heart by the Spirit of God."[16] After all, the greatest testimony to Christ is the lives of His people, and the greatest handicap is the lives of those who profess more than their character warrants. We are open letters to commend or condemn the witness given to Christ, the Lord.

The gospel has not ordinarily been translated by great men, but by thousands of common disciples who through the centuries have represented Christ where they are. Here is the true genius of the missionary task, the authentic mark of gospel ministry.

The Superiority of the New Covenant

2 Corinthians 3:4-11

> 4   And such trust have we through Christ to God-ward:
> 5   Not that we are sufficient of ourselves to think any thing as of ourselves; but our sufficiency is of God;
> 6   Who also hath made us able ministers of the new testament; not of the letter, but of the spirit: for the letter killeth, but the spirit giveth life.
> 7   But if the ministration of death, written and engraven in stones, was glorious, so that the children of Israel could not stedfastly behold the face of Moses for the glory of his countenance; which glory was to be done away:
> 8   How shall not the ministration of the spirit be rather glorious?
> 9   For if the ministration of condemnation be glory, much more doth the ministration of righteousness exceed in glory.
> 10   For even that which was made glorious had no glory in this respect, by reason of the glory that excelleth.
> 11   For if that which is done away was glorious, much more that which remaineth is glorious.

The remark in v. 3 calls to mind one of the differences between the old covenant and the new. The confidence that is Paul's is not of himself, but of God. It is God who has made Paul an able minister of the New Testament. Therefore he speaks with full trust of that difference wrought through the Spirit.

This adequacy "is its superiority as a ministry of the new covenant—a ministry of the Spirit."

1. *Superior, as life is more glorious than death* (5-6). The old covenant was grounded in a written code. It could only "incite and condemn sin" (Rom. 7:7-25), since it defined man's duty but gave him no power to obey (Rom. 8:3). Paul is not rejecting the law but describing how it can only lead to death ("the letter killeth," 6). He recognized the Old Testament as scripture, but saw the deadly effect of the law without life.

While the letter can only lead to death, "the Spirit gives *life*" (RSV). Frank Carver summarizes the thought superlatively when he observes:

But the "Spirit of life in Christ Jesus" (Rom. 8:2;

cf. 3:17; I Cor. 15:45) is able to engrave the will of God on the heart (3:3; Acts 15:9), enabling the Christian to fulfill the righteous requirements of a holy God (3:9; Rom. 8:4). The Law, however, was not invalidated, for "the law is holy" (Rom. 7:22). Rather it is established (Rom. 3:31) or fulfilled (Rom. 13:8-10; Gal. 5:14) when by the power of the constant presence of the Spirit of Christ (Rom. 8:2-9) faith operates through love *(agape)* in the ethical concern of the Christian (Gal. 5:6). The sufficiency of Paul's calling is that it is anchored in a superior ministry, the ministry of a transforming Spirit (3:18).[17]

The Spirit changes a man's life in love, not by imposing a new ethical code, but by changing his heart and making him a new man in Christ. The new covenant not only told a man what to do, but gave him the strength to do it through the Spirit of Christ. "With its commandments, it brought its power."

2. *Superior, as righteousness is more glorious than condemnation* (7-9). Paul is describing his ministry. He has declared it fully accredited through the call of Christ and the transformed character of his converts. He now exhibits its glory by comparing the gospel of Christ with the law of Moses.

This comparison was not by chance. Paul is declaring the heart of Christian ministry. He must remove from the minds of the Corinthian Christians the suspicions inspired by his enemies who were insisting on the preservation of the ceremonial law.

It is with this in mind that the apostle describes the triumphant nature of his ministry. He was not adulterating the gospel with the ingredients of the law.

To make his point, Paul refers to the glorious law of Moses as the "ministration [dispensation] of death, written and engraven in stones." But even that glory was to be done away. It was a "fading" (RSV) glory which radiated from his face.

The Law of Moses was a key to the inauguration of a

new nation. It was indeed so glorious that the face of Moses shone with such splendor that the children of Israel could not look upon him. Yet the glory was transient; it was a means to the end rather than the end itself. In comparison, the new covenant exceeded it in glory. The former was the dispensation of *condemnation* because it condemned the lawbreaker. The gospel of the Spirit in Christ is the dispensation of *righteousness* because it proclaims the "righteousness of God through faith in Jesus Christ for all who believe" (Rom. 3:22, RSV), as a free gift of grace.

John Calvin in a magnificent passage says, "The office of the law is to show us the disease, in such a way as to show us at the same time, no hope or cure; the office of the gospel is to bring a remedy to those who were past hope."[18]

While the law could only end in death, the gospel of Christ could only end in righteousness because it witnesses to a love relationship between a Father and His sons. It changes a man's life, not by giving him new laws to follow, but by transforming his heart and making him a new person in Christ. The labor of servantship is transformed into the glory of sonship.

No wonder the dispensation of condemnation was outshone by the dispensation of righteousness. Legality gave way to a new transforming relationship of "faith working through love" (Gal. 5:6, RSV). It makes a tremendous difference whether a man is laboring under law or serving Christ in love.

3. *Superior, as the permanent is more glorious than the uncertain* (11). The apostle declares the third and last difference. "For if what faded away came with splendor, what is permanent must have much more splendor" (RSV).

The brightness of the law soon faded. Its transient glory was but a passing symbol of what was to come in the surpassing "splendor" of the dispensation of the new covenant. The latter was of such a "permanent" nature that it could never be outshone.

The Glorious Hope of the Gospel

2 Corinthians 3:12-18

> 12 Seeing then that we have such hope, we use great plainness of speech:
>
> 13 And not as Moses, which put a vail over his face, that the children of Israel could not stedfastly look to the end of that which is abolished:
>
> 14 But their minds were blinded: for until this day remaineth the same vail untaken away in the reading of the old testament; which vail is done away in Christ.
>
> 15 But even unto this day, when Moses is read, the vail is upon their heart.
>
> 16 Nevertheless when it shall turn to the Lord, the vail shall be taken away.
>
> 17 Now the Lord is that Spirit: and where the Spirit of the Lord is, there is liberty.
>
> 18 But we all, with open face beholding as in a glass the glory of the Lord, are changed into the same image from glory to glory, even as by the Spirit of the Lord.

Paul turns with great confidence and boldness to the openness of plain speech. "We have nothing to conceal," he says. "We are not like Moses." The fading of his glory was a symbol of impermanence, and the children of Israel have grown dull in their "spiritual perception" to this day. When the Old Testament is read that they might see, a veil of blindness, ignorance, and unbelief is upon their heart. "Nevertheless when it [the Jew] shall turn to the Lord, the veil shall be taken away" (16).

Paul, then, in v. 17 breaks out into one of the great joyful expressions of insight which is so characteristic of his prose. "Now the Lord is that Spirit: and where the Spirit of the Lord is, there is liberty." The passage teaches three areas of liberty.

1. *In Christ the Christian has freedom of access to the presence of God* (15-16). When Moses is read, a "veil lies over their minds," but "when a man turns to the Lord the veil is removed" (RSV). The hindrances to access to God are removed as one turns to Christ, who is the only Means of that access.

One cannot but remember the majestic experience of Isaiah when he saw the "Lord . . . high and lifted up" in the Temple (Isa. 6:1); or the veil of the Temple "torn in two from top to bottom" (Matt. 27:51, RSV), that man should no longer be kept from the Divine Presence (cf. Heb. 10:19-22).

It is the glorious gospel of Christ which has made such access to God possible. The crucified-resurrected Son of God in love introduces us to God himself.

2. *In Christ the Christian has freedom of access to the deep needs of his own heart* (17-18). Christlikeness is not a human achievement but a door opened by the "creative power of the Spirit." "For it is God who is at work in you, both to will and to work for His good pleasure" (Phil. 2:13, NASB). And while we must "work out our own salvation," it is all in response to the work of God's Spirit in our lives.

There is no issue the Spirit cannot probe and help. There is no problem the Spirit cannot resolve—perhaps not from our perspective, but for His glory (cf. Rom. 8:28). Change is the radical expression of God's grace in the lives of His people. Why? Because we stand with "unveiled face" (RSV) in His presence and are "being changed into his likeness from one degree of glory to another; for this comes from the Lord who is the Spirit" (RSV).

We are open to that divine aid by the purification of the heart, effected by the life-giving presence of the Holy Spirit. This comprehends freedom from sin (Rom. 6:6-7), death (Rom. 6:21-23), and condemnation (Rom. 8:1). It is the freedom of sonship (Rom. 8:14-16), the possession of the prospect of "the glorious liberty of the children of God" (Rom. 8:21).

3. *In Christ the Christian has freedom of access to the sure hope of the glory of God forever* (18). Even as Moses reflected the divine glory of God, so Christians beholding the surpassing glory of Christ reflect that glory, being "changed into the same image from glory to glory, even as by the Spirit of the Lord."

If we gaze at Christ long enough, we will reflect Him. The change is both critical and gradual. The transformation is wrought by the Spirit of the Lord, or "from the

Lord, the Spirit" (NASB), and is wrought from glory to glory. Hering suggests that "from glory" speaks of the source of that glory; while "to glory" is its result, to be revealed at the resurrection to come.

Here is our hope. God has opened the door of salvation through Christ. That great crisis event begins a change which is continuous until the "day of our Lord." Within that development is the further crisis of heart cleansing, which prepares a man for "God's great future" revealed and released through the person and work of Jesus Christ. Such is the new covenant.

> *Oh, perfect life of Christ, my Lord!*
> *I want to be like Jesus.*
> *My recompense and my reward,*
> *That I may be like Jesus.*
>
> *His Spirit fill my hung'ring soul,*
> *His power all my life control;*
> *My deepest pray'r, my highest goal,*
> *That I may be like Jesus.*

—THOMAS O. CHISHOLM

2 CORINTHIANS 4

The Glory of God in Jesus Christ

2 Corinthians 4:1-6

1 Therefore seeing we have this ministry, as we have received mercy, we faint not;

2 But have renounced the hidden things of dishonesty, not walking in craftiness, nor handling the word of God deceitfully; but by manifestation of the truth commending ourselves to every man's conscience in the sight of God.

3 But if our gospel be hid, it is hid to them that are lost:

4 In whom the god of this world hath blinded the minds of them which believe not, lest the light of the glorious gospel of Christ, who is the image of God, should shine unto them.

5 For we preach not ourselves, but Christ Jesus the Lord; and ourselves your servants for Jesus' sake.
6 For God, who commanded the light to shine out of darkness, hath shined in our hearts, to give the light of the knowledge of the glory of God in the face of Jesus Christ.

In this section Paul resumes the theme opened in 3:12, namely, the frankness and openness with which he has preached the gospel. He has been accused of dishonesty, duplicity, and deceit. Once again he establishes his sincerity, truthfulness, and integrity, testifying to the fullness of the revelation of the glory of God in Christ.

1. *The glory of the gospel through Paul's ministry* (1-2). The antecedent to "this ministry" is the one he has just described as a ministry of life, righteousness, liberty, and glory. It is only on this basis that he has received mercy. His was the consciousness of a great task grounded in the mercy he had received. He would spend a whole life in response to the love given in Christ. The concept was beyond his comprehension—a mystery. That God in His mercy had shared His righteousness as a gift made Paul immeasurably grateful.

It is this mercy that undergirds the integrity of Paul's ministry. It was his only boast, his only ground of confidence (cf. 3:4). On this basis alone, he concludes, "We faint not" or "We do not lose heart" (NASB). So glorious was the commission from Christ that it outweighed all the distressing experiences that he might have undergone to discharge it.

He is not driven to despair. The dignity of his ministry is dependent upon God's power rather than his own ability. He will, therefore, not lose heart. For this reason he has "renounced disgraceful, underhanded ways" and refused to "tamper with God's word," willing always to commend himself "to every man's conscience in the sight of God." The gospel gives both confidence and openness.

2. *The condition of those who are unable to see the glory of that ministry* (3-4). The unspoken criticism suggested in v. 3 relates to those who maintained that Paul's mes-

sage was obscure and lacked "the perspicuity of true revelation." The inference was that Paul himself was not open —an accusation he vehemently denies.

It is true, Paul observes, that for some the message is hid; but it is because there is a "veil" over their minds (cf. 3:14). Their lostness is the reason for their lack of comprehension. Just as a veil concealed from the children of Israel the light through which Moses' face was shining, so unbelief blinds some men from the truth. As a result they fail to see the "light of the glorious gospel of Christ." Paul describes them as lost, for Satan has blinded their minds. They fail to see in the glorious gospel the "Christ, who is the image of God," the Embodiment of all perfection.

3. *The source of that glory is Jesus Christ our Lord* (5-6). What a marvelous conclusion to his argument! *"We preach not ourselves, but Christ Jesus the Lord;* and ourselves your servants for Jesus' sake." Paul felt no need for subterfuge or deceit. No true preacher need hide nor seek power for himself. His whole endeavor is not for himself, but for his Master. The heart of the ministry is to help men to submit themselves to Christ as Lord.

It is fascinating that in v. 5 he concludes with the human title, Jesus, indicating His humility and Paul's own submission as servant (literally, bondslave) for Jesus' sake.

Thus, as in the preceding paragraph, Paul again sets forth the glory of the gospel—a message that comes through the mercy of God. There is no personal gain for the apostle. He is so wrapped up in the wonder of the new covenant, the light that shines out of darkness, the "knowledge of the glory of God in the face of Jesus Christ," that his whole vision is bathed in the light of his Lord.

God's Treasure in Earthen Vessels

2 Corinthians 4:7-18

7 But we have this treasure in earthen vessels, that the excellency of the power may be of God, and not of us.

8   We are troubled on every side, yet not distressed; we are perplexed, but not in despair;
9   Persecuted, but not forsaken; cast down, but not destroyed;
10   Always bearing about in the body the dying of the Lord Jesus, that the life also of Jesus might be made manifest in our body.
11   For we which live are alway delivered unto death for Jesus' sake, that the life also of Jesus might be made manifest in our mortal flesh.
12   So then death worketh in us, but life in you.
13   We having the same spirit of faith, according as it is written, I believed, and therefore have I spoken; we also believe, and therefore speak;
14   Knowing that he which raised up the Lord Jesus shall raise up us also by Jesus, and shall present us with you.
15   For all things are for your sakes, that the abundant grace might through the thanksgiving of many redound to the glory of God.
16   For which cause we faint not; but though our outward man perish, yet the inward man is renewed day by day.
17   For our light affliction, which is but for a moment, worketh for us a far more exceeding and eternal weight of glory;
18   While we look not at the things which are seen, but at the things which are not seen: for the things which are seen are temporal; but the things which are not seen are eternal.

1. *Earthen vessels and God's power* (7). "I have this treasure in a mere earthen jar, to show that its amazing power belongs to God and not to me" (Goodspeed). The metaphor may be speaking of the custom of the Romans, who actually carried their treasures in earthen vessels, or it may just as well be speaking of small clay receptacles which were fragile and easily shattered.

In either case, a Christian is shown to be mortal, subject to weakness, disability, and death. He is still involved in the human situation over which he has very little control.

There is much to keep a follower of Christ from pride. Barclay wrote, "We talk a great deal about the power of God, and about the vast forces which he now controls. But the real characteristic of man is not his power but his weakness. As Pascal said, 'a drop of water or a breath of air can kill him.'"[19]

Paul recognized his weakness, but he was also aware of the power of God. The metaphor of the earthen vessel served to protect the truth that salvation is of God and not of us. In Paul's weakness he was entrusted with this treasure.

The apostle's physical disabilities were apparent to all. The "ugly little Jew" was a study in contempt (10:10). He was subject to a recurrent malady—"a thorn in the flesh" (12:7) which prayer did not remove. He had suffered shipwreck, stoning, and beating (11:24-27). Add to that the anxiety he felt for his churches, and you have the picture of human existence in perplexity apart from the grace of God.

That weakness was spiritual as well as physical. Paul was always aware that the spiritual journey was a struggle —a fight until the end. The moral and spiritual ambiguities of his life because of imperfect insight were at times personally overwhelming.

By this superlative metaphor Paul shows that "the transcendent power belongs to God and not to us" (RSV). The vessel is of clay, but it holds the excellency of God's power. "God hath chosen the foolish things of the world . . . to confound the things which are mighty" (1 Cor. 1:27). Men with great weakness have been enabled to do wonderful feats of ministry for Christ—but it has always been *in Christ.* The power of God triumphs through the weakness of man.

We have all seen men who have ended the possibility of ministry through a spirit of self-sufficiency. But the Church has also been blessed with rare men who are so saturated and filled with the power of God that human considerations seem relatively unimportant.

2. *Four great Pauline paradoxes* (8-9). These two famous verses are no "fitful rhapsody of troubled feeling." They move in personal witness from confusion to cohesion, from self-enchantment to Christ, to holiness, and finally to the hope of heaven. The apostle pours himself out with candor and sacrifice. It is the incarnational pattern of Another.

a. *"Troubled, yet not distressed"* (8). "Hard-pressed on every side, we are never hemmed in" (NEB). The NASB puts it, "We are afflicted in every way, but not crushed" (cf. 7:5; 6:12; Gal. 4:20). Here, with the following three contrasts, is an illustration of Paul's weakness and God's power. In a series of present participles (present experience), the earthen vessel is represented by the first of each pair, and the divine power of God by the second.

b. "Perplexed, but not in despair" (8). If we preserve the relation between the words of the original, we have: "Put to it, but not utterly put out." Barclay paraphrases the thought, "We are persecuted by men, but never abandoned by God."

Pure minds are not adequate enough to satisfy our questions. But in the midst of that despair there is a Hand that reaches out to save us from complete despair. It is Kierkegaard's qualitative leap of faith. It is Augustine's freedom in Christ. It is Wesley's Aldersgate. In Christ there is the inevitable point where perplexity, however confounding, discovers faith in response to God's call.

c. "Persecuted, but not forsaken" (9). "Routed, but not abandoned" (Goodspeed). Or as Phillips has it, "We never have to stand it alone." We are not left in enemy hands! There are times in the life of a Christian when he cannot see the future, but he knows that there is One in his future. There are times when touch is more important than sight, when we are pursued by the enemy without any letup; yet we are steadied by the faith that we are not abandoned.

d. "Cast down, but not destroyed" (9). "Struck down" (RSV), but never "knocked out" (Barclay). The blow is never fatal for the Christian; he rises again, and again, and again! He may lose many of the battles, but in Christ the campaign is already won.

When the enemies of Paul seemed to have him in their power, God delivered him. This occurred so often it was crystal clear it was of God and not of man. Paul's own resources were not enough apart from God—and neither are ours! He was a combatant who was pressed, then hemmed in, pursued, and finally cast down. His life was a succession of indignities and sufferings. The aristocracy of his early life was succeeded by an existence akin to the suffering Christ.

3. *The secret of victory* (10-18). After stating the four great paradoxes in life, Paul goes on to share the secret of his own victory—the "why" of his triumph in Christ.

a. A servant of the Servant (10-11). That "why" is discovered as a life of dying with the Lord Jesus in order that the life of Jesus might also be revealed in his body. The apostle was convinced that the same process of dying which culminated on the Cross was the life that would ripen in the resurrection of Jesus. That "resurrection-life" was revealed in the life that bore the marks of Jesus (cf. Gal. 6:17). Because the apostle shares in "the death that Jesus died," he shares also in "the life that Jesus lives" (NEB).

Carver reminds us that vv. 10-11 speak four times of the name of Jesus, showing "how closely Paul linked the career of Jesus with that of his own as a servant of the Servant. The mark of a true apostle (and minister) is that 'he is, like Jesus, a suffering and dying figure, whose work and power and victory arise from his weakness and infirmity and defeat.'"

b. An example and promise to the faithful (12-18). It is through these distresses which wear at the bodies of Christ's servants and bring them to share in Christ's death that the faith of God's people is strengthened. "So it is death that operates in my case, but life that operates in yours" (Goodspeed). Paul faced every emergency with the conviction that his sufferings would lead others into the light and love of God.

It is said that 300 lives were lost in the clearing and rehabilitation of the Suez canal in 1974-75. They died that the nations of the world might have ready access to the markets of the world. Their sacrifice was not useless but purposeful.

Paul's sacrificial life in a greater sense was also purposeful activity. His dying brought others to Christ. Barclay remarks, "When a man has the complete conviction that what is happening to him is happening literally for Christ's sake he can face and bear anything."

Faith in the resurrection, then, sustained both Paul and the congregation through his example and witness. In vv. 13-15 the apostle mentions four factors that held him steady in hard and perilous work.

(1) He was reassured by the Psalmist's declaration: "I believed, and so I spoke" (Ps. 116:10, RSV). He returned to the foundation upon which his faith rested—the resurrection of Jesus through the power of God.

(2) He was supported by the conviction that regardless of what happens in this life, he too with all faithful believers shall be resurrected through Christ and be presented with Him before God. "Knowing" (14) is a causal participle, "because we know." So as in 1 Cor. 15: 23-28, personal confidence in bodily resurrection is founded upon faith in Christ's resurrection. Because He rose, we shall also rise with Him. Paul is very closely bound to his churches. His faith can be theirs as well (cf. 1:14; 1 Thess. 2:19-20; Phil. 4:1).

(3) That confidence led to the third reason for Paul's poise. Whatever he does is for their sakes "so that, as the abounding grace of God is shared by more and more, the greater may be the chorus of thanksgiving that ascends to the glory of God" (15, NEB). His constant concern for his church supported him in all his baffling experiences.

(4) The fourth support was found in the divine purpose: "in order that" grace might "increase thanksgiving to the glory of God" (15, RSV). Giving glory to God along with bearing concern for the community strengthened Paul in his sufferings for Christ.

It is no wonder he says again, "We faint not." He is well aware that the outward man is wasting away, but he is also experiencing daily inner renewal (16). While the physical energies run down, the spiritual energies spent for Christ are restored in beauty and power. Neither old age nor anticipated death can destroy the inner man which is being renewed day by day.

To that thought is added the assurance that our "slight momentary affliction" (17, RSV) is preparing for us "an eternal weight of glory far beyond all comparison" (NASB). *Affliction* is transmuted to *glory.*

Paul can say this because he is not looking "at the things which are seen," but the eternal dimension of the "things which are not seen." "What is seen is transitory, but what is unseen is eternal" (Goodspeed). His eyes are fixed on that eternal city which wasteth not away. His motives are purged, and his convictions have crystallized in a mature understanding of the gospel.

The decay of a godless man is a "melancholy spectacle," for it is the disintegration of everything. "The way of the wicked is like darkness," but the path of the Christian "is like the light of dawn, that shines brighter and brighter until the full day" (Prov. 4:18-19, NASB). The Christian lives by "the blessed hope" of Christ's second coming (Titus 2:13). Carver suggests, however, that the ultimate goal does not minimize the importance of daily life in the Spirit which "affects one's outward look on life" both morally and psychologically. To know Christ is worth everything, Paul cries, both here and in the hereafter.

2 CORINTHIANS 5

The Realities of the Future

2 Corinthians 5:1-10

> 1 For we know that if our earthly house of this tabernacle were dissolved, we have a building of God, an house not made with hands, eternal in the heavens.
> 2 For in this we groan, earnestly desiring to be clothed upon with our house which is from heaven:
> 3 If so be that being clothed we shall not be found naked.
> 4 For we that are in this tabernacle do groan, being burdened: not for that we would be unclothed, but clothed upon, that mortality might be swallowed up of life.

5 Now he that hath wrought us for the selfsame thing is God, who also hath given unto us the earnest of the Spirit.

6 Therefore we are always confident, knowing that, whilst we are at home in the body, we are absent from the Lord:

7 (For we walk by faith, not by sight:)

8 We are confident, I say, and willing rather to be absent from the body, and to be present with the Lord.

9 Wherefore we labour, that, whether present or absent, we may be accepted of him.

10 For we must all appear before the judgment seat of Christ; that every one may receive the things done in his body, according to that he hath done, whether it be good or bad.

While Paul has been speaking of his sufferings, he has not forgotten the consolations in Christ. Someday death can only bring victory. This is not only a hope of heaven, but also a condition of a happy, healthy existence here and now. This passage breathes with such Christian hope and happiness.

1. *The Christian's confidence* (1, 6, 8). Three times Paul explicitly expresses his Christian confidence. In v. 1 he declares, "We know." In 6 he concludes, "Therefore we are always confident." Again, in 8, he says, "We are confident." From what does all this assurance arise? Where is its source?

While that confidence is his own, it is actually a faith that all believers share. Paul does not look forward to his death. It remains a mystery, even for the man of faith. Death is a step into the dark. The Scriptures are never explicit as to its nature. However, Paul had no doubt about the outcome. "If the earthly tent we live in is destroyed, we have a building from God, a house not made with hands, eternal in the heavens" (1, RSV).

The second expression of confidence arises from the fact that God has given us the "earnest of the Spirit" (5; cf. 1:22). The Spirit is the Source of our life in Christ here and now and also a pledge of the life to come. His personal indwelling in our hearts is a guarantee that the process of our salvation will be completed. "So we are always of good courage," Paul adds. "We know that while we are at home in the body we are away from the Lord, for we walk by faith and not by sight. We are of good courage, and we would rather be away from the body and at home with the Lord" (6-7, RSV). The reiterations of his confidence do not mean he is dissatisfied to be "in the body"; his constant hope nevertheless is for the day when he will be "present with the Lord."

2. *The Christian's desire* (2-4). Paul's strong desire to be at "home with the Lord" is expressed negatively in v. 3—a Hebraism which reveals the strong Old Testament aversion to a disembodied spirit. The Bible rejects Greek dualism and looks upon the self as a psychophysical unity. So Paul looks expectantly to bodily resurrection. His hope is "that being clothed we shall not be found naked" (in an intermediate state). He longs to receive his spiritual body as soon as possible. While in this life "we sigh with anxiety," in that life we shall put on our heavenly body. The whole passage reveals Paul's strong desire to be "at home with the Lord."

3. *The Christian's faithfulness* (4-7). The oft-quoted phrase, "We walk by faith and not by sight," is a passing parenthesis to support the preceding observation in v. 6. Charles Hodge paraphrases the thought, "We are absent from the Lord, for we now, in this life, walk by faith" (cf. Rom. 8:24). Our present life is a matter of faith and not of fruition. It is a life of faith without the objects of faith. Thus, we run with patience, walk by faith, and hope continually for the "building of God not made with hands."

Since the hope of the new covenant is conditioned on his "continuing in the faith" (Col. 1:23), it is imperative that he labor now to be accepted of the Lord then. Longing to be with Christ produces the desires and secures the effort to be found acceptable of Him now. "Everyone who thus hopes purifies himself as he is pure" (1 John 3:3, RSV). It is such responsiveness to grace which leads a follower of Christ to be obedient "all the days of his life." The one aim of the Christian is to please Christ. His commandments are never out of mind. His hope is our hope—as we wait patiently to do His will.

4. *The Christian's hope in judgment* (10). While the prospect of the judgment gives motivation to obedience, it is not the prime motive. Nevertheless Paul's expectation of the return of the Lord, of bodily resurrection, and of future judgment had a practical bearing on his life. These great mysteries made his suffering bearable and hopeful. He did not view them with fear, but saw in them an inspiring possibility.

These "blessed realities of the future" are largely veiled from us, but enough is revealed to comfort our hearts. We may "see through a glass darkly," but we do see through.

Life, says Charles Erdman, should be lived with these solemn truths in view. We should so abide in Christ "that if he should be manifest, we may have boldness, and not be ashamed before him at his coming."

Motivated to Serve Both God and Man

2 Corinthians 5:11-13

> 11 Knowing therefore the terror of the Lord, we persuade men; but we are made manifest unto God; and I trust also are made manifest in your consciences.
> 12 For we commend not ourselves again unto you, but give you occasion to glory on our behalf, that ye may have somewhat to answer them which glory in appearance, and not in heart.
> 13 For whether we be beside ourselves, it is to God: or whether we be sober, it is for your cause.

Throughout the Epistle in one way or another, Paul's thought moves paradoxically between the treasure of the gospel and the "earthen vessel" in which it is contained; between the authority of the apostle and his humility; between the sonship and ignominy of Christ. All of these paradoxes are set out in the present paragraph and are clearly related to the preceding materials and the arguments that follow.

Paul is moved to a beautiful liturgical style, but what he writes is clearly associated with what he has said and as surely with what will follow.[20] As he returns to his life and work as an apostle, he wants to help his converts to defend his conduct against critics who judge merely by appearances.

1. *His transparency before God* (11a). Paul, like all Christians, must stand before God (10). "Knowing the fear of the Lord" (RSV) is to be interpreted in the same context. Fear is not "terror" as the KJV translates the word, but the "reverential awe" which every man feels in the presence of God's holiness. James Reid observes that "the judgment of holy love is more terrible to face than the judgment of one who does not care about us."

Paul appeals to the knowledge of God for his defense. "What we are is known to God" (11, RSV). Whatever men may say of us, "we stand open to God." Paul is confident that his aims and motives are clearly revealed to God now as they will be on the day of judgment. He was defending himself in order that he might defend the gospel. Once again he is saying that a minister must be absolutely circumspect for the gospel's sake.

2. *His transparency before men* (11b). Paul was not only responsible before God but, in a sense, before men. His prayer was, "I hope they [our lives] also lie open to you in your heart of hearts" (NEB). His earnest prayer was that his motives might be as transparent to his readers as they were to God and be made known to their consciences. He is confident that when they think seriously, they will know that he is sincere.

3. *His appeal to integrity* (12). Paul's approach may sound to his readers like conceit. It is not! This is not self-flattery. He is not beginning to commend himself again to them. His desire is that they glory in his behalf. That is, he would give them a defense against those who "pride themselves on a man's position and not on his heart" (RSV). "Appearance" *(prosopon)* indicates that "man is centered upon himself" (the ground of carnal-mindedness), while "heart" *(kardia)* suggests "man centered on God." Paul's enemies are interested in their own gain rather than a min-

istry of suffering. Their "pride is all in outward show and not in inward worth" (NEB).

4. *An appeal to motive* (13). The apostle concludes by speaking to a criticism. There were those who said he was out of his mind. He does not deny that there were times in his experience when oneness with God soared mystically. Jesus was accused of being "beside himself" (Mark 3:21). Francis of Assisi was called mad. The early Christians were accused of "turning the world upside down" (Acts 17:6). All he has to say is that his moments of ecstacy are affairs between God and himself. Whatever he has done, "it is for your cause" (the Corinthians). Since Paul's critics professed to be Christians, they should not pass judgment on worldly standards, but seek Christian standards, divining his motives and testing his integrity. In the final analysis, our only defense is the transparency of a life entirely open to both God and man.

The Word of Reconciliation

2 Corinthians 5:14-19

> 14 For the love of Christ constraineth us; because we thus judge, that if one died for all, then were all dead:
> 15 And that he died for all, that they which live should not henceforth live unto themselves, but unto him which died for them, and rose again.
> 16 Wherefore henceforth know we no man after the flesh: yea, though we have known Christ after the flesh, yet now henceforth know we him no more.
> 17 Therefore if any man be in Christ, he is a new creature: old things are passed away; behold, all things are become new.
> 18 And all things are of God, who hath reconciled us to himself by Jesus Christ, and hath given to us the ministry of reconciliation;
> 19 To wit, that God was in Christ, reconciling the world unto himself, not imputing their trespasses unto them; and hath committed unto us the word of reconciliation.

In Christ, God has reconciled men to himself. This is the grand theme Paul now introduces. In so doing he touches the very heart of the gospel.

1. *The love of Christ constrains us* (14). Only in the Authorized Version is the full emotional depth of this passage communicated. It has been quoted again and again

for more than 350 years from thousands of pulpits. Paul's mind and heart are under the control of Christ. He cannot deviate from the course. Notice that it is not Paul's love, but Christ's love that "controls" (RSV) him. Our love is always a response to His love. We are to be held (restricted) within the bounds of Christ's love for us.

> The genitive *of Christ* is exclusively subjective (cf. Rom. 8:35, 39). This is indicated by the immediate reference to Christ's death: *One died for all.* For Paul the death of Christ is "the self-giving of Christ without limit." It genuinely manifests the love of God: "God demonstrates His own love toward us, in that while we were yet sinners, Christ died for us" (Rom. 5:8, NASB). The practical result is that "the love of God has been poured out within our hearts through the Holy Spirit who was given unto us" (Rom. 5:5, NASB). This is the love that holds Paul captive, a "love which originates and ends with God in Christ" (cf. Rom. 8:28-30).[21]

2. *The motive for Christ's identification with all mankind* (15). Convinced that One died for all, Paul immediately gives the objective of that atoning death: "That those who live might live no longer for themselves but for him" (RSV) who died for them and rose again. In Christ we experience the "new order" in which our old, self-centered personality comes to an end.

This means that "justification reaches out to involve sanctification." Christ died that we might be freed from self as the focus of interest. Paul, in writing to the Romans, says, "Our old self was crucified with Him . . . that we should no longer be slaves to sin. . . . Now if we have died with Christ, we believe that we shall also live with him . . . for the death that He died, He died unto sin, once for all; but the life that He lives, He lives to God in Christ Jesus" (Rom. 6:6-11, NASB). For Paul, "to live is Christ" (Phil. 1:21; cf. Phil. 2:5-18).

There is a radical change in this "crisic-process" (as Rob Staples puts it), from living for self to the new life in Christ. From the old sinful self as a center of reference, the scene changes to the new life centered in Another—not just on *any* other, but the *One* other, the Lord Jesus Christ. The resurrection cannot be divorced from the crucifixion. Celebration cannot be separated from suffering in the lifestyle of the authentic Christian.

> *Thee may I set at my right hand,*
> *   Whose eyes mine inmost substance see,*
> *And labour on at Thy command,*
> *   And offer all my works to Thee.*
>
> *Give me to bear Thy easy yoke,*
> *   And every moment watch and pray,*
> *And still to things eternal look,*
> *   And hasten to Thy glorious day.*
>
> *For Thee delightfully employ*
> *   Whate'er Thy bounteous grace hath given,*
> *And run my course with even joy,*
> *   And closely walk with Thee to heaven.*
>
> —Charles Wesley

3. *The Person in that identification* (16). There was a time when Paul had judged Christ "from a human point of view" (RSV), from the perspective of race, social status, wealth, and title. His view was Phariasic. He had failed to recognize Jesus as Messiah and expected Him to fit into his ideas of political and military leadership.

Just as he evaluates no man by how he first sees him, he now sees Christ as the divine, risen, and glorified Son of God. It is upon this Christ that his thoughts center. The change was radical for Paul and will be for all those who move in faith from self-interest to Christ-centeredness. The object of Christian faith is the Lord Jesus Christ!

4. *The result of that identification* (17-19). "If any man be in Christ, he is a new creature." Because of Christ, the change is radical and vital. The old considerations are no longer pertinent but have given way to the new life of integrity in Christ. "Behold the new has come" (RSV),

praise God! The human Jesus, viewed from a natural perspective, cannot make this difference; only the divine, glorified, living Christ can make one "a new person" (Phillips).

Nor must we allow this last term to tease, discourage, or distress us. The new order includes both a crisis and a process. When we accept the lordship of Christ, we begin to live in Him. Many of the familiar things become sordid and shameful. The new life-style is a new world which progressively becomes more actual. The new man in Christ sees the change here—he sees the final fruition in that One who sits on the throne and says, "Behold, I make all things new" (Rev. 21:5). It is no wonder that Barclay said, "I am saved, I am being saved, and I will be saved."

The new life is possible because of the *word of reconciliation.* The Lord's death stands in a place that is "mysteriously unique." Paul had learned that he could not reconcile himself to God. He could not bring about by benevolent friendship what God did in Christ, for he was the enemy (sinner) and was banished from God's presence. But in Christ he found the Answer. The apostolic Good News is that God in Christ has done what man could not do for himself. In His love He has reconciled us to himself by Jesus Christ. This gospel must be proclaimed before it can do its saving work. It was this gospel that was given to Paul as "the word of reconciliation." It was this Good News he believed, lived for, and upon which he staked his very existence.

The Ministry of Reconciliation

2 Corinthians 5:20—6:2

> 20 Now then we are ambassadors for Christ, as though God did beseech you by us: we pray you in Christ's stead, be ye reconciled to God.
> 21 For he hath made him to be sin for us, who knew no sin; that we might be made the righteousness of God in him.
> 1 We then, as workers together with him, beseech you also that ye receive not the grace of God in vain.
> 2 (For he saith, I have heard thee in a time accepted, and in the day of salvation have I succoured thee: behold, now is the accepted time; behold, now is the day of salvation.)

After stating the heart of "the word of reconciliation," Paul reminds us that, with others, he has been given the urgent apostolic ministry of earnestly proclaiming this word to others.

1. *Ambassadors of the Good News* (20-21). Paul and his colleagues are acting on behalf of a sovereign Ruler. The word "ambassador" points to his authority and responsibility. Paul is acting on behalf of Christ. He is out to further His cause.

a. In a real sense every minister is Christ's ambassador. His task is one of honor and responsibility. He speaks at all times in the name of his Lord. When his dealings are in sensitive areas, it is important that he represent and interpret his Lord rightly. "He is not responsible for the message he delivers, only for transmitting it rightly."

b. The message is the word of reconciliation from God to man. Of itself it makes us willing to be reconciled. It is an enabling message that puts us straightforward in a decision-making role. James Reid observes that the spirit in which the *ambassador* transmits the message is all-important:

> He is one who pleads. . . . He must not only lift up the Cross; he must carry it. If he must warn or rebuke, he will do it as one who sorrows over sin. . . . He will, like Jesus, be filled with compassion (Matt. 9:36). . . . When he is tempted to condemn the obstinate narrow-mindedness or bigotry of some religious people, he will remember how Jesus longed to draw such people to himself. . . . Their blindness and self-righteousness will not plant a thorn in his side, but a cross in his heart. His reactions to what men do or say will always be dictated by love. . . . His aim must be to produce a personal encounter with God. His insistent appeal is, *Be reconciled to God.*[22]

c. Paul concludes this section by returning to his motif of how reconciliation is made possible. Christ "knew no sin" that was His own doing (cf. Matt. 4:1-13; John 8:46; Acts 3:14; Heb. 4:15; 1 Pet. 2:22; 1 John 3:5). The proper word order is stressed by the NASB, "He made Him who knew no sin to be sin on our behalf that we might become the righteousness of God in Him" (21).

Although Christ was sinless, enjoying unbroken fellowship with the Father, nevertheless God "made him to be sin for us." He suffered temptation, alienation (Mark 15:34), and death. He experienced the consequences of sin and its punishment in death (Rom. 6:23). And because of His voluntary acceptance on our behalf of the penalties of wrongdoing, the broken relationship between God and ourselves is restored.

It is upon this acceptance that Paul can say that we have in Christ "become the righteousness of God." It is beyond our comprehension to enter into the full meaning of these two verses. The Cross was the only way by which God could deal with rebellion and turn it to repentance.

Christ took upon himself the full burden of our sin—its shame, judgment, and guilt. But in Christ we see the miracle of both the root and fruit of reconciliation. By identification with His death, the power of the Resurrection becomes life indeed in us!

> *Wounded for me, wounded for me,*
> *There on the Cross He was wounded for me.*
> *Gone my transgressions, and now I am free,*
> *All because Jesus was wounded for me.*
>
> *Dying for me, dying for me,*
> *There on the Cross He was dying for me.*
> *Now in His death my redemption I see,*
> *All because Jesus was dying for me.*
>
> *Risen for me, risen for me,*
> *Up from the grave He has risen for me.*
> *Now evermore from death's sting I am free,*
> *All because Jesus has risen for me.*

—W. G. Ovens and Gladys Roberts

2. *Working together with Him* (1-2). As an ambassador Paul is impressed by the importance of cooperation and submission to God's work in Christ. He knows that the relationship of the new order cannot be automatically maintained. The Corinthians must be urged not to receive the grace of God in vain. "Do not let it go for nothing," the NEB translates it.

This phrase might be interpreted in several ways. It may warn against an intellectual acceptance of the gospel without a yieldedness of one's heart to the love of the Saviour. It may urge against the acceptance of the "letter" without realizing the freedom of the Spirit (3:6). Theological knowledge does not necessarily produce yieldedness.

The phrase reminds us that we may be thrilled by the spectacle of the gospel without living by its power. James Reid remarks that Niagara Falls was only a "wonderful spectacle" until engineers captured its power to energize cities and light homes. The cross of Christ can be "merely a moving spectacle without subduing the will to obedience." Jesus said: "Why do you call me 'Lord, Lord' and not do what I tell you?" (Luke 6:46, RSV). Unless the Cross produces both the desire and the power to do God's will, we receive the grace of God in vain.

This intriguing phrase, "working together with him" (RSV), cautions against resting content in conversion without exploring the full commitment of sonship in the life in the Spirit. There are many who have not opened their hearts to His full sanctifying grace, without which growth is stunted and development is arrested. They are like a plant which grows without flowering. The potential is there, but the promises are not fulfilled. The central theme of the Corinthian correspondence comes alive in the phrase "Do not let it go for nothing." Ye are saints by calling—now act like it!

A familiar parenthesis follows which speaks of the

urgency of the apostolic message: "Behold, now is the accepted time; behold, now is the day of salvation." Paul enforces the appeal by a striking quotation from Isa. 49:8, which foretells the blessed time when reconciliation will be accomplished in the One to come. In Christ, reconciliation has been accomplished; therefore the Corinthians should accept God's grace and take advantage of the "full salvation" provided through Christ's death and resurrection.

Proving Our Ministry

2 Corinthians 6:3-10

> 3 Giving no offence in any thing, that the ministry be not blamed:
> 4 But in all things approving ourselves as the ministers of God, in much patience, in afflictions, in necessities, in distresses,
> 5 In stripes, in imprisonments, in tumults, in labours, in watchings, in fastings;
> 6 By pureness, by knowledge, by longsuffering, by kindness, by the Holy Ghost, by love unfeigned,
> 7 By the word of truth, by the power of God, by the armour of righteousness on the right hand and on the left,
> 8 By honour and dishonour, by evil report and good report: as deceivers, and yet true;
> 9 As unknown, and yet well known; as dying, and, behold, we live; as chastened, and not killed;
> 10 As sorrowful, yet alway rejoicing; as poor, yet making many rich; as having nothing, and yet possessing all things.

Paul has explained the provision for reconciliation to God in Christ (5:14-19). He has faithfully and urgently entreated the unreconciled to accept the gracious welcome (5:20—6:2). Now he witnesses to the fact that he so acted that he "put no obstacle in any one's way" (RSV) but worked untiringly and steadfastly to fulfill his mission in the face of extreme persecution and hardship (cf. 11:23-28).

The moving recital that follows is a magnificent display of God's grace. Paul commends himself with much patience or "great endurance" (4, RSV) only because this is the sign of the Master's working in him.

His logical mind breaks the impassioned utterances into three general divisions, each with three specifications which express the endurance of the apostle. He concludes with a noble poetic insight which expresses all that has gone before—"having nothing, yet possessing all things."

1. *Manifold trials of the new man in Christ* (4-5).

a. Paul first speaks of general problems: afflictions, necessities, and distresses (4). "Afflictions" speak of physical, mental, and spiritual pressures which Paul might otherwise have avoided. The word used here originally expressed "sheer physical pressure on a man"—the pressures of the demands of life. Paul believes that triumphant "endurance" *(hupomonē)* can cope with it all. Barclay, after speaking of Chrysostom's great discourse on *hupomonē*, calls this triumphant Christian endurance, the "alchemy which transmutes tribulation to glory and strength." Paul has triumphantly endured affliction.

"Necessities" is concerned with the times when a man is taxed to the utmost—the "inescapable pains of life," the things which define a man's very existence. There are some elements in life that are real by definition and must be endured—triumphantly! They do not pass away. They may come as sorrow, disappointment, discouragement, and finally death, but they are a part of man's human situation. But thank God, Paul says, they can be endured with patience.

The "distresses" or anxieties of life ("dire straits," NEB) represent relationships from which there is no escape. The Greek word literally means "too narrow a place" from which to break loose.

These are the conditions which are to be borne patiently and triumphantly. As long as a man is in this life, he will face them. Christ does not promise exemption from these three kinds of trials, but assures us triumphant endurance in and through them.

b. The outward tribulations of life (5*a*). First, Paul mentions "stripes" ("beatings," RSV). His spiritual suffering was complemented by physical suffering. Five times he took "forty stripes save one" for the sake of the gospel—195 lashes altogether.

Such persecution is not unknown today. The Church behind the iron curtain is undergoing great persecution for Christ's sake. One author has suggested that more Christians have died for their faith since World War II than in the first 400 years of Christian history.

There were imprisonments. Paul was in prison no less than seven times. He was in prison both before and following the Corinthian correspondence. He knew what he was talking about; yet he was not shaken in his resolve.

He did not face the law as much as he did the violence of the mob ("tumults"). Many a Christian hero has faced the murdering intent of a hostile crowd—but with inward poise.

Today it is not the mob as much as the mockery, contempt, and indifference of the crowd against which the Christian must stand firm.

The word "tumult" in the New Testament usually means a disorder or lawless outbreak (Luke 21:9). Paul was frequently exposed to these outbursts, as in Antioch in Pisidia (Acts 13:50), at Lystra (14:19), at Philippi (16:19), and at Jerusalem (21:30).

c. The conditions to be borne by the Christian (5*b*). Paul suddenly turns from the tribulations to the disciplines of the Christian life. "Labours" spoke of his own vocation in which he made the "gospel of no expense." But more than that, he was speaking of the demands upon his time, including travelling and caring for the sick, the poor, and the general interests of the church (cf. 11:23, 27; 1 Thess. 2:9).

"Watchings" represent a way of life involving prayer and anxiety in the face of peril. Paul was always a watchman in the tower of the Lord (cf. 11:27).

"Fastings" does not seem to indicate deliberate self-denial as much as the times of hunger Paul endured through his ministry. This spirit of self-discipline runs through this whole passage. Abstinence was in keeping with his obedience and loyalty to the Saviour (cf. 11:27; Phil. 4:12).

2. *Graces and gifts of the new man in Christ* (6-7). Having finished with the "manifold trials" suffered with trium-

phant endurance, Paul turns to enumerate nine spiritual characteristics consistent with the virtue of patience (4).

a. Purity, knowledge, and longsuffering (6a). These God-given qualities of the mind reveal the new order in Christ of which Paul was a part.

"Purity" suggests he kept his life chaste and his motives single. Purity is "freedom from every stain of flesh and spirit." It is that grace which ushers a man into the very presence of God (Matt. 5:8). It is a complete integrity of life.

"Knowledge" is the spiritual understanding of what God has done in Jesus Christ (cf. 8:7; 11:6; 1 Cor. 2:6-12), both in one's own life and its implications for all men. It is the knowledge of God in living, personal experience. It is a knowledge *of* God rather than *about* God. It is not only intellectual but deeply spiritual.

"Longsuffering" denotes patience with people—a tolerant spirit toward those whose conduct exasperates. It is the ability to be patient in the face of ill-treatment without irritation or retaliation.

b. Kindness, *by love unfeigned (6b).* Paul is sympathetically kind and sweet-tempered. He tried to make no difference between the friendly and the hostile. Even in the heat of the Corinthian correspondence, one could always count on his spirit. Kindness *(chrestotēs),* says Barclay, is one of the great New Testament words. It is "the sympathetic kindness or sweetness of temper which puts others at their ease and shrinks from giving them pain" (see Gen. 26:17-22 for illustration).

The Holy Spirit was on display in any list of Paul's graces and gifts. He was the Power by which all virtues were exhibited. If the proper noun, Holy Ghost, seems out of place, a "spirit of holiness" was certainly consistent with the Person behind the apostle's disposition.

The word Paul uses for "love" in "love unfeigned" is the familiar *agape,* which means a spirit of giving without a demand for compensation—"an unconquerable benevolence and good-will."

Love is the greatest of all virtues (1 Corinthians 13), the heart of the Christian ethic, a divine gift and command for all the followers of Christ. It has to do with the mind as well as the emotions. It is the principle by which a Christian lives. It also has to do with the will. We are bidden to "love our enemies," and no one can love his enemies apart from divine grace.

> *Agape* is the spirit which says "no matter what a man does to me, I will never seek to do harm to him; I will never set out for revenge; I will always seek nothing but his highest good." That is to say, Christian love, *agape,* is unconquerable benevolence, invincible goodwill. It is not simply a wave of emotion; it is a deliberate policy of the life; it is a deliberate achievement and conquest and victory of the will. It takes all of a man to achieve Christian love; it takes not only his heart; it takes his mind and will as well.[23]

c. *The word of truth, the power of God, and the armor of righteousness* (7). These are the elements of equipment given for the preaching of the good news of God in Christ.

"Truthful speech" (RSV) is a vital imperative for every preacher. People must have confidence in both the integrity of the proclaimer and the truth of the proclamation. The preacher must be strictly honest. His interpretation of the Word must carry a truth-impulse which is God-given. Jesus, in rebuking the Pharisees, said, "It is your words that will acquit you, and your words that will condemn you" (Matt. 12:37, Phillips). How important it is that we handle revelation with care! (Cf. Eph. 1:13; Col. 1:5.)

"The power of God" meant everything to Paul. He was Christ's servant open to God's movings. That power of God was expressed in different ways. "He that wrought effectually in Peter to the apostleship of the circumcision," he said, "the same was mighty in me towards the Gentiles" (Gal. 2:8). That power was displayed in his conversion and in the preparation for and exercise of his apostleship. It was the enabling power of God that made the man what he was. His attacks on unrighteousness were girded by the word of truth and the power of God.

"The weapons of righteousness" were both "for the right hand and the left" (RSV). Calvin and many others see the "armour of righteousness" as the armor that personal integrity affords—a moral rectitude. But it seems more in keeping with the passage to interpret it as the "righteousness of faith" or the divine armor that righteousness provides.

The Christian is enforced both on the right hand with the "sword of the Spirit" (Eph. 6:17) and on the left with the "shield of faith" (Eph. 6:16). On his head is the helmet of salvation (Eph. 6:17).

It was not Paul's honesty which was his armor but the resources which came as a result of his relationship to God. He was fully equipped with both defensive and offensive weapons.

3. *Diverse circumstances of good and evil report for the new man in Christ* (8-10). All of these verses are closely intertwined. In the first set (4-5), the Greek preposition *en* is used in a local sense. That is, by patience *in* afflictions, *in* necessities, etc. In the second group *en* is used in its instrumental sense, *by* pureness, *by* knowledge, etc. In this triad the preposition *dia* again has a local sense— through, or in the midst of. Paul maintained his integrity in the midst of all the circumstances that plagued him. The beauty of the paradoxical language is in its striking truthfulness.

a. In honor and dishonor or, as the RSV has it, "in ill repute and good repute, . . . as imposters, and yet . . . true." In the eyes of his enemies, the apostle was held in dishonor. By "evil report" he was labeled "dishonest." And yet he was approved as honorable, of good repute, and truthful both by God and the "consciences" of those who knew him as a man of God.

b. As unknown, and yet well known; as dying and living; as chastened, yet not killed. In the minds of many,

Paul and his associates were nonentities. They counted for nothing. Yet for those who really counted, they were "well known" (RSV) and were becoming better known.

They were constantly exposed to death, yet Christ gave them strength to live in the midst of their afflictions (4:11; 1 Cor. 15:31). Paul "died daily" and yet he lived. God always seemed to deliver him for His cause. Shipwrecked, beaten, stoned, God brought him back to proclaim His truth until on the *Via Ostiensis* he took him home to life indeed. "Chastened" in this sense seems to be a synonym of affliction. He was "punished, and yet not killed" (RSV).

c. *As sorrowful, yet always rejoicing; as poor, yet making many rich; as having nothing, and yet possessing everything* (10, RSV). The final three circumstances in this lyrical passage express most fully the antitheses of the Christian life. The followers of Jesus have more true joy in sorrow than the world can either comprehend or afford. They would not change places with the wealthiest men in the world, for the love of God supports them in the direst of circumstances. So many who are poor in this world's goods, can impart to many, the riches of God's grace.

Paul and his associates had nothing. They had given their all to Christ, yet they were conscious of "possessing everything" (RSV). In belonging to Christ, they held the whole world in their hands.

Now put yourself in the arena of human existence. From the perspective of the world we may be dishonorable, deceiving, nonentities, living in the fear of death perpetually, suffering, etc. But heaven sees things differently. The faithful Christian is held in high honor, is true, renewed day by day, joyful. He is not smart enough to know that he has nothing, for in Christ he has everything! He has access to heavenly treasures which nothing can ever touch or take away. Alan Redpath remarks, "When I read this great passage I realize that Paul has left me behind. I can't keep up with him." And for all of us, this is true. But, as Redpath adds, "I am following in his track."

An Appeal for Holiness

2 Corinthians 6:11—7:1

> 11 O ye Corinthians, our mouth is open unto you, our heart is enlarged.
> 12 Ye are not straitened in us, but ye are straitened in your own bowels.
> 13 Now for a recompence in the same, (I speak as unto my children,) be ye also enlarged.
> 14 Be ye not unequally yoked together with unbelievers: for what fellowship hath righteousness with unrighteousness? and what communion hath light with darkness?
> 15 And what concord hath Christ with Belial? or what part hath he that believeth with an infidel?
> 16 And what agreement hath the temple of God with idols? for ye are the temple of the living God; as God hath said, I will dwell in them, and walk in them; and I will be their God, and they shall be my people.
> 17 Wherefore come out from among them, and be ye separate, saith the Lord, and touch not the unclean thing; and I will receive you,
> 18 And will be a Father unto you, and ye shall be my sons and daughters, saith the Lord Almighty.
> 1 Having therefore these promises, dearly beloved, let us cleanse ourselves from all filthiness of the flesh and spirit, perfecting holiness in the fear of God.

In this tremendously open passage, Paul stands "naked" before the church and the world—and that transparency proves the integrity of the apostle. Paul is confirmed by both God and his converts.

1. *An appeal for fellowship* (11-13). The apostle is himself surprised at his openness in his dictation of the letter and in the candid exposure of his life and motives. In rare fashion he metaphorically expresses his love for the church: "Our mouth is open to you," or, "Our heart is wide" (11, RSV). Here we glimpse Paul's generous and compassionate spirit.

The success of a Christian minister depends, to a large extent, on his love and compassion for his people. Paul's appeal is for an unrestricted confidence. He asks for a like response from the Corinthians.

Communication has broken down. Frank confession is in order (cf. 1 John 1:7). Paul opens the door and now is waiting for their reciprocal spirit of fellowship and confidence. "In return—I speak as to children—widen your hearts also" (RSV).

There are those, however, who are afraid of openness, at least to the degree that Paul is speaking of ("You are restricted in your own affections" [12, RSV]). There are Christians who "shrink from having too much of God." Paul was attempting to clear the barriers in order that the ministry of reconciliation might have its day. "For Christ's sake we must sometimes wear our hearts on our sleeve. It is a risk. But results are not in our hands, and often we can break barriers between us and others in no other way."

2. *An exhortation to holy living* (6:14—7:1). Rather abruptly after the burst of affection comes admonition for "a radical separation of the church from its pagan environment." How does this come about?

God's love is inclusive, possessive, if you please. It was for the sake of their preservation and well-being that God marked the Israelites as a separated people. He wanted no other rivals because of what those rival gods could do to His people. God calls for a holy people.

The New Testament takes up the theme. Jesus declared, "If the world hate you, ye know that it hated me before it hated you. If you were of the world, the world would love its own: but because ye are not of the world, but I have chosen you out of the world, therefore the world hateth you" (John 15:18-19; cf. Luke 9:23; Heb. 13:12-13; Jas. 1:27; 4:4). Both Jesus and Paul were indignant at the possibility of their followers' compromising with the world (Gal. 6:14, 17). The Christian is to reckon himself "dead indeed unto sin, but alive unto God through Jesus Christ our Lord" (Rom. 6:11).

Alan Redpath represents that commitment to Christ by declaring that:

Separation is investing every moment of your day, wherever you may be, in the ministry or in secular life (and this is a ministry anyway), to the glory of God in a commitment to His authority and power in your life without reservation. . . .

It is not a question of simply trying to empty your heart and life of every worldly desire—what an awful responsibility! It is rather opening your heart wide to all the love of God in Christ, and letting that love just sweep through you and exercise its expulsive power till your heart is filled with love. . . . Surely the all-sufficient incentive for a holy life is not legalism but grace. . . . [It is] not saying to a young Christian, "Thou shalt not" . . . [but] "Do you not recognize what God has done for you in Jesus Christ? . . . You are the Temple of the living God."[24]

a. The demand for a holy life (14-16*a*). The theme of this passage is holiness of life which results from the acceptance of the "word of reconciliation." Paul's metaphor speaks of the incompatibility of righteousness with unrighteousness. Light and darkness are mutually exclusive; so are righteousness and unrighteousness. This is specifically the prohibition of a Christian's entering into wedlock with an acknowledged unbeliever: "Do not be mismated with unbelievers" (RSV). But included in the sweep of this injunction is the command for Christians to separate themselves completely from the spirit and practices of their pagan environment.

Following his usual practice, the apostle does not lay down rules but sets down one grand universal principle inferred from the believer's relationship to Christ—separation from the world (cf. 1 Cor. 6:12-20). "What concord hath Christ with Belial?" (15).

One would think that Bible-believing Christians should never need such a warning as Paul gives these Corinthians, but they do! We must be consistently reminded that we are to be what we are called—the temple of God (16). "What agreement hath the temple of God with idols?" Paul asks. As Jesus cleansed the Temple of the money changers, so we must separate ourselves from every sinful practice and relationship. God's temple must be kept holy!

b. The motivation for a holy life (16*b*-18). Our strongest motivation for holy living lies in the conditional promise of the indwelling Spirit of God. If believers remember that they are indeed the temple of the living God, God promises, "I will dwell in them, and walk in them; and I will be their God, and they shall be my people" (16).

This is not a call for a migration to Jerusalem or Mecca, or for a pilgrimage to Rome! It is a call to live free of all relationships which might ally us with idolatry. The call is to live in the world, right where we are, without becoming a part of it (cf. 1 Cor. 5:9-11).

These Corinthians were urban Christians, fighting the temptations of an idolatrous, lascivious city. The cities of our modern world present inducements to evil and vice which are excessive beyond what many of us can imagine. How appropriate for urban believers is Paul's call to holiness:

> *Therefore come out from them,*
> *and be separate from them, says the Lord,*
> *and touch nothing unclean* (17, RSV).

The inducement for such separation is found in the promises of this passage:

> *I will be a Father to you,*
> *and you shall be my sons and daughters,*
> *says the Lord Almighty* (18, RSV;
>   cf. 2 Sam. 18:14).

While the soul of the Christian is tempted until the article of death, his only rest is in turning to God and finding in Him true life and joy. Paul's call may suggest that a holy life may even mean a break with home and family (cf. Matt. 10:34-37). In such a situation God will be a Father, even if the natural father is alienated by our commitment to Christ.

c. The appeal to a holy life (7:1). This great, climactic verse is both negative and positive.

(1) The negative appeal: "Since we have these promises, beloved, let us cleanse ourselves from every defilement of body and spirit" (RSV). Such cleansing is something for which the believer is responsible. The ethical cleavage with the "old way" is both decisive ("cleanse" is in the aorist tense, which demands a complete act of severance) and comprehensive ("from all defilement of flesh and spirit," NASB). Flesh and spirit represent man's total existence—all his acts and attitudes which would compromise his single-minded devotion to his Lord.

The verb "to cleanse" *(katharizein)* is used by Paul only three times (2 Cor. 7:1; Eph. 5:26; Titus 2:14). The reason, Richard Howard says, is that the metaphor of slavery and freedom was "far more meaningful in the Gentile and pagan world where Paul labored."[25] However, the truth comes home decisively. The believer's death with Christ breaks the power of sin (Rom. 6:1-10). In view of this death which we underwent at our conversion, we must now cleanse ourselves from all vestiges of the old way of life.

The New Testament Christian faced a hostile world, and separation was often excruciatingly painful. Frequently it meant the loss of vocation, alienation from friends and family. Whatever pain he suffered, there were certain things he could not do as a Christian. Regardless of the suffering involved, his new relationship to Christ demanded a loyalty which was exclusive—a cleansing from all defilement. Does the gospel not still demand such all-out devotement to Christ?

(2) The positive appeal. Christ never demands a negative action without issuing a corresponding call to positive action. And if Paul urges a cleansing from "all

defilement," he completes this by calling for a "perfecting [of] holiness in the fear of God." Frank Carver draws out the radical implications of this phrase:

> The break is not only decisive (6:17) but is also to characterize all of their living (6:14; Rom. 12:2). *Let us cleanse ourselves* is further interpreted by the nominative present participle, *perfecting holiness in the fear of God.* The term *perfecting (epitelein)* means "to bring to a goal," and the durative tense should be taken as repetitive: "We cleanse ourselves effectively when in every instance that presents itself we turn from the stain of flesh and spirit." We are to continue moment by moment to attain the goal of the proper ethical response to a holy God. Clarke would define this process of completing sanctification as "getting the whole mind of Christ brought into the soul . . . [which is] the grand object of a genuine Christian's pursuit." . . .
>
> There is a paradox here. Those who have been brought into a sanctified relationship to God in Jesus Christ (cf. I Cor. 1:2, 30; Heb. 2:11; 10:1, 14, 29; 13:12), must ever reach for the ethical ideal of that relationship; holiness is both a gift and a task. It means, Become what you are! Such an actualized attitude to life (cf. Phil. 3:12-15) is the respect and reverence we owe to God.[26]

What does all this mean? While the focus of the passage is not on the crisis of entire sanctification as such, the actualization of the Christian ethic presupposes the crisis. It means that God has opened the door for us to be what He has called us to be. We are daily to go about the business of "perfecting holiness in the fear of God." We are not only to practice but to complete holiness, carry it on to perfection (cf. 8:6, 11; Phil. 1:6).

James Denney puts Paul's thought succinctly:

> The puritanism of the New Testament is no harsh, repellent thing, which eradicates the affections and makes life bleak and barren; it is the condition under which the heart is opened to the love of God, and filled with all comfort and joy in obedience. With Him on our side—with the promise of the indwelling Spirit to sanc-

tify us—shall we not obey the exhortation to come out and be separate, and to cleanse ourselves from all that defiles, to perfect holiness in His fear?[27]

An Apostle's Heart Exposed

2 Corinthians 7:2-16

> 2 Receive us; we have wronged no man, we have corrupted no man, we have defrauded no man.
> 3 I speak not this to condemn you: for I have said before, that ye are in our hearts to die and live with you.
> 4 Great is my boldness of speech toward you, great is my glorying of you: I am filled with comfort, I am exceeding joyful in all our tribulation.
> 5 For, when we were come into Macedonia, our flesh had no rest, but we were troubled on every side; without were fightings, within were fears.
> 6 Nevertheless God, that comforteth those that are cast down, comforted us by the coming of Titus;
> 7 And not by his coming only, but by the consolation wherewith he was comforted in you, when he told us your earnest desire, your mourning, your fervent mind toward me; so that I rejoiced the more.
> 8 For though I made you sorry with a letter, I do not repent, though I did repent: for I perceive that the same epistle hath made you sorry, though it were but for a season.
> 9 Now I rejoice, not that ye were made sorry, but that ye sorrowed to repentance: for ye were made sorry after a godly manner, that ye might receive damage by us in nothing.
> 10 For godly sorrow worketh repentance to salvation not to be repented of: but the sorrow of the world worketh death.
> 11 For behold this selfsame thing, that ye sorrowed after a godly sort, what carefulness it wrought in you, yea, what clearing of yourselves, yea, what indignation, yea, what fear, yea, what vehement desire, yea, what zeal, yea, what revenge! In all things ye have approved yourselves to be clear in this matter.
> 12 Wherefore, though I wrote unto you, I did it not for his cause that had done the wrong, nor for his cause that suffered wrong, but that our care for you in the sight of God might appear unto you.
> 13 Therefore we were comforted in your comfort: yea, and exceedingly the more joyed we for the joy of Titus, because his spirit was refreshed by you all.
> 14 For if I have boasted any thing to him of you, I am not ashamed; but as we spake all things to you in truth, even so our boasting, which I made before Titus, is found a truth.
> 15 And his inward affection is more abundant toward you, whilst he remembereth the obedience of you all, how with fear and trembling ye received him.
> 16 I rejoice therefore that I have confidence in you in all things.

We have considered a pause in Paul's message. He now resumes his previous appeal: "Open your hearts to us . . . for I said before that you are in our hearts, to die together and to live together" (2-3, RSV; cf. 6:11-13). He goes on to mention once again his joy in tribulation and then passes on to the happy occasion of Titus' arrival and the report of improving relations between the apostle and his Corinthian converts.

The coming of Titus was like "the passing away of a storm" when nature never looked so beautiful—like the fresh bosom of the world after a rain. The scripture is particularly moving, affectionate, and unrestrained. The "coin has turned" and Paul is grateful.

1. *There is a claim that we can make* (2). Paul's life is without reproach. A man who is backed by a life of integrity can speak out against wrong. Paul has so spoken.

He says he has wronged no man. Is he answering accusations concerning his labors (12:14-18) and allegations of the misuse of authority? Is he writing about the shady business dealings of some Christians who had wronged others (cf. 1 Cor. 6:4-8)? He is not finding fault. On the contrary his desire for mutual love and confidence is so deep and moving that he can say, "We hold you so close in our hearts that nothing in life or in death can part us from you" (3, Knox; cf. 1:6-7; 3:2, Phil. 1:7).

He has corrupted no one by bad example or teaching. He has "taken advantage" (RSV) of no one. He sharply denies that he has been involved in any sharp business practices. His hands are clean!

2. *There is a compassion we should feel* (3). For fear his converts may again feel the lash of his words, he hastens to add in most intimate terms, "I speak not to condemn you: for I have said before, that ye are in our hearts to die and live with you." Paul is vitally bound to his converts in Christian fellowship and love. The bond is permanent. It will last as long as life lasts. His glory in them is two-pronged. He is speaking of his identification with the church in community. He is also speaking of that day when they shall rise to be with the Lord when He returns.

> 'Mid toil and tribulation,
> And tumult of her war,

She waits the consummation
Of peace forevermore;
Till, with the vision glorious,
Her longing eyes are blest,
And the great Church victorious
Shall be the Church at rest.

—Samuel J. Stone

3. *There is a comfort that we can enjoy* (4-12). Paul is both encouraged and amazed to hear that his stern rebuke has borne fruit. It is obvious he has been concerned whether his admonitions would produce hostility rather than repentance. His anxiety shows through until he hears the good news through Titus (5). The church has indeed repented with "fervent zeal"—and for that Paul rejoices.

a. Paul is encouraged by the way that God works (6). The unspeakable relief in Titus' return confirms his faith that God was at work, even though he had anguished over the possibility of a complete fracture of relations (8). Now he is nearly beside himself with joy.

b. He sees again the miracle of *godly sorrow* ("grief," RSV) leading to repentance and life (10). The pain God allows deepens the awareness of sin. It brings us under the judgment of God. It creates an antipathy toward the sin we have indulged in and "sets us free from its power to tempt or bemuse the mind."

Godly sorrow is more than the sorrow of the world. The latter can only lead to death (cf. Rom. 6:23; 7:13), for it is merely remorse for the painful consequences of one's misdeeds. Only godly sorrow produces repentance unto salvation. True repentance is a "turning around," a radical change of attitude: sin is recognized, disliked, and finally disowned.

Mark the words that Paul uses in v. 11 to describe their repentance: "carefulness," "clearing," "indignation," "desire," "zeal," and "revenge." What "earnestness" (RSV)!

Such repentance makes it possible for their pastor to reveal his real object in writing the letter (12). He was not thinking chiefly of the offender (such as the flagrant sinner of 1 Cor. 5:1-5) but the church as a whole. His desire was that he should draw out from them an expression of concern for himself so that a pastoral relationship might be restored. It was a delicate way to approach a sensitive subject. But now Paul is "comforted in their comfort" (13). He lets "bygones be bygones." The passage helps us to see that bitter stock can yield sweet and wholesome fruit.

Carver points out that as their "father of the faith," Paul is concerned for their spiritual well-being. So much, in fact, that he is willing to cause them pain though he is not the less pained (8-9). Such pain when used of God effects the repentance that leads to salvation and to the correction of the difficulties within the church (10-12).

4. *There is a confidence that a Christian may experience* (13-16). The repentance of the Corinthians authenticates their faith. Paul's love has always thought the best of them, and he has boasted of his confidence. Now he can write, "Our boasting before Titus has proved true" (14, RSV).

His strategy is sound. His openness has led to faith and faith to repentance and the restoration of mutual trust. The church and the world are crying for display of such confidence. Perhaps this is one reason the first of "The Four Spiritual Laws" has made such an impact upon university campuses around the world: "God loves you and has a plan for your life." He loves us even in spite of our sins.

> For His great love has compassed
> Our nature, and our need
> We know not; but He knoweth,
> And He will bless indeed.
> Therefore, O Heavenly Father,
> Give what is best to me;

And take the wants unanswered,
As offerings made to Thee.
                    —Author Unknown

The Grace of Christian Giving
2 Corinthians 8:1—9:15

The eighth and ninth chapters of the Second Epistle of Paul to the Corinthians form a great classic on the grace of giving. All that a Christian should know about Christian benevolence is set forth in this important passage. "It is a complete summary of the motives and methods of church support and church benevolences." If the contemporary church would follow the principles described, church boards would never have to search for funds.

The occasion was Paul's desire that the collection be complete in Corinth before he arrived. His letter indicates that the Corinthians' repentance made the time ripe for an exhortation to liberality on behalf of their brethren in Jerusalem.

The brethren in Jerusalem were feeling the pangs of persecution. Their social and vocational ostracism left many with no means of support—and welfare and social security were not even dreams. Their experiment in "Christian communism" had also failed. They were dependent upon the brethren for support.

Paul had taken a keen interest in raising money for the widows and the poor of Jerusalem. There were a number of reasons for his eagerness in their behalf. (1) He could not forget his part in their persecution prior to his conversion. (2) There is the common grace of Christian charity which leads all followers of Christ to sympathize with needy brethren both within and without the Church. (3)

Those in need were Jewish Christians, "his kinsmen after the flesh," his brethren in Christ. (4) At the Conference of Jerusalem, Paul had been specially instructed to "remember the poor—the very thing I also was eager to do" (Gal. 2:10, NASB).

There was, of course, the one supreme reason—a union of sympathy and understanding between the Jew and Gentile in the body of Christ. Nothing would help more to seal that union than for the Christian churches to express their love in material form to the mother church in Jerusalem.

2 CORINTHIANS 8

The Example of Macedonia

2 Corinthians 8:1-6

> 1 Moreover, brethren, we do you to wit of the grace of God bestowed on the churches of Macedonia;
> 2 How that in a great trial of affliction the abundance of their joy and their deep poverty abounded unto the riches of their liberality.
> 3 For to their power, I bear record, yea, and beyond their power they were willing of themselves;
> 4 Praying us with much intreaty that we would receive the gift, and take upon us the fellowship of the ministering to the saints.
> 5 And this they did, not as we hoped, but first gave their own selves to the Lord, and unto us by the will of God.
> 6 Insomuch that we desired Titus, that as he had begun, so he would also finish in you the same grace also.

1. *They gave in the face of great affliction and deep poverty.* Phillips translates v. 2, "Somehow, in most difficult circumstances, their joy and the fact of being down to their last penny themselves, produced a magnificent concern for other people." Affliction, however, speaks more of the ill-treatment from non-Christians. Poverty was nothing new. It was quite common among the apostolic communities.

The Macedonian churches were suffering because of their faith. Rome had abstracted most of the province's wealth. The source of their income was gone. But God wrought a miracle in their hearts. Their suffering for the sake of Christ turned to generosity for their brethren. It always does!

2. *They gave according to their means* (3, RSV). While the grace of tithing is not mentioned in the New Testament, it is strongly suggested (cf. Heb. 7:8; 1 Cor. 16:2). They did not decide the amount of their gift by what others gave but by the strength of their own means.

3. *They gave beyond their means* (3b, RSV). Their giving went far beyond their responsibility. They gave to the point of sacrifice—until it hurt. Giving of this nature speaks to the Christian stewardship of money. Alan Redpath says that the "principle of the Cross lies at the very heart of heaven's missionary program." When Christ captures our heart with complete yieldedness, we begin to see His poverty and our wealth and count all things loss for Christ. The missionary program of the church will prosper when we catch a vision of Christ.

4. *They gave of their own free will* (3, RSV). They actually begged (with "much entreaty") to be part of the project in the "support of the saints" (NASB). It was the poor who helped the poor because they knew what poverty was like.

Paul uses the language of paradox. First, they gave what was expected but then gave far beyond that—and of their own free will. The apostle might have hesitated to ask in Macedonia at all because of their poverty, but they entreated him to accept their gifts. They had caught some of the great insights of Christian truth. Both fellowship *(koinonia)* and ministry *(diakonia)* spoke to their hearts (4).

5. *They gave of themselves to Christ* (5). The Macedonian generosity could only be understood in the light of their giving of "their own selves to the Lord." They knew that all they had belonged to God (cf. 5:15). They were giving Him only what was His.

Since the apostle was the representative of Christ, they partially repaid their debt to Christ by giving to him for the needy in Jerusalem. They had sorted out their priorities. Their love for Christ made them rich in all things. They would share what they had with the brethren because they were His.

The phrase "gave themselves" implies a costly giving, as it does in Gal. 1:4 where the same language is used of Christ's death. Giving in the name of Christ is gracious giving. "It reveals the grace of God in action."

These Christian brethren were not arguing about a tithe. They gave far more than a tithe. They responded not because of a human appeal, but in the giving of self to Him and in service to the church.

The spirit of the Macedonians is expressed by James Allen in his essay "Perfect Love":

> Perfect Love is perfect Trust. He who has destroyed the desire to grasp can never be troubled with the fear of loss. Loss and gain are alike foreign to him. Steadfastly maintaining a loving attitude of mind toward all, and pursuing, in the performance of his duties, a constant and loving activity, Love protects him and evermore supplies him in fullest measure with all that he needs.[28]

Anne Sexton caught some of this thought in her poem "Welcome Morning":[29]

> *There is joy*
> *in all:*
> *in the hair I brush each morning,*
> *in the Cannon towel, newly washed,*
> *that I rub my body with each morning,*
> *in the outcry from the kettle*
> *that heats my coffee,*
> *each morning,*
> *in the spoon and the chair,*
> *that cry "Hello there, Anne"*
> *each morning,*
> *in the Godhead of the table*
> *that I set my silver, plate, cup upon,*
> *each morning.*

All this is God,
right here in my peagreen house
each morning
and I mean,
though often forget,
to give thanks,
to faint down by the kitchen table
in a prayer of rejoicing
as the holy birds at the kitchen window
peck into their marriage of seeds.

So while I think of it,
let me paint a thank you on my palm
for this God, this laughter of the morning,
lest it go unspoken.

The joy that isn't shared, I've heard
dies young.

(Pulitzer prize for poetry, 1967)

The Criteria for Christian Giving

2 Corinthians 8:7-15

7 Therefore, as ye abound in every thing, in faith, and utterance, and knowledge, and in all diligence, and in your love to us, see that ye abound in this grace also.

8 I speak not by commandment, but by occasion of the forwardness of others, and to prove the sincerity of your love.

9 For ye know the grace of our Lord Jesus Christ, that, though he was rich, yet for your sakes he became poor, that ye through his poverty might be rich.

10 And herein I give my advice: for this is expedient for you, who have begun before, not only to do, but also to be forward a year ago.

11 Now therefore perform the doing of it; that as there was a readiness to will, so there may be a performance also out of that which ye have.

12 For if there be first a willing mind, it is accepted according to that a man hath, and not according to that he hath not.

13 For I mean not that other mean be eased, and ye burdened:

14 But by an equality, that now at this time your abundance may be a supply for their want, that their abundance also may be a supply for your want: that there may be equality:

15 As it is written, He that had gathered much had nothing over; and he that had gathered little had no lack.

The central appeal toward generosity is not on the ground of authority (8), but on the gracious example of Christ (9). Giving in the name of Christ is gracious giving. It is the grace of God at work. Paul had commended his converts on their faith and utterance and knowledge, their diligence and their love (7). Now, he would commend them to the virtue of sharing with their brethren in need. His commendation suggests three criteria for Christian giving.

1. *The magnitude of the grace of Christ* (7-9). The final appeal to their generosity was the "ethic of the incarnation." In James Stewart's words, "this is using a 'sledgehammer to crack a nut!'"[30] The "grace of God" is now defined as the "grace of our Lord Jesus Christ." The Corinthians well knew that for their sakes, the One who was rich had become poor. It was a personal example for every one of them and at the same time was at the heart of Paul's ministry. "Paul knew no distinction between dogma and ethic; for him the most difficult doctrines of all, the Incarnation and the atonement, belonged at the heart of the practical ethic of every Christian. The center of our faith must be applied to its every circumference or we are unfaithful servants."[31]

Paul had been speaking of the grace of sacrifice illustrated by the Macedonians, but thinking of the sacrifice that was exercised by Christ. He was "antecedently and eternally wealthy," when he stooped to take the creaturely nature with its obligations and its limitations.

When one catches a glimpse of that grace, it awakens an undying gratitude. But how can that debt be paid? It can be paid only by our love for those for whom Christ died (Matt. 25:40). This personal gratitude is the supreme motive of our liberality. Chesterton sums it all up: "It is the highest and holiest of the paradoxes that the man who really knows he cannot pay his debt will be forever paying it. . . . He will be always throwing things away into a bottomless pit of unfathomable thanks."[32]

> *Thrice blessed will all our blessings be,*
> *When we can look through them to Thee;*
> *When each glad heart its tribute pays*
> *Of love and gratitude and praise.*
>
> —JANE COTTERILL

2. *The extent of material blessing* (10-12). The Corinthian church was foremost in nearly everything. They had been blessed with all material blessings. They were the first of the churches to give and enjoyed a strong desire to share. Paul now challenges them to give out of what they have in completing what was first begun. He is challenging them to their best—not to give of what they have *not,* but from what they *have.* It would be a sad thing if the church which was first in the beginning should not now complete the project.

They were not asked to sacrifice as the Macedonians had sacrificed, but to give out of the abundance of what they had. Paul could not ask anything less. It enunciated the principle that God judges all men on their ability to give.

There is a fine line of insight which unites will with performance, compassion with deed, desire with action. One of the tragedies of life is that so many of us start out with great ambition but fall sadly short of our ideal.

3. *The measure of the needs of the body of Christ* (13-15). Some Corinthians had evidently objected to the collection on the ground that others would be eased while they were burdened. Paul replies that life has a strange way of keeping accounts in balance. He enforces the idea by quoting Exod. 16:18. In that day enough manna and no more was given to each family. He uses this figure to show that those who have should share with their less fortunate brothers.

The whole passage is a reflection of the Christian ethic of Jesus in Matt. 6:33. "Generous impulses ought not to be checked by faithless fear of future want." Anxieties about our own security should not inhibit us from sharing with others.

Paul's Plan for the Collection

2 Corinthians 8:16—9:15

16 But thanks be to God, which put the same earnest care into the heart of Titus for you.

17 For indeed he accepted the exhortation; but being more forward, of his own accord he went unto you.

18 And we have sent with him the brother, whose praise is in the gospel throughout all the churches;

19 And not that only, but who was also chosen of the churches to travel with us with this grace, which is administered by us to the glory of the same Lord, and declaration of your ready mind:

20 Avoiding this, that no man should blame us in this abundance which is administered by us:

21 Providing for honest things, not only in the sight of the Lord, but also in the sight of men.

22 And we have sent with them our brother, whom we have oftentimes proved diligent in many things, but now much more diligent, upon the great confidence which I have in you.

23 Whether any do enquire of Titus, he is my partner and fellowhelper concerning you: or our brethren be enquired of, they are the messengers of the churches, and the glory of Christ.

24 Wherefore shew ye to them, and before the churches, the proof of your love, and of our boasting on your behalf.

1 For as touching the ministering to the saints, it is superfluous for me to write to you:

2 For I know the forwardness of your mind, for which I boast of you to them of Macedonia, that Achaia was ready a year ago; and your zeal hath provoked very many.

3 Yet have I sent the brethren, lest our boasting of you should be in vain in this behalf; that, as I said, ye may be ready:

4 Lest haply if they of Macedonia come with me, and find you unprepared, we (that we say not, ye) should be ashamed in this same confident boasting.

5 Therefore I thought it necessary to exhort the brethren, that they would go before unto you, and make up beforehand your bounty, whereof ye had notice before, that the same might be ready, as a matter of bounty, and not as of covetousness.

6 But this I say, He which soweth sparingly shall reap also sparingly; and he which soweth bountifully shall reap also bountifully.

7 Every man according as he purposeth in his heart, so let him give; not grudgingly, or of necessity: for God loveth a cheerful giver.

8 And God is able to make all grace abound toward you; that ye, always having all sufficiency in all things, may abound to every good work:

9 (As it is written, He hath dispersed abroad; he hath given to the poor: his righteousness remaineth for ever.

10 Now he that ministereth seed to the sower both minister bread for your food, and multiply your seed sown, and increase the fruits of your righteousness;)

11 Being enriched in every thing to all bountifulness, which causeth through us thanksgiving to God.

12 For the administration of this service not only supplieth the want of the saints, but is abundant also by many thanksgivings unto God;

13 Whiles by the experiment of this ministration they glorify God for your professed subjection unto the gospel of Christ, and for your liberal distribution unto them, and unto all men;
14 And by their prayer for you, which long after you for the exceeding grace of God in you.
15 Thanks be unto God for his unspeakable gift.

1. *Human instruments in liberality* (8:16-24). God works through human instruments in developing all the Christian graces. Liberality is no exception. Here the principle of cultivation and harvest is involved in the apostolic plan of computing the collection.

Titus is the first partner and brother mentioned by Paul. He was with Paul in Macedonia and brought him the good news from Corinth of the healing of the defection. He heads the delegation with an earnest care and ambition to fulfill the task.

The names of the other two brethren are not given. One is spoken of as "the brother whose praise is in the gospel throughout all the church." He (perhaps Luke) had also accompanied Paul to Jerusalem with the former collection for the poor. Their confidence delighted Paul, for he knew that the integrity of the mission was dependent upon the confidence that the churches had in the collectors. He was more than careful to administer the trust funds with adequate precaution and care. Church finances should always be handled in the same manner. They are a trust given to church leaders from the fellowship in Christ.

The third member of the commission was a "brother" Paul trusted implicitly. He had often been "tested and found earnest in many matters" (22, RSV). Furthermore, he had great confidence in the Corinthians which, by inference, they reciprocated.

The committee was impeccable by reputation (22). Paul concludes his appeal once again by a challenge to the church to give proof of their love and of his boasting in their behalf.

It probably never occurred to Paul to identify the two "brothers in Christ" who were accompanying Titus. The first was well known by the churches. The second is spoken of as "diligent in many things" (22). At least their credentials were impeccable.

Paul's approach is intensely practical. He knows that there are critics and provides the assurance that he will not use the monies collected for any other purpose than intended. Barclay observes that the same apostle who spoke as a theologian and "lyric poet" could also speak as an accountant.

2 CORINTHIANS 9

2. *In preparation for giving* (9:1-7). Regardless of what had been said before, it was obvious that Paul was not over-confident about the Corinthian response. Asking for money was a very delicate matter after the disturbances of the previous year. It is natural and expedient that he should write with great care and tactfulness. We need great grace in dealing with others. The apostle, as usual, not only approaches the subject with tact but also includes elements of the gospel in application. There are some important lessons in the passage.

a. Zeal as an incentive to others (2-6). The generosity of the Macedonians had already been commended along with the earnestness of the Corinthians in initiating the offerings. Both were congratulated by Paul for different reasons. The zeal of the Corinthians encouraged the Macedonians. Paul wanted this to be known to the former. Their zeal had provoked (stirred) many to giving.

The apostle was very careful to remind the Corinthians that "he had staked the integrity of his word on their performance" (1-4). He had boasted of them, and that boasting was a gentle prod to action. His planning, however, was both careful and meticulous. Their giving must be intelligent, conscientious, and deliberate.

There are times when an offering may be an emotional outpouring of love. But this plan was the kind which represents the sustaining income of the church. Real generosity is habitual and systematic. That generosity Paul states in the form of a principle: "He which soweth sparingly shall reap also sparingly; and he which soweth bountifully shall reap also bountifully." Thus, the rewards of giving are in direct proportion to the degree of giving.

b. The rewards of giving. That reward may or may not be material as indicated in v. 7. The blessing is primarily spiritual; only incidentally is it material. In some form or other our giving comes back to us. Jesus said, "The measure you give will be the measure you get" (Matt. 7:2, RSV). James Reid has expressed the thought superlatively:

> Yet no deed of genuine love or liberality can ever be done for the sake of a return in kind. There is little more in that case than a commercial transaction, which often defeats itself. Jesus urged the giving that expects nothing in return, and the hospitality which is shown to those who cannot afford to repay it. He did not however condemn the natural expectation that sacrifice for his sake would be rewarded. When his disciples asked what they would get for what they had given up, he expressly said "a hundredfold," and "now in this time" (Mark 10:30). Even a cup of cold water in his name would not go forgotten (Matt. 10:42). The world is a moral order. The desire that justice be done, and that all things will eventually make sense, is reasonable. The rewards may not be in kind. The real rewards of goodness are in the spirit. Love's true return is not even the love of others; it is the increased capacity to love. A generous-hearted man looking back on his life remarked, "I have loved more than I have been loved. I have trusted more than I have been trusted, but the balance remains with me." The reward of generosity is the generous heart which rejoices in giving and seeks no return. But the law of returns remains. We reap what we sow.[33]

c. The nature of giving (7).

(1) Giving must be the result of thought and deliberation: "as he purposeth in his heart." Every man is to give as he has decided ahead of time to give.

(2) Giving ought to be as liberal as possible and with a good spirit *("not grudgingly")*. The spirit in giving is supremely important. A gift that is "reluctantly" (RSV) made has no value. But a gift given not under "compulsion" (RSV) is a "sweet smelling savour" to our Heavenly Father. Our confidence is that our giving will not impoverish us but that God will supply our needs.

(3) Giving ought to be made with a willing spirit. This thought pervades the whole passage. Paul was praying that the willing desire of the Corinthians would characterize the collection. "Not of necessity" implies delight in the giving—a delight shared by God, "for God loveth a cheerful giver."

3. *The blessing of liberality* (9:8-15). As Paul closes his message concerning the collection for the poor, he presents motives that are applicable to Christians everywhere and in all generations. He has already shown the enrichment that can come to a Christian's life through giving (6-7).

a. Giving increases the resources of the Christian (8-10). God is able to provide those means in order that His people might have enough for their own needs and some for others as well. His abounding grace to us makes it possible for us to be abounding in good works. This provision reflects the word of the Psalmist: "He hath dispersed abroad; he hath given to the poor: his righteousness remaineth forever" (Ps. 112:9).

"The spring of His bounty" is not dried up by giving to others. It is actually enhanced. "He who supplies seed to the sower and bread for food will supply and multiply your resources and increase the harvest of your righteousness" (10, RSV). Those who give liberally may expect their opportunities for charity to be increased because of the increase of their resources. They will be enriched in everything so they can be generous at all times. The rule is not without exception, but it is general enough to encourage every Christian to exercise this grace.

b. Giving bears fruit in the lives of those who are recipients of the gift (12). Paul does not dwell on the second motive of liberality because of the obvious. The one who gives not only reaps a harvest in his own life but also aids in alleviating the poverty, pain, and anxiety of others.

c. Giving also calls forth thanksgiving (12). It "overflows in many thanksgivings to God" (RSV). Goodspeed renders v. 12, "For the rendering of this service does more than supply the wants of God's people; it results in a wealth of thanksgiving to God." So, as one gives to the suffering, he not alone receives a blessing but also invokes a great flood of thanksgivings to God from those who are helped.

More far-reaching than the immediate results of the collection were the thanksgivings given to God from the poor and the widows. Paul's thrust is then twofold. He sought to convince the Jerusalem Christians of the genuineness of the Gentile believers, and he desired that both should express their unity in Christ. It is this last burden that provides the fourth motive for liberality.

d. The unity of the fellowship in Jesus Christ (13-15). The expression "by the experiment of this ministration" is better translated "under the test of this service" (RSV). The service will provide a means of testing the sincerity of the Corinthians in their giving. On the other hand, the Judean Christians would not only unite in thanksgivings for the generosity of their Gentile friends, but would also pray for them, recognizing the "exceeding grace of God" in them. Both the generosity of the Gentile and the thanksgiving and prayers of the Judean Christians would provide a *koinonia,* a unity in Christ for which Paul was exceedingly thankful. It is no wonder that he should conclude this chapter by crying: "Thanks be unto God for his unspeakable gift."

After all Paul has said, his burden is in the supreme gift of God in Christ. What that gift means is beyond his power to express. Christ was God's Expression of love. Here are all the motives personified in one Person. God's grace, mercy, and goodness are united in Jesus Christ. "In him is found the true motive for all charity. He is the final embodiment and source of all grace, and for him thanks should be given to God, who is the Giver of every good and perfect gift."[34]

> *What Thou hast given, Thou canst take,*
> *And when Thou wilt new gifts can make.*
>   *All flows from Thee alone;*
> *When Thou didst give it, it was Thine;*
> *When Thou retook'st it, 'twas not mine.*
>   *Thy will in all be done.*
>
> —JOHN AUSTIN

Spiritual Vindication in Christ
2 Corinthians 10:1—13:14

___

2 CORINTHIANS 10

___

The Process of Victory in a Ministry for Christ

2 Corinthians 10:1-18

1 Now I Paul myself beseech you by the meekness and gentleness of Christ, who in presence am base among you, but being absent am bold toward you:
2 But I beseech you, that I may not be bold when I am present with that confidence, wherewith I think to be bold against some, which think of us as if we walked according to the flesh.
3 For though we walk in the flesh, we do not war after the flesh:
4 (For the weapons of our warfare are not carnal, but mighty through God to the pulling down of strong holds;)
5 Casting down imaginations, and every high thing that exalteth itself against the knowledge of God, and bringing into captivity every thought to the obedience of Christ;
6 And having in a readiness to revenge all disobedience, when your obedience is fulfilled.
7 Do ye look on things after the outward appearance? If any man trust to himself that he is Christ's, let him of himself think this again, that, as he is Christ's, even so are we Christ's.
8 For though I should boast somewhat more of our authority, which the Lord hath given us for edification, and not for your destruction, I should not be ashamed:
9 That I may not seem as if I would terrify you by letters.
10 For his letters, say they, are weighty and powerful; but his bodily presence is weak, and his speech contemptible.
11 Let such an one think this, that, such as we are in word by letters when we are absent, such will we be also in deed when we are present.
12 For we dare not make ourselves of the number, or compare ourselves with some that commend themselves: but they measuring themselves by themselves, and comparing themselves among themselves, are not wise.
13 But we will not boast of things without our measure, but according to the measure of the rule which God hath distributed to us, a measure to reach even unto you.
14 For we stretch not ourselves beyond our measure, as though we

reached not unto you: for we are come as far as to you also in preaching the gospel of Christ:

15 Not boasting of things without our measure, that is, of other men's labours; but having hope, when your faith is increased, that we shall be enlarged by you according to our rule abundantly,

16 To preach the gospel in the regions beyond you, and not to boast in another man's line of things made ready to our hand.

17 But he that glorieth, let him glory in the Lord.

18 For not he that commendeth himself is approved, but whom the Lord commendeth.

There is a transition here as Paul turns to deal with a recalcitrant minority in Corinth who have not listened to him. Instead, they have given attention to the claims of false pastors who have intruded into their loyalties. Since it is Paul's authority that they question, he abandons the plural with Timothy and stands alone in his appeal, "Now I Paul myself beseech you . . ." (cf. Gal. 5:2; 3:1; Philem. 19).

The men who opposed Paul were Jews who claimed to be apostles of Christ (11:13). Evidently they established themselves for a short time and proceeded to take all the credit owed to Paul (10:12-18). They were arrogant, tyrannical and boastful men (10:12; 11:18, 20). The apostle faces their charges by answering, "For though we walk in the flesh, we do not war after the flesh" (3). "His weapons are spiritual (1-6), his authority is consistent (7-11) and his boasting legitimate (12-18)."

Paul's spiritual victory in the issue was achieved because of consistent Christian service. Any ministry must walk in the footsteps of the Saviour as illustrated by Paul.

1. *It must be consistent with the principles of the Cross in method and technique* (1-6).

a. Meekness and gentleness: attitudes of the Cross (1-2). Paul sought to walk with all "meekness and gentleness," reflecting the One whom he was commissioned to serve (Matt. 9:29). "Meekness" *(prautēs)* is an inward virtue (Matt. 5:5) which accepts life as it is without responding with hostility to its ills. Paul's self-will has been crucified. He looks at the whole of life as purposive within the will of God. He certainly does not take everything "sitting down," as we would say. His opposition to evil is firm, but it is not carnal. "I have learned to be content, whatever the circumstances might be," he writes elsewhere. "I know how to live when things are difficult and I know how to live when things are prosperous. In general and particular I have learned the secret of facing either plenty or poverty" (Phil. 4:11-12, Phillips).

The word "gentleness" *(epieikeia)* "is used by Aristotle to describe the clemency exercised by the judge who is good as well as just, and who recognizes that circumstances alter cases and that adherence to the strict letter of the law may sometimes result in the perpetration of moral wrong" (cf. Ps. 86:5; John 8:1-11).

Paul takes for granted that ministers should seek to be gentle in their dealings with men. He is most reluctant to use methods and attitudes which bear the stamp of severity. On the other hand, he does not want his gentleness to be confounded with timidity. He demands the Corinthians' respect. And if necessary he will show such confidence (2) toward those who misrepresent him, suspecting him to act "in worldly fashion."

b. Spiritual weapons: the strategies of the Cross (3-4). Paul immediately admits that he is a man of weakness. But he does not "war after the flesh." He is not at the mercy of a fleshly nature. He does not use carnal weapons, but spiritual weapons empowered through the Holy Spirit to "destroy strongholds" (RSV) which are in opposition to Jesus Christ. It is through spiritual warfare that every thought must be led "into captivity . . . to the obedience of Christ" (cf. 1 Cor. 2:16). The Christian will always fight a losing battle if he fights in his own strength. "Not by might, nor by power, but by my spirit, saith the Lord of hosts" (Zech. 4:6).

Our "weapons" are "love" and "truth" and "righteousness" which in the end can conquer evil in the hearts of men. No wonder Paul tells the Ephesians to be "strong in the Lord, and in the power of his might" (Eph. 6:10). Weakness drives the Christian to dependence. But it is not a debilitating dependence that uses God as a crutch. It is an enabling dependence which arises through prayer. As someone has wisely said, "A man cannot be beaten who, when he falls, falls on his knees."

c. Carnal attitudes: enemies of the Cross (5-6). Tasker defines these carnal weapons as "human cleverness or ingenuity, organizing ability, eloquent diatribe, powerful propaganda, or reliance on charm or forcefulness of personality." These are all "in themselves quite unavailing" in the battle against entrenched evil.[35] Such carnal weapons may win temporary battles, as well they did in Corinth, but they will never win the warfare against Satan. Fire only fuels fire, it does not put it out.

But, thank God, spiritual weapons can penetrate the strongholds of Satan and bring every thought under the control of the Spirit. The proof of the gospel is the changed lives who are led by the "foolishness of the Cross" into utter submission to the Saviour.

Paul closes with a promise to "punish every disobedience" (5, RSV), but he first desires to win those on the fringe who have not as yet committed themselves wholeheartedly to the truth. "A minister can deal with a recalcitrant minority only when he has the loyal backing of a faithful group."

Paul's weapons were the weapons of the Cross—meekness and gentleness which he drew from the life of Christ. Robertson describes the spirit beautifully when he says:

> So it ever is: humility, after all, is the best defense. It disarms and conquers by the majesty of submission. To be humble and loving—that is true life. Do not let insult harden you, nor cruelty rob you of tenderness. If men wound your heart, let them not embitter it; and then yours will be the victory of the Cross. You will conquer as Christ conquered, and bless as he blessed. But remember, fine *words* about gentleness, self-sacrifice, meekness, are worth very little. Talking of the nobleness of humility and self-surrender is not believing in them. Would you believe in the Cross and its victory? Then live in its spirit—act upon it.[36]

2. *It must be consistent with the integrity and quality of one's calling in Christ* (7-11). The scripture seems to indicate that Paul is addressing himself to "Christ's" party (1 Cor. 1:12) which was convinced of its spiritual superiority to other members of the congregation. They arrogated to themselves a unique authority, applying their own criteria to others which would discredit even the apostle. Paul replies that if they are confident, so also is he.

a. Paul is consistent in his commitment to Christ (7). The question of commitment is a burning issue with the apostle. His desire is to meet his arrogant opponents face-to-face. Their spiritual egoism shocks him. He knows that the gospel of Christ is for all men and that the spiritual haughtiness of his critics is not in line with the spirit of Christ.

"Look at what is before your eyes," Paul says, "so I must open my life to your scrutiny. I have nothing to hide" (7, RSV). We do not know what these men were implying about Paul. Were they still talking about his persecution of the early Christians? Were they reflecting on his claim to apostleship? Were they jealous of his leadership and trying to destroy him through innuendo? Such actions and attitudes are characteristic of those who claim a special holiness and look down on others rather than keep their eyes on Christ. "There can be no finer definition of the church than a *fellowship of forgiven sinners,*" Barclay observes. When a man realizes that he belongs to such a fellowship, there is no longer any room for pride. The arrogant Christian feels that Christ belongs to him rather than that he belongs to Christ. We must never forget that we are "sinners saved by grace." That should make us thankful rather than arrogant.

Paul turns to the logic of his critics to authenticate his own position: "If any one is confident that he is Christ's, let him remind himself that as he is Christ's so are we" (ASV). It is important to him to establish the integrity of his relationship to Christ.

b. Paul is consistent in his commitment to build

rather than to destroy (8). He seems to pause for a moment to see if he has boasted too much of his authority. He must be careful not to claim too much for himself, as he had accused his critics of doing. His confidence in his calling to apostleship gives him the authority to edify, but not to destroy.

It is no idle boast that he should glory in his personal relationship to Christ and his "jurisdiction" given by the Master. He is, however, careful to explain that the gifts were given to build up rather than to tear down (cf. 12:9; 1 Cor. 8:1; 14:26). The proof is right before his critics' eyes. It is only "arguments and every proud obstacle" (RSV) that he is attempting to tear down—attitudes that set themselves up against the "knowledge of God." His critics, notwithstanding, are tearing down the fabric of love and unity which define the true fellowship of Christ (12:20).

c. Paul is consistent in his conduct among Christians (9-11). The charge made in vv. 9-10 is contemptible. His critics are taking advantage of Paul's absence by accusing him of hypocrisy and weakness. Weymouth paraphrases the passage, "Let it not seem as if I wanted to frighten you by my letters. For they say, 'his letters are weighty and forcible, but his personal appearance is feeble, and his speech contemptible!'"

Paul replies that what he says he is in writing when absent, he is when he is present. His enemies' criticism was tremendously painful to him. In modern vernacular, "it got to him." His answer is beautifully incisive: "My deeds are consistent with my words."

Though the emphasis is parenthetical, Paul's critics were also speaking of his personal appearance: "His bodily presence is weak and his speech of no account" (RSV). He has been described variously as "an ugly little Jew, bald, squat of stature, bandy legged, with bowed shoulders." He was also thought to have been the victim of humiliating infirmities such as ophthalmia and epilepsy. It was difficult for some of the Greek Sophists to accept profound thoughts from such a mean vessel. But Christ saw the power of this man. His personal integrity and that of his message was his authority.

Dr. Clovis Chappel, the great biographical expositor, was like Paul in this respect. He was small of stature and possessed a high, penetrating voice. He stood *by* the pulpit in St. Luke's in Oklahoma City rather than peep *over* its top. Anyone listening to him for the first time would be tempted to say, "What has this man got to make him the preacher his reputation says he is?" But one soon forgot both stature and voice in the marvel of his characterization of biblical personalities. He made them step out of the pages of the Bible and live again for his listeners.

Paul must have been like that! His life spoke louder than appearance or word.

> *Make me patient, kind and gentle,*
> *Day by day;*
> *Teach me how to live more nearly*
> *As I pray.*

> —SHARPE'S MAGAZINE

3. *It must be consistent with an attitude of humility which labors only in obedience and gives all credit for its successes to the Lord* (12-18).

a. Paul's boasting is within limits (12-17). His confidence is that the church will find his acts correspond to his words. Paul adds that those who measure themselves by themselves "are without understanding" (RSV). His standard of measurement is within the "limits God has apportioned to us" (RSV). The word *kanon* means literally *"reed"* or *"rod."* In this context it means a rule or limit, or an assigned region. Paul is saying that God has assigned him his region of work including Corinth. Therefore he will act with proper authority in preaching the gospel among the Corinthians. Here was the province of his boasting.

His standard is not found in himself or in others, but only in Christ. The church is not to be a "mutual admiration society," but a community which lives constantly under God's judging word in Christ.

b. Paul's boasting is within a given perspective (14-17). His philosophy of ministry includes two principles exhibited in vv. 14-15.

(1) He will not compete with others in a worldly fashion. His critics were boasting of other men's labors, not their own. Paul was the first to come to Corinth with the gospel. The fruit was his through Christ. His critics were feeding on his work.

It is a tragedy to see congregations competing with one another in proselyting converts from other churches. Our God-given task is to reach others "first . . . with the gospel of Christ" (14, RSV). Our boasting then will not be in other men's labors but rather in what Christ has done in reaching the lost through us. Even so, we will say with Paul, "I laboured . . . : yet not I, but the grace of God which was with me" (1 Cor. 15:10).

(2) His view of church growth is to see a flourishing congregation like the Corinthian church, not as an end in itself but as a base for future operations. His hope is that as their faith increases, he will be enabled to enlarge his own field of evangelistic endeavor so that he may "preach the gospel in the regions beyond" rather than boast in what has been accomplished "in another's field" (16, RSV).

c. Paul's boasting is really in the Lord (17-18). His cry in 17 (a quotation from Jer. 9:24) was often on his lips and permeates the whole passage: "Let him who boasts, boast in the Lord" (RSV; cf. 1 Cor. 1:30-31; Gal. 6:14; *et al.*). He always insists that there is only one rule of praise. All praise belongs to Christ through whom alone we have any success.

This perspective is all-inclusive in the apostle's writings. Christ does not approve of those who commend themselves, but commends those who glory in Him (cf. 5:9; 1 Cor. 4:15). It is as though he says, "After all, apostolic authority is not really safe in my hands. God's recommendation is the only mark of genuineness" (Strachan).[37] Paul boasts, not that he is an apostle, but that God has made him one. The servant of Christ, says Carver, can boast only of what God has done, what He is doing, and what He has promised to do. Paul's great desire was to have God's approval always. "The standards a man applies to himself may be faulty or even dishonest, but God can see all the way through him."

2 CORINTHIANS 11

Paul's Defense of His Apostolic Authority

2 Corinthians 11:1-15

1 Would to God ye could bear with me a little in my folly: and indeed bear with me.
2 For I am jealous over you with godly jealousy: for I have espoused you to one husband, that I may present you as a chaste virgin to Christ.
3 But I fear, lest by any means, as the serpent beguiled Eve through his subtilty, so your minds should be corrupted from the simplicity that is in Christ.
4 For if he that cometh preacheth another Jesus, whom we have not preached, or if ye receive another spirit, which ye have not received, or another gospel, which ye have not accepted, ye might well bear with him.
5 For I suppose I was not a whit behind the very chiefest apostles.
6 But though I be rude in speech, yet not in knowledge; but we have been throughly made manifest among you in all things.
7 Have I committed an offence in abasing myself that ye might be exalted, because I have preached to you the gospel of God freely?
8 I robbed other churches, taking wages of them, to do you service.
9 And when I was present with you, and wanted, I was chargeable to no man: for that which was lacking to me the brethren which came from Macedonia supplied: and in all things I have kept myself from being burdensome unto you, and so will I keep myself.
10 As the truth of Christ is in me, no man shall stop me of this boasting in the regions of Achaia.
11 Wherefore? because I love you not? God knoweth.
12 But what I do, that I will do, that I may cut off occasion from them which desire occasion; that wherein they glory, they may be found even as we.
13 For such are false apostles, deceitful workers, transforming themselves into the apostles of Christ.
14 And no marvel; for Satan himself is transformed into an angel of light.
15 Therefore it is no great thing if his ministers also be transformed as the ministers of righteousness; whose end shall be according to their works.

Paul has just condemned all self-commendation, yet here he is forced to do what has the appearance of the same spirit he has previously rebuked. It was distressing to him that the church whom he loved was alienated in affection, faith, and belief. It is no wonder that the apostle was greatly upset by the false teachers from Jerusalem who were undermining the faith of the fellowship in the gospel.

The task was repugnant to him, and yet it seemed quite necessary to present the grounds by which he spoke with authority. He finds it difficult to do what he feels he must do. It is within this context that he introduces his deep concern by stating, "I wish you would bear with me in a little foolishness. Do bear with me!" (1, RSV).

1. *A justification for divine jealousy* (2-3). Paul's feeling is a "hallowed passion," a paradox which expresses itself in love on the one hand and "sanctified scorn" on the other.

He was the agent of a spiritual betrothal. He has arranged a marriage to one husband, even to Christ. He has presented the church as a chaste virgin. This is a familiar Old Testament metaphor (Isa. 54:5; 62:5; Hos. 2:19), which Paul reemploys in Eph. 5:23-24. It occurs again in the Book of Revelation where the Church is referred to as the bride of Christ (Rev. 21:9). Betrothal was always a sober relationship carrying with it the demand for faithfulness. It was a testing time between the betrothed.

Even as Satan enticed Eve, Paul is concerned lest by "craftiness" (NASB) the church "should be corrupted from the simplicity that is in Christ." He is jealous for the attitude that sees Christ as the sole Way of salvation, the ultimate Object of desire, and the unstained Exemplar of perfect love.

His fear is justified by the attention the church is giving to a message quite different from the one he had introduced.

His jealousy for them is to be expected. It arose from

the purest of motives (2-3) and was unmixed with selfish or mercenary interest. He yearns to save them from the tragedy of infidelity. His one desire is that the Corinthian church should remain faithful to their vows so that they might be presented to Christ "a glorious church, not having spot, or wrinkle," on that great day (Eph. 5:27). His dread is that they should be rejected and condemned, as a woman unfaithful to her vows.

2. *The proclamation of a false gospel* (4). Paul realizes that his critics are learned men, articulate in expression, convincing and persuasive. He contrasts their oratory with his "unskilled" speech and yet declares himself "not the least inferior to these superlative apostles" (5, RSV). His anxiety is not a concern over the skills of communication, but over the substance of theology. The opponents are leading the Corinthians away from the fundamentals, and Paul is jealous in behalf of the truth.

a. They presented "another Jesus" (14*a*). Seducers were preaching a different teacher than the one Paul had introduced. The issue was crucial. It still is! The Christian faith is grounded in the historical Jesus, the Son of God, who became "flesh and dwelt among us," who was crucified, resurrected, and who now reigns as Lord at the right hand of the Father. He is coming again in glory.

The false prophets were teaching a Jesus who was a descendent of David, head of the Jewish family, teacher, and reformer—the best of humankind. What they said of Him was noble, but it was a profile foreign to the Christian faith.

b. They presented "another spirit" (4*b*). Commentators do not agree as to whether Paul means the Holy Spirit or an attitude of mind and heart. Both interpretations fit. In Christ, through His Spirit, the church had received a spirit of freedom and joy, not a spirit of bondage and fear.

F. F. Bruce suggests that it was "a different spirit" (RSV) than the Spirit whom the Christians received when they believed (1:22; 5:5; cf. 1 Cor. 12:13). Those who proclaimed another Jesus might have been "spiritual" men, but they were not energized by the Holy Spirit of God.

The spirit of legalism which Paul fought all of his life was of "another kind" than the spirit of surrender to the lordship of Christ which came through the Spirit of God.

When a church, caught in the shackles of secularism, denies, for all practical purposes, the lordship of Christ, they are already on the road to "another Jesus" and "another spirit."

c. They preached "another gospel" (4c). The message of the Judaizers was an alien gospel. It demanded that Christians submit to certain Jewish rites and accept the responsibility of keeping the Jewish law. Paul describes this gospel in Gal. 1:7: "Not that there is another gospel, but there are some who trouble you and want to pervert the gospel of Christ" (RSV).

It was the news of a Christ who was stripped of His glory as the incarnate Son of God. As a result, He is not a Christ who can meet us in our personal needs.

3. *The sharing of a genuine concern* (5-15).

a. The key verse is 11: "And why? Because I do not love you? God knows that I do!" (RSV). Paul admits his inferiority in certain areas. He is less eloquent (6). He is untrained in sophisticated oratory. He may not have the tricks of "beguiling and falsifying speech," but in the essential truths of the gospel he is not at a loss. His work among them was his proof.

b. Even though it was a subject of irritation to the church, Paul had not received any income from them (7). He held an attitude of independence in order that he might not be in any man's debt (1 Cor. 9:18). And while he fully realized that "the Lord commanded those who proclaim the gospel should get their living by the gospel" (1 Cor. 9:14, RSV), he was determined to preach without any obligation to any man. In regard to the Corinthian situation, "Paul was only wise."

The association of preaching with money is always a

danger. The called man of God preaches because of an inner compulsion, never for what he receives. Other churches had contributed to Paul's support, but it was important to him that he stand alone in Corinth. Too much was at stake to open such a Pandora's box in this situation.

This is the backdrop of Paul's sob, "God knows that I love you!" His gratuitous preaching is the real reason for his glorying. His unselfishness is very real, his critics deceptive. He is unwilling to compromise. They are "sham apostles," their work is fraudulent, their image is false. "Even Satan," he says, "disguises himself as an angel of light" (14, RSV). So it is not strange that his ministers should act in like fashion.

Religious prejudice, race, and party loyalty blinded these men to the truth, and Paul would have nothing of it. "Their end will correspond to their deeds" (15, RSV).

It is well to backtrack and look at this passage once again. Paul pauses to apologize for the unusual course he is taking. He is indeed compelled to boast. But he does so, knowing full well that boasting is folly and that the Corinthians must tolerate it rather than follow it as an example. It is a method of defense, a strategy of irony through which the apostle attacks all that is not exemplary of the spirit of Christ. It is a boasting of infirmities and a glorying in the grace of God.

Through it all Paul is saying, "God loves you and I love you. I will give my life for Christ and the gospel if it takes that to hold your loyalty to Him."

The Credentials of the Apostle

2 Corinthians 11:16—12:10

16 I say again, Let no man think me a fool; if otherwise, yet as a fool receive me, that I may boast myself a little.
17 That which I speak, I speak it not after the Lord, but as it were foolishly, in this confidence of boasting.
18 Seeing that many glory after the flesh, I will glory also.
19 For ye suffer fools gladly, seeing ye yourselves are wise.
20 For ye suffer, if a man bring you into bondage, if a man devour you, if a man take of you, if a man exalt himself, if a man smite you on the face.

21 I speak as concerning reproach, as though we had been weak. Howbeit whereinsoever any is bold, (I speak foolishly,) I am bold also.
22 Are they Hebrews? so am I. Are they Israelites? so am I. Are they the seed of Abraham? so am I.
23 Are they ministers of Christ? (I speak as a fool) I am more; in labours more abundant, in stripes above measure, in prisons more frequent, in deaths oft.
24 Of the Jews five times received I forty stripes save one.
25 Thrice was I beaten with rods, once was I stoned, thrice I suffered shipwreck, a night and a day I have been in the deep;
26 In journeyings often, in perils of waters, in perils of robbers, in perils by mine own countrymen, in perils by the heathen, in perils in the city, in perils in the wilderness, in perils in the sea, in perils among false brethren;
27 In weariness and painfulness, in watchings often, in hunger and thirst, in fastings often, in cold and nakedness.
28 Beside those things that are without, that which cometh upon me daily, the care of all the churches.
29 Who is weak, and I am not weak? who is offended, and I burn not?
30 If I must needs glory, I will glory of the things which concern mine infirmities.
31 The God and Father of our Lord Jesus Christ, which is blessed for evermore, knoweth that I lie not.
32 In Damascus the governor under Aretas the king kept the city of the Damascenes with a garrison, desirous to apprehend me:
33 And through a window in a basket was I let down by the wall, and escaped his hands.
1 It is not expedient for me doubtless to glory. I will come to visions and revelations of the Lord.
2 I knew a man in Christ above fourteen years ago, (whether in the body, I cannot tell; or whether out of the body, I cannot tell: God knoweth;) such an one caught up to the third heaven.
3 And I knew such a man, (whether in the body, or out of the body, I cannot tell: God knoweth;)
4 How that he was caught up into paradise, and heard unspeakable words, which it is not lawful for a man to utter.
5 Of such an one will I glory: yet of myself I will not glory, but in mine infirmities.
6 For though I would desire to glory, I shall not be a fool; for I will say the truth: but now I forbear, lest any man should think of me above that which he seeth me to be, or that he heareth of me.
7 And lest I should be exalted above measure through the abundance of the revelations, there was given to me a thorn in the flesh, the messenger of Satan to buffet me, lest I should be exalted above measure.
8 For this thing I besought the Lord thrice, that it might depart from me.
9 And he said unto me, My grace is sufficient for thee: for my strength is made perfect in weakness. Most gladly therefore will I rather glory in my infirmities, that the power of Christ may rest upon me.
10 Therefore I take pleasure in infirmities, in reproaches, in necessities, in persecutions, in distresses for Christ's sake: for when I am weak, then am I strong.

Paul again finds himself in a situation he does not like but from which he cannot escape. His words are apologetic but bite with irony: "Accept me as a fool, so that I too may boast a little" (16, RSV). His argument which follows is, he says, "not with the Lord's authority" (RSV). He is using the weapons of his enemies to refute their own arguments (16-21). He is both decisive and convincing.

In the passage (11:22—12:10) are found the credentials for his apostolic teachings. Nothing in the New Testament compares in richness and interest with this characterization of his life. It is told with a "tantalizing brevity," and no one can read the verses without recognizing that Paul is baring his soul. His opponents have drawn him into this exposé. Phillips paraphrases v. 22, "This is a foolish game, but look at the list."[38] In that list is found the life story and character of a great man.

1. *His pedigree* (22-23). He is speaking racially, culturally, and spiritually. His background is as prestigious as his critics! "If they say they are Hebrew, *so am I!* If they say they are Israelites and descendents of Abraham, *so am I!* If they even claim to be ministers of Christ (I speak as a fool), *I am more."*

2. *His labors* (23). "I have worked harder than any of them." Paul was not afraid of work. His day extended from sunup to sunset. Work was his vocation and his hobby. He knew nothing else. It was his glory to be spent for his Lord.

3. *His persecutions* (23-25).
   "I have served more prison sentences!
   "I have been beaten times without number.
   "I have faced death again and again.
   "I have been beaten the regulation thirty-nine stripes by the Jews five times.
   "I have been beaten with rods three times.
   "I have been stoned once" (Phillips).

4. *His dangers* (25-27)
   "I have been shipwrecked three times.
   "I have been twenty-four hours in the open sea.

"In my travels I have been in constant danger from rivers and floods, from bandits, from my own countrymen, and from pagans. I have faced danger in city streets, danger in the desert, danger on the high seas, danger among false Christians. I have known exhaustion, pain, long vigils, hunger and thirst, doing without meals, cold and lack of clothing" (Phillips).

5. *His leadership concerns* (28-29). Paul leaves the externals and moves on to "the daily pressure upon me of concern for all the churches" (NASB). The preceding enumeration was not exhaustive, but he turns quickly to his enervating official duties which come upon him daily. His is a spirit of identification (29). He shares in the weakness of every Christian. In empathetic identification, he lives "in them" as well as "with them." Their victory is his victory. Their failure, caused by others, makes him indignant.

Plummer describes Paul's heart as "ablaze with pain." Robertson depicts him as "set on fire with grief."

6. *His dependence upon God* (30-33). The apostle finishes his autobiographical picture by saying, "If I must needs glory, I will glory of the things which concern my infirmities." The verse leads to the narrative of the incident in Damascus (32-33) which illustrates his weakness and may have given rise to a charge of cowardice.

Rather than revealing cowardice, however, it showed what Christ could do through a weak and broken vessel. In v. 31 Paul places himself on an oath that this is true. He came to Damascus with all the pomp and pride of the Sanhedrin; he left slinking away like a hunted thief. Could anything be more humiliating from the human viewpoint? His first trial may have been his most difficult. However, he still feels impelled to boast. He has accepted suffering for Christ's sake. The Cross has transformed all his values. Only the grace of Christ could take an arrogant Pharisee and make him a suffering servant of Jesus Christ.

7. *His spiritual insight* (12:1-6). Paul still feels impelled to "boast," but it is out of his weakness rather than his strength. Though boasting is personally distasteful, it is necessary to justify his apostleship against his vindictive opponents. He fights back for the sake of his own leadership and the ongoing of the church.

Paul lays no great stress on his ecstatic experiences and under other circumstances probably would have said nothing about them. His conversion experience (Acts 9:3-6) and his call to Macedonia (Acts 16:9-10) were probably his two most outstanding experiences, but there were others which he relates here.

The principal thing to remember is that his experiences were not counterfeit; they were of the Lord. And while visions and ecstatic revelations were quite common in the several religious cultures of New Testament times, Paul describes his visions and revelations against the backdrop of weakness (his "thorn in the flesh").

The passage is a corrective as well as a witness. Too often we enjoy our special experiences without giving credit as to their Source.

a. Paul identifies the Source of his mystical experiences (1). His visions and revelations came from the Lord. They were not self-glorifying but Christ-exalting experiences.

b. He reveals the spirit of his witness (2-3). He speaks of a man in Christ, not in the first but in the third person. He is completely objective in recounting this ecstatic experience. So "absorbed" is he in Christ, he loses sight of himself.

c. He reveals the place of the experience (3-4). He was caught up into paradise where God dwells. He was taken out of himself into the very throne room of heaven. This was not ecstasy for ecstasy's sake; it was a revelation of God for the comfort, encouragement, and inspiration of Christ's servant. While this beatific vision is not for the many, Paul's report brings heaven a little nearer earth.

> *Father! replenish with Thy grace*
> *This longing heart of mine;*
> *Make it Thy quiet dwelling-place,*
> *Thy sacred, inmost shrine.*
>
> —JOHANN SCHEFFLER

d. These revelations came by means of a Voice (4). Paul heard "things which could not be told" (RSV). The words were unspeakable but he heard! He glories in the Voice. A scriptural vision or revelation is always accompanied by a Voice (Isa. 6:8; Ezek. 1:28; Luke 9:35; Rev. 1:10). The vision is but a prelude to a divine communication. This distinguishes a true revelation from Quietism. A heavenly vision motivates, sets us on our feet, commissions us to serve!

8. *His humility* (7). To keep him from being "unduly elated" (NEB), God gave His servant a "thorn in the flesh." Paul speaks of it as "a messenger of Satan to hurt and bother me, and prick my pride" (TLB).

We do not know the nature of Paul's thorn. It was not a moral or spiritual disorder. It was probably a physical disease, "humiliating, incurable, so terrible indeed, that it could be described as devilish." The Greek word may be rendered "stake," stuggesting the agony barbarians inflicted by impaling their captives.

The thorn has been variously understood as a repulsive physical appearance (10:10), or epilepsy (Gal. 4:14), or severe and penetrating headaches (Tertullian and Jerome), or eye trouble (Acts 9:9; Gal. 4:15; 6:11), or virulent malaria. Whatever it was, Paul, in God's providence, does not tell us. Now every sufferer can in some measure identify with the apostle.

9. *His resignation* (8-10). Three times Paul cries for relief from his suffering. God's reply comes not as a direct answer of deliverance but as a promise of sustaining grace

and a statement of divine promise: "And he said unto me, My grace is sufficient for thee: For my strength is made perfect in weakness. Most gladly therefore will I rather glory in mine infirmities, that the power of Christ may rest upon me."

"My grace is sufficient!" The tense of the verb indicates that the supply of grace is continuous. The divine assistance and comfort is, and will continue to be, more than a compensation for the thorn. God's grace will enable Paul to carry out his ministry in spite of his problem. It is sufficient for all the trials of the journey, all the temptations of the road, all the disabilities of frail humanity.

The principle is the same as in 4:7 ff. The "transcendent power" (RSV) is God's, not Paul's. This realization moves him to glory in his infirmities. He even welcomes these sufferings, along with the indignities which accompany his apostleship (cf. 11:23 ff.). Thank God, in our weakness we find His strength!

The Signs of an Apostle

2 Corinthians 12:11-19

> 11 I am become a fool in glorying; ye have compelled me: for I ought to have been commended of you: for in nothing am I behind the very chiefest apostles, though I be nothing.
> 12 Truly the signs of an apostle were wrought among you in all patience, in signs, and wonders, and mighty deeds.
> 13 For what is it wherein ye were inferior to other churches, except it be that I myself was not burdensom to you? forgive me this wrong.
> 14 Behold, the third time I am ready to come to you; and I will not be burdensome to you: for I seek not yours, but you: for the children ought not to lay up for the parents, but the parents for the children.
> 15 And I will very gladly spend and be spent for you; though the more abundantly I love you, the less I be loved.
> 16 But be it so, I did not burden you: nevertheless, being crafty, I caught you with guile.
> 17 Did I make a gain of you by any of them whom I sent unto you?
> 18 I desired Titus, and with him I sent a brother. Did Titus make a gain of you? walked we not in the same spirit? walked we not in the same steps?
> 19 Again, think ye that we excuse ourselves unto you? we speak before God in Christ: but we do all things, dearly beloved, for your edifying.

Paul has concluded his "boasting." His critics have

compelled him to resort to a self-defense he considers foolish. They should have been his protectors. Instead, these "marvelous fellows" (TLB) have stolen away his friends' hearts and imperiled the body of Christ. "I have been a fool! You forced me to it, for I ought to have been commended by you. For I am not at all inferior to these superlative apostles, even though I am nothing" (11, RSV).

1. *Miracles as Signs* (12-13). To carry the title "apostle," one must have seen the risen Christ. This was considered the "absolute requirement" of apostleship. But an apostle also was attested "by signs and wonders and various miracles" (cf. Heb. 2:1-4, RSV). So Paul can say here, "The signs of a true apostle were performed among you in all patience, with signs and wonders and mighty works" (12, RSV).

It is not known whether Paul intends these "signs and wonders and mighty works" to be grouped together or considered separately. At any rate, these miraculous events had taken place before the very eyes of the Corinthians. How then can they doubt his authority?

It would seem that the three terms describe the same thing—a miracle in its various aspects. A "sign" points to the power of God at work; a "wonder" suggests the awe in the one who views the miracle. A "mighty deed" is powerful because it is performed by the power of God.

Paul speaks parenthetically (13) to remind the Corinthians that as an apostle he has received nothing from them. He reminds them that they are inferior only in that he has not been burdensome to them.

2. *Love as the chief sign* (14-19). Paul has seen the risen Jesus; he exhibits the apostolic power to perform miracles —but the final and conclusive sign of his apostleship is caring love for his converts.

a. "I seek not what is yours but you," he assures them (14, RSV). He is planning a third visit. When he arrives, he will not seek anything from the Corinthians, "for children ought not to lay up for their parents, but parents for their children" (RSV). As a parent freely gives himself for his children, so Paul, their father in Christ, will gladly spend and be spent for their souls (15).

b. He will love them even in the face of their ingratitude and hostility (15*b*-18). Those who give themselves for the good of others must be prepared for such an attitude. "I was crafty, you say, and got the better of you by guile" (16, RSV). It is hard to understand such a reaction, but Christ's ministers often discover that those they love sometimes misunderstand their motives. "Did I take advantage of you through any of those whom I sent to you? . . . Did Titus take advantage of you? Did we not act in the same spirit? Did we not take the same steps?" Paul plaintively asks (18, RSV). Should not self-sacrifice and service be rewarded by trust and appreciation? Should it be used by one's enemies to arouse suspicion concerning his sincerity?

c. Nevertheless, the apostle will not take advantage of these Corinthians (19). "Have you been thinking all along that we have been defending ourselves before you?" he asks. "It is in the sight of God that we have been speaking in Christ, and all for your upbuilding, beloved" (RSV).

From the beginning Paul's dealings with the Corinthians have sprung from a spirit of love and self-sacrifice. His only motive has been to serve them in Christ's grace. All things have been for their edification. To be able to make such a claim is the final mark of authentic Christian ministry.

Final Warnings and Appeals from a Concerned Pastor

2 Corinthians 12:20—13:14

> 20 For I fear, lest when I come, I shall not find you such as I would, and that I shall be found unto you such as ye would not: lest there be debates, envyings, wraths, strifes, backbitings, whisperings, swellings, tumults:
> 21 And lest, when I come again, my God will humble me among you, and that I shall bewail many which have sinned already, and have not repented of the uncleanness and fornication and lasciviousness which they have committed.
> 1 This is the third time I am coming to you. In the mouth of two or three witnesses shall every word be established.
> 2 I told you before, and foretell you, as if I were present, the second

time; and being absent now I write to them which heretofore have sinned, and to all other, that, if I come again, I will not spare:

3 Since ye seek a proof of Christ speaking in me, which to you-ward is not weak, but is mighty in you.

4 For though he was crucified through weakness, yet he liveth by the power of God. For we also are weak in him, but we shall live with him by the power of God toward you.

5 Examine yourselves, whether ye be in the faith; prove your own selves. Know ye not your own selves, how that Jesus Christ is in you, except ye be reprobates?

.6 But I trust that ye shall know that we are not reprobates.

7 Now I pray to God that ye do no evil; not that we should appear approved, but that ye should do that which is honest, though we be as reprobates.

8 For we can do nothing against the truth, but for the truth.

9 For we are glad, when we are weak, and ye are strong: and this also we wish, even your perfection.

10 Therefore I write these things being absent, lest being present I should use sharpness, according to the power which the Lord hath given me to edification, and not to destruction.

11 Finally, brethren, farewell. Be perfect, be of good comfort, be of one mind, live in peace; and the God of love and peace shall be with you.

12 Greet one another with an holy kiss.

13 All the saints salute you.

14 The grace of the Lord Jesus Christ, and the love of God, and the communion of the Holy Ghost, be with you all. Amen.

Paul brings his passionate defense of his apostolic ministry to a conclusion with a series of solemn warnings and passionate appeals. Unless there is evidence of repentance and reformation among the Corinthians, he will be forced to exercise his authority in discipline. He prays that such a course will be unnecessary. On his second visit to Corinth his forbearance was interpreted as weakness. He vows this will not happen again. "When I come this time, I will show no leniency" (13:2, NEB). His fear is that he will be ashamed of the church when he stands among them. He has no wish to experience the personal humiliations which disrupted his relationship to them on his last journey.

1. *The marks of a carnal fellowship* (12:20). "I fear that perhaps I may come and find you not what I wish," he writes, "and that you may find me not what you wish" (RSV). He then proceeds to enumerate the carnal attitudes which were marring their life as a professed community of Christ:

a. Strife and jealousy (NASB). The KJV translates the first word *debates*. It is the Greek *eris,* the name of the goddess of discord. *Zelos* is the other word, the twin of strife. The original means "zeal," but it is a zeal for one side against another. It is the spirit of a mean and little mind.

b. Angry tempers, disputes (NASB). The outbursts of angry temper among the Corinthians were expressions of "personal rivalries" (NEB) which existed among them (cf. 1 Cor. 3:1-4). This latter word was found only in the writings of Aristotle prior to the New Testament; it means "a self-seeking pursuit of political office by unfair means." By its sectarian spirit the Corinthian church turned the community of Christ into a political convention of angry name-callers!

c. Slanders, gossips (NASB). The first word represents a loud-mouthed, open attack upon a rival. The second might be described as a whispering campaign—"the discreditable tale passed on as a spicy secret." One can deal with the first because it is open; he is helpless in the face of the second.

d. Arrogance, disturbances (NASB). Here is what Barclay calls "democracy run mad." The worldly spirit of Greek individualism has brought the church to the very brink of ruin. The seamless robe of Christ has become a tatter of rags!

2. *The marks of a backslidden spirit* (12:21). Once again the apostle voices his profound misgivings about the Corinthians. "I am afraid that, when I come again, my God may humiliate me in your presence, that I may have tears to shed over many of those who have sinned in the past and have not repented" (NEB).

Paul then characterizes the sins of these backslidden church members: "uncleanness and fornication and lasciviousness." The first word is a general term for impurity of life. Technically, "fornication" refers to immorality among the unmarried, but here as elsewhere in the New Testament it has the broader meaning of illicit sexual intercourse between any two parties. Several modern versions translate it simply "immorality." "Lasciviousness" is a lustful defiance of public decency.

That such immoralities could creep into the fellowship of Jesus Christ is difficult to accept. "But the Christian faith does not rest on sentimental belief in human goodness. It rests on the knowledge of the inherent sinfulness of human nature apart from redeeming grace. The fact makes the gospel both credible and necessary."[39]

On his second visit to Corinth the apostle faced up to these evils within the Corinthian fellowship and called for repentance—an open confession of wrongdoing and a complete change of conduct. Now he fears that such repentance has not occurred. These scandalous sinners should have humiliated themselves long ago. The fact that apparently they have not means personal defeat for the apostle, for he has been unable to draw them back to Christ and purity of life. "Their ruin is his defeat." If such is the case, he will "mourn" (RSV) over them as spiritually lost and dead. His unspoken conclusion is that, as an apostle, he will be forced to use his apostolic authority to save the church.

2 CORINTHIANS 13

3. *The authority of the apostolic ministry* (13:1-4). "I warned those who sinned before and all the others," Paul now writes, "and I warn them now while absent, as I did when present on my second visit, that if I come again I will not spare them—since you desire proof that Christ is speaking in me" (13:1-2, RSV).

Paul's tender forbearance, which had accompanied his former warning, had been taken by these persons as a sign of personal weakness. It was rather intended to bring them to repentance (cf. Rom. 2:4-5). But if his second visit had been a day of mercy, the third was to be a day of judgment!

In Paul's mind, the difference is between the first and second comings of Christ—His humiliaton and His exaltation. In His first advent, Christ was crucified in weakness, but He was resurrected and now lives by the power of God (4). The powerful Christ will be acting in Paul when the apostle returns on his third visit! For the sinning Corinthians, judgment is at hand. In the power of Christ, Paul will be strong when he comes to them! "I am weak as he was weak," he says, "but I am strong enough to deal with you for I share his life by the power of God" (4, Phillips).

4. *The Christian test* (13:5-14). Paul's enemies in Corinth have been hypercritical and vocal in their attacks upon him. They have stopped at nothing in their effort to discredit and destroy him in the eyes of the congregation. While these critics, joined by the carnal and backslidden elements within the church, were only a minority group, they had succeeded in bringing their pastor to a place of personal embarrassment and humiliation.

Having exhausted his patience and longsuffering, Paul now "turns the tables" on these persons. "Examine yourselves," he writes, "to see whether you are holding to your faith. Test yourselves" (5a, RSV). Phillips paraphrases the last sentence, "It is yourselves that you should be testing, not me."

Here Paul is clearly echoing Jesus, who said, "Judge not, that ye be not judged" (Matt. 7:1). Rather than straining to find the speck in Paul's eye, these hypercritical Corinthians should have removed the log from their own eye! Rather than being judgmental toward others, we must keep ourselves under God's judgment.

And what is the final test of being Christian? Listen to Paul: "Know ye not your own selves, how that Jesus Christ is in you, except ye be reprobates?" Dietrich Bonhoeffer writes: "The only criterion for self-examination is Christ himself." The mark that I am a Christian is that *Christ himself lives in me.* "Not I, but Christ" (Gal.

2:20) is the only valid test. If I am a Christian, Jesus Christ occupies exactly the space which was once occupied by my sinful ego. "Now if any man have not the Spirit of Christ, he is none of his" (Rom. 8:9). This Spirit is the Spirit of God who brings Christ to make His home in my heart, so that my existence becomes an expression of Him. "We realize that our life in this world is actually his life lived in us" (1 John 4:17, Phillips).

This is the test Paul wants the Corinthians to pass. "And when you have applied your test, I am confident that you will soon find that I myself am a genuine Christian. I pray God that you may find the right answer to your test, not because I have any need of your approval, but because I earnestly want you to find the right answer, even if that should make me no real Christian. For, after all, we can make no progress against the truth; we can only work for the truth" (6-8, Phillips).

The objective referent is "the truth" (8). He does not mean that all opposition to truth is futile. What he is suggesting is that it will be impossible for him to discipline the Corinthians merely as an exercise of authority. His personal vindication must give way before the truth. Nothing, not even his own interests, can stand in the way of the gospel. "What we pray for is your improvement" (9b, RSV).

"This also we wish, even your perfection," the KJV translates this last sentence. The Greek word is *katartisis,* elsewhere used for the mending of nets (Matt. 4:21). A few sentences later Paul uses the verb form of the word: "Be perfect" (13:11). This means simply, "Mend your ways" (RSV, NEB). As a bone specialist "perfects" a broken arm by setting it and restoring it to a proper functioning, so Paul would see the wrongs in the Corinthian church put right. He longs and prays for a rectifying and restoration of this congregation to its pristine love for Christ and one another. He yearns to see them clean, healthy, and strong for the witness of the gospel. Nothing else matters. In relation to this, his own reputation is a trifle!

"And now, my friends, farewell. Mend your ways; take our appeal to heart; agree with one another; live in peace; and the God of love and peace will be with you. Greet one another with the kiss of peace. All God's people send you greetings.

"The grace of the Lord Jesus Christ, and the love of God, and the fellowship of the Holy Spirit, be with you all" (11-14, NEB).

Reference Notes

THE CORINTHIAN CORRESPONDENCE

1. William Baird, *The Corinthian Church—A Biblical Approach to Urban Culture* (New York: Abingdon Press, 1964), p. 28. A review of the Corinthian culture and the place of the church can be found in most commentaries and expositional studies. See also the *Beacon Bible Commentary;* the *International Critical Commentary;* William Barclay, *The Letters to the Corinthians,* The Daily Study Bible Series; J. G. O'Neel, *Ancient Corinth,* Johns Hopkins University Studies in Archaeology, No. 8.

2. *Ibid.*

3. Rollo May, *New York Times,* March 26, 1971, Sec. 6.

4. Baird, *Corinthian Church,* p. 27.

1 CORINTHIANS

1. Charles Hodge, *An Exposition of 1 and 2 Corinthians* (Wilmington, Del.: Sovereign Grace Publishers, 1972), p. 9.

2. Clarence Tucker Craig, "1 Corinthians" (Introduction), *Interpreter's Bible,* ed. George A. Buttrick (New York: Abingdon Press, 1953), 10:9-10.

3. Clarence Tucker Craig, "I Corinthians" (Exegesis), *Interpreter's Bible,* 10:16.

4. John Calvin, *Commentary on the Epistle of Paul the Apostle to the Corinthians,* trans. by Rev. John Pringle (Grand Rapids, Mich.: William B. Eerdmans Publishing Co., 1948), 1:52.

5. William Barclay, *The Letters to the Corinthians,* "The Daily Study Bible" (Philadelphia: Westminster Press, 1954), p. 12.

6. *Worship in Song* (Kansas City: Lillenas Publishing Co., 1972), p. 421.

7. Alan Redpath, *The Royal Route to Heaven* (London: Pickering and Inglis, Ltd., 1960), p. 19.

8. Quoted by Barclay, *Corinthians,* p. 16.

9. Hodge, *Corinthians,* p. 18.

10. Sören Kierkegaard, *On Authority and Revelation,* trans. by Walter Lowrie (Princeton: Princeton University Press, 1955), p. 105.

11. As quoted by Baird, *Corinthian Church,* p. 44; Heinz D. Wendland, *Die Briefe an die Korinthe, Neue Testament Deutsch* (Göttingen: Vandenhoeck and Ruprecht, 1954), p. 19.

12. *Ibid.,* p. 44.

13. F. F. Bruce, *Introduction to I Corinthians* (Greenwood, S.C.: Attica Press, 1971), p. 37.

14. F. W. Robertson, *Expository Lectures on St. Paul's Epistles to the Corinthians* (London: Kegan, Paul, Trench and Co., 1855), p. 37.

15. Hodge, *Corinthians,* p. 26.

16. *Ibid.,* p. 33.

17. *Ibid.,* p. 34.

18. Bruce, *I Corinthians,* p. 42.

19 *Ibid.,* p. 44.

20. Quoted from Lycidas by Craig, "I Corinthians," *Interpreter's Bible,* 10:48.

21. *Ibid.,* p. 57.

22. Baird, *Corinthian Church,* pp. 58-60.

23. J. Robertson McQuilkin, "Whatever Happened to Church Discipline?" *Christianity Today* (April 17, 1974), pp. 8 ff.

24. Gordon Poteat, *We Preach Not Ourselves* (New York: Harper and Bros., 1944), p. 103.

25. Baird, *Corinthian Church,* p. 80.

26. John Short, "I Corinthians" (Exposition), *Interpreter's Bible,* 10:81.

27. F. F. Bruce, *I Corinthians,* p. 73.

28. Barclay, *Corinthians,* p. 75.

29. Redpath, *Royal Route,* p. 80.

30. Barclay, *Corinthians,* p. 75.

31. Charles R. Erdman, *The First Epistle of Paul to the Corinthians* (Philadelphia: The Westminster Press, 1966), p. 108.

32. Short, *Interpreter's Bible,* 10:118.

33. As quoted by Short, *Ibid.*

34. As quoted by Baird, *Corinthian Church,* p. 113; from Leroy E. Loemker, *The Nature of Secularism,* p. 11.

35. *Ibid.,* p. 114.

36. Dietrich Bonhoeffer, *Prisoner for God: Letters and Papers from Prison,* Eberhard Bethge, trans. by Reginald H. Fuller (New York: The Macmillan Co., 1954), p. 57.

37. Baird, *Corinthian Church,* p. 114.

38. Bonhoeffer, *Prisoner for God,* p. 57.

39. Margaret E. Thrall, *The First and Second Letters of Paul to the Corinthians* (Cambridge: Cambridge University Press, 1965), p. 79.

40. Bruce, *I Corinthians,* p. 107.

41. Erdman, *First Corinthians,* p. 147.

2 CORINTHIANS

1. As quoted by Gene E. Bartlett, *The Audacity of Preaching,* The Lyman Beecher Lectures, Yale Divinity School, 1961 (New York: Harper and Brothers, 1961), p. 17.

2. As quoted by James Reid in "The Second Epistle to the Corinthians," *Interpreter's Bible* (Exposition) (New York: Abingdon Press, 1953), 10:277. From *Within* (London: Williams and Norgate, 1912), p. 88.

3. Frank Carver, "II Corinthians," *Beacon Bible Commentary* (Kansas City: Beacon Hill Press of Kansas City, 1968), 8:500 ff.

4. *Worship in Song* (Kansas City: Lillenas Publishing Co., 1972), No. 304.

5. Reid, *Interpreter's Bible,* 10:278.

6. William Barclay, "The Letters to the Corinthians," *The Daily Study Bible* (Philadelphia: The Westminster Press, 1956), p. 190.

7. Carver, *BBC,* 8:502 ff.

8. *Ibid.,* p. 505.

9. Handley C. G. Moule, *The Second Epistle to the Corin-*

thians (London: Pickering and Inglis Ltd., 1962), pp. 8 ff. This fine section is the heart of Moule's discussion on "God's Promises."

10. *Ibid.*

11. Margaret E. Thrall, *The First and Second Letters of Paul to the Corinthians* (Cambridge: University Press, 1965), p. 126.

12. Carver, *BBC,* 8:510 ff. See the exegetical study and footnotes; also the expositional outline that follows.

13. See Charles Hodge, *An Exposition of 1 and 2 Corinthians* (Wilmington: Sovereign Grace Pub., 1972), for an excellent discussion of Paul's universal application of God's redemptive work in Christ, p. 219.

14. Floyd V. Filson, (Exegesis), *Interpreter's Bible,* 10:273.

15. Carver, *BBC,* 8:519. See expository suggestions.

16. William Baird, "Letters of Recommendation: A Study of II Corinthians 3:1-3," *Journal of Biblical Literature,* Vol. 80 (June, 1961), p. 168.

17. Carver, *BBC,* 8:530.

18. John Calvin, *Commentary on the Epistles of Paul the Apostle to the Corinthians,* trans. by John Pringle (Grand Rapids, Mich.: Wm. B. Eerdmans Publishing Co., 1948), 2:178.

19. Barclay, *Daily Study Bible,* p. 190.

20. C. K. Barrett, *A Commentary on the Second Epistle to the Corinthians* (New York: Harper and Row Publishers, 1973), p. 163.

21. Carver, *BBC,* 8:550 ff.

22. Reid, *Interpreter's Bible,* 10:343.

23. William Barclay, *New Testament Words* (Philadelphia: Westminster Press, 1974), pp. 21-22.

24. Alan Redpath, *Blessings out of Buffetings, Studies in II Corinthians* (Westwood, N.J.: Fleming H. Revell Co., 1965), p. 128.

25. Richard Howard, *Newness of Life* (Kansas City: Beacon Hill Press of Kansas City, 1975), p. 106.

26. Carver, *BBC,* 8:566 ff.

27. James Denny, *The Second Epistle to the Corinthians* (New York: Eaton and Mains, n.d.), p. 247.

28. James Allen, *As a Man Thinketh* (Kansas City: Hallmark Cards, 1971), p. 41.

29. Anne Sexton, "Welcome Morning," as quoted from the *Bostonia,* summer, 1975, Vol. 49, No. 2 (Boston University Office of Publications), p. 48. Used by permission.

30. Quoted by Carver, *BBC,* 8:580.

31. *Ibid.*

32. Quoted by Reid, *Interpreter's Bible,* 10:117, from *St. Francis of Assisi.*

33. *Ibid.,* p. 376.

34. Charles R. Erdman, *St. Paul's Second Epistle to the Corinthians* (Philadelphia: Westminster Press, 1928), p. 90.

35. R. V. C. Tasker, *The Second Epistle of Paul to the Corinthians* (Grand Rapids, Mich.: Wm. B. Eerdmans Publishing Co., 1958), p. 132.

36. Frederick W. Robertson, *Expository Lectures on St. Paul's Epistles to the Corinthians* (London: Kegan Paul, Trench & Co., 1885), p. 416.

37. As quoted by Carver, *BBC,* 8:599.

38. Phillips is used through this entire section.

39. Reid, *Interpreter's Bible,* 10:416.

A Selected Bibliography
with Annotations

ARNDT, WILLIAM F., AND GINGRICH, F. WILBUR. *A Greek-English Lexicon of the New Testament and Other Early Christian Literature*. Chicago: The University of Chicago Press, 1957. Perhaps the best modern lexicon of New Testament Greek.

BAIRD, WILLIAM. *The Corinthian Church—A Biblical Approach to Urban Culture*. New York: Abingdon Press, 1964. A beautifully written study of Pauline ethics based on careful exegesis.

BARCLAY, WILLIAM. *New Testament Words*. Philadelphia: The Westminster Press, 1974. The British scholar examines pivotal Greek words in popular style.

———. *The Letters to the Corinthians*. Philadelphia: The Westminster Press, 1964. A rich source for historical and illustrative material.

BARRETT, C. K. *A Commentary on the First Epistle to the Corinthians*. New York and Evanston: Harper and Row Publishers, 1968. Contains a new translation of the Epistle and a discerning commentary on the text.

———. *A Commentary on the Second Epistle to the Corinthians*. New York and Evanston: Harper and Row Publishers, 1973. (See above comment.)

BERNARD, J. H. "The Second Epistle to the Corinthians." *The Expositor's Greek Testament*, Vol. III. Edited by W. Robertson Nicoll. Grand Rapids, Mich.: Wm. B. Eerdmans Publishing Co., reprint edition. One of the classical commentary sets with special emphasis on grammatical and linguistic exegesis.

BRUCE, F. F. "1 and 2 Corinthians," *New Century Bible*. Greenwood, S.C.: Attic Press, Inc., 1971. A superb treatment of Paul's letters with particular emphasis upon exegesis.

————. *Paul and His Converts*. London: Lutterworth Press, 1962. A British scholar's short interpretations of the Corinthian correspondence along with his treatment of First and Second Thessalonians.

CALVIN, JOHN. *Commentary on the Epistles of Paul the Apostle to the Corinthians*, Vol. I. Translated by John Pringle. Grand Rapids, Mich.: Wm. B. Eerdmans Publishing Co., 1948. A rich source of biblical interpretation by the French theologian.

CARVER, FRANK G. "The Second Epistle of Paul to the Corinthians." *Beacon Bible Commentary*. Kansas City: Beacon Hill Press of Kansas City, 1968. A superlative exegetical study of the Second Epistle with expository suggestions.

CRAIG, CLARENCE TULDER. "Exegesis of the First Epistle to the Corinthians." *The Interpreter's Bible*, Vol. X. George A. Buttrick, editor. New York: Abingdon-Cokesbury Press, 1956. The accompanying exposition by John Short is particularly helpful.

DENNY, JAMES. *The Second Epistle to the Corinthians*. New York: Eaton and Mains, n.d. This is a part of *The Expositor's Bible*, edited by W. Robertson Nicoll. It combines popular exposition with exegetical excellence.

DODS, MARCUS. "The First Epistle to the Corinthians." *The Expositor's Bible*. Edited by W. Robertson Nicoll. London: Hodder and Stoughton, n.d. A rich source for materials.

EARLE, RALPH, *et al. Exploring the New Testament*. Kansas City: Beacon Hill Press, 1955. A college text written as an overview of the New Testament.

EERDMAN, CHARLES R. *The First Epistle of Paul to the Corinthians*. Philadelphia: The Westminster Press, 1928. Reprinted in 1966. A popularly written exposition of First Corinthians.

————. *The Second Epistle of Paul to the Corinthians*. Philadelphia: The Westminster Press, 1929. A popular exposition.

FINDLAY, G. G. "St. Paul's First Epistle to the Corinthians." *The Expositor's Greek Testament*, Vol. II. W. Robertson Nicoll, editor. Grand Rapids, Mich.: Wm. B. Eerdmans Publishing Co. Reprint edition. Part of the classic set of commentaries, usually a rich source of linguistic information.

FILSON, FLOYD V. "Exegesis of the Second Epistle to the Corinthians." *The Interpreter's Bible,* Vol. X. George A. Buttrick, editor. New York: Abingdon-Cokesbury Press, 1956. The accompanying exposition by James Reid is particularly helpful.

FISHER, FRED. *Commentary on I and II Corinthians.* Waco, Tex.: Word Books, Publisher, 1975. An illuminating verse-by-verse study written in the language of the "educated layman." Its bibliography is thorough.

GLEN, J. STANLEY. *Pastoral Problems in First Corinthians.* Philadelphia: The Westminster Press, 1964. An analysis of the Epistles from a pastoral perspective.

GOSHEIDE, F. W. *Commentary on the First Epistle to the Corinthians.* Grand Rapids, Mich.: Wm. B. Eerdmans Publishing Co. 1953. A careful exegesis by a conservative scholar.

GUDER, EILEEN. *To Live in Love.* Grand Rapids, Mich.: Zondervan Publishing House, 1967. Devotional essays from First Corinthians.

HERING, JEAN. *The First Epistle of St. Paul to the Corinthians.* Translated by A. W. Heathcote and P. I. Allcock. London: The Epworth Press, 1962. A good example of Protestant French scholarship.

———. *La Seconde Epitre de Saint Paul aux Corinthians.* "Commentaire du Nouveau Testament," Vol. VIII. Paris: Velachaux and Niestle, 1958.

HODGE, CHARLES. *An Exposition of the Second Epistle to the Corinthians.* New York: Robert Carter and Brothers, 1868. Reprinted by Wilmington, Del.: Sovereign Grace Publishers, 1972. One of the classical conservative studies.

HOWARD, RICHARD E. *Newness of Life.* Kansas City: Beacon Hill Press of Kansas City, 1975.

HUGHES, PHILLIP E. *Paul's Second Epistle to the Corinthians.* Grand Rapids, Mich.: Wm. B. Eerdmans Publishing Co., 1962. A careful exegesis based on the English translation but with reference to the Greek text.

LENSKI, R. C. H. *The Interpretation of St. Paul's First and Second Epistles to the Corinthians.* Columbus, Ohio: Wartbury Press, 1946. Combines critical exegesis with popular application.

LIGHTFOOT, J. B. *Notes on the Epistles of St. Paul.* Grand Rapids, Mich.: Zondervan Publishing House, 1895. Notes published posthumously.

MCPHEETERS, JULIAN C. "The Epistles to the Corinthians." *Proclaiming the New Testament.* Ralph G. Turnbull, editor. Grand Rapids, Mich.: Baker Book House, 1964. The former president of Asbury Theological Seminary treats the epistles homiletically.

METZ, DONALD S. "The First Epistle of Paul to the Corinthians." *Beacon Bible Commentary.* Kansas City: Beacon Hill Press of Kansas City, 1968. A warmhearted exegetical study with selected expositions.

MOFFATT, JAMES. *The First Epistle of Paul to the Corinthians.* New York: Harper and Brothers Publishers, n.d. Based on his translation. Provides excellent background material.

MORRIS, LEON. "The First Epistle of Paul to the Corinthians." *Tyndale New Testament Commentaries.* R. V. G. Tasker, editor. Grand Rapids, Mich.: Wm. B. Eerdmans Publishing Co., 1958. Excellent and well-understood commentaries for. the questing Bible student.

MOULE, HANDLEY C. G. *The Second Epistle to the Corinthians.* London: Pickering and Inglis Ltd., 1962. The distinguished bishop of Durham has written a beautiful translation, paraphrase, and exposition of the Epistle.

PLUMMER, ALFRED A. *A Critical and Exegetical Commentary on the Second Epistle of St. Paul to the Corinthians.* London: T. & T. Clark, 1915. A classic commentary based on the Greek text.

POTEAT, GORDAN. *We Preach Not Ourselves.* New York: Harper and Brothers, 1944. Sermons from the Corinthian letters.

REDPATH, ALAN. *Blessings out of Buffetings: Studies in II Corinthians.* Westwood, N.J.: Fleming H. Revell Co., 1965. The former pastor of Moody Memorial Church in Chicago and Charlotte Chapel in Edinburgh.

———. *The Royal Route to Heaven.* Westwood, N.J.: Fleming H. Revell Co., 1966. A series of probing sermons on First Corinthians.

RENDELL, KINGSLEY G. *Expository Outlines from 1 and 2 Corinthians.* Grand Rapids, Mich.: Baker Book House, 1969. Suggestive expository outlines.

ROBERTSON, A. T. *Word Pictures in the New Testament.* Vol. IV, *The Epistles of Paul.* New York: Harper and Brothers Publishers, 1931. Strong in its treatment of word meanings and grammatical constructions.

ROBERTSON, ARCHIBALD; AND PLUMMER, ALFRED. *A Critical and Exegetical Commentary on the First Epistle of St. Paul to the Corinthians.* Edinburgh: T. & T. Clark, 1914 (second edition). A classic example of thorough exegesis.

ROBERTSON, FREDERICK W. *Expository Lectures on St. Paul's Epistles to the Corinthians.* London: Kegan Paul, Treveh & Co., 1885. The great preacher's expositions on the Corinthian correspondence.

SCHLATTER, D. ADOLF. *Die Korintherbrief.* Stuttgart: Calwer Vereinsbuchhandlung, 1928. Combines scholarly excellence with popular appeal.

STRACHEN, R. H. *The Second Epistle of Paul to the Corinthians.* New York: Harper and Brothers Publishers, n.d. A part of the Moffatt commentary series. Valuable for background studies.

TASKER, R. V. G. *The Second Epistle of Paul to the Corinthians.* Grand Rapids, Mich.: Wm. B. Eerdmans Publishing Co., 1958. A popular but scholarly treatment of the Epistle in the Tyndale series.

THRALL, MARGARET E. "The First and Second Letters of Paul to the Corinthians." *The Cambridge Bible Commentary.* Cambridge: The University Press, 1965. A short commentary based on *The New English Bible.*

WAGNER, C. PETER. *A Turned-on Church in an Up-tight World.* Grand Rapids, Mich.: Zondervan Publishing House, 1971. Popular lectures based on the Corinthian correspondence.

WESLEY, JOHN. *Explanatory Notes upon the New Testament.* London: Epworth Press, 1958 (reprint). Rich insights into the Corinthian correspondence.